CHARLES DICKENS

GREAT EXPECTATIONS

Charles Dickens

GREAT EXPECTATIONS

[Edited with Complete Introduction, Author's Background, Textual Analysis, Study Questions and Critical Essays]

Aditya Nandwani

B.A. English (Hons) , Delhi University;

M.A. (English), IGNOU; Print Journalism (English) YMCA

ANMOL PUBLICATIONS PVT. LTD.

NEW DELHI - 110 002 (INDIA)

ANMOL PUBLICATIONS PVT. LTD.

H.O.: 4374/4B, Ansari Road, Darya Ganj,
New Delhi-110 002 (India)
Ph.: 23278000, 23261597

B.O.: No. 1015, Ist Main Road, BSK IIIrd Stage
IIIrd Phase, IIIrd Block
Bangalore - 560 085 (India)

Visit us at: www.anmolpublications.com

Great Expectations

First Published, 2009

PRINTED IN INDIA

Printed at Mehra Offset Press, Delhi.

Contents

Preface

Charles Dickens (7 February 1812 – 9 June 1870), one of the most popular Victorian Era's English novelists. He was also a great social activist. He is one of the most renowned and greatest writers, known for his amazing story telling and some memorable characters. During his lifetime, he had attained huge critical acclaim from all across the world. Charles Dickens is known for catering the world of English Literature with some of the best novels and short stories. He was born in Landport, Portsmouth in Hampshire. A few popular works of Charles Dickens are A Tale of Two Cities, Little Dorrit, The Adventures of Oliver Twist etc.

Great Expectation is a beautifully narrated story of a young orphan boy, Pip, whose encounter with a frightening man on Christmas Eve is one of the most significant incident of his life. His sister and husband were taking care of him. This man was a convict and escaped from prison. He forced Pip to steal some food, as he was very hungry. He also asked young Pip to get a file for grinding away his leg shackle. To know more about little, read the story.

Author

Chapter 1

Introduction

Dickens reworks his own childhood once again as a first-person narrative in *Great Expectations*, his thirteenth novel but only his second use of this highly subjective narrative point-of-view — the first being *David Copperfield* (1849-50), which incorporates the autobiographical fragment that Dickens never published. Unlike his earlier picaresque young heroes such as Nicholas Nickleby and Martin Chuzzlewit, Pip (more properly, Philip Pirrip) and David are fully developed, 'round' characters. Just as a child would, Dickens divides his settings and characters in both novels into the categories of "secure" and "threatening." But Dickens continues to prize distinctiveness in the drawing of the supporting characters. Uniqueness of identity in both major and minor characters makes the relatively 'flat' hero and heroine seem normal by comparison to such odd ducks as Orlick and Wemmick. As in the earlier, looser works such as *The Pickwick Papers* (1837), Dickens uses natural dialogue to reveal character subtly and indirectly.

Critics such as biographer Fred Kaplan have repeatedly pointed out that Pip and David are portraits of the novelist as a young man, something that the initials of the novelist hero of the 1851 novel suggest. The futile love affair with Estella — bright, and distant, and cold as the stars for which he has named her — reflects young Dickens' own hopeless infatuation with a banker's daughter, Maria Beadnell. Significantly, in the original ending Dickens did not reward Pip for his struggles by arranging the traditional happy ending for the lovers.

In his novels Dickens sees the chief problem in life as being people's failing to understand one another clearly, to see the emotional and spiritual reality beneath the surface. This problem is reflected in such matters as the harshness of employers, the disinterestedness of government, the biases of the penal and justice systems—in short, the sheer inhumanity of British social institutions. "What is a gentleman, what is true gentility?" are the questions Dickens poses before his reader in *Great Expectations*. He shows the development of Pip from an innocent, unsophisticated orphan to a pseudo- aristocrat and snob tinged by the taint of the prison house.

The desire of the animalistic and brutal Orlick for personal vengeance reflects what Dickens sees as the fearful revolutionary potentialities of the masses so well exemplified by that tigress Madame Defarge in his previous novel in *All the Year Round, A Tale of Two Cities* (1859). Estella, cold and distant as the stars that hold the mysteries of our fates, makes Pip painfully aware of his humble condition and motivates him to strive to be something better, worthier of her love (which she can never bestow). Perhaps both learn their social-climbing at Satis House, and then demonstrate that they have unlearned those childhood lessons in the final scene there, in the revised ending that novelist Sir Edward G. D. Bulwer-Lytton and Dickens's mistress, Ellen Ternan (perhaps a model for Estella) preferred.

Wholesale trade was finally considered genteel in the second half of the nineteenth century—as is the case with the proud, haughty Miss Havisham, a brewery heiress who fancies herself an aristocrat. Pip begins with iron chains at Joe's forge but yearns for golden chains, those that also bind Miss Havisham to her past and her thirst for vengeance. At the close of Chapter 19 Pip changes clothes (an act symbolic of his changing class) and leaves his true friends, Biddy and Joe, for the vain and superficial society of London.

Like Martin Chuzzlewit in the 1843 picaresque novel, Pip leaves the unspoiled countryside for a city of filth, crime, and oppression. However, Pip becomes a gentleman only in the true sense when he learns from the mouth of his benefactor the actual source of his great expectations; he proves his fundamental humanity by deciding to assist Magwitch, his greathearted fairy- godfather who is to Pip what Miss Havisham is to Estella. Abel Magwitch, victim of the aristocratic and depraved Compeyson (Cain?), is Dickens' s indictment of nineteenth-century British society's callous disregard for the welfare of the lower orders. From him Pip unlearns the lessons of Miss Havisham, Jaggers, and Wemmick; once again he values people for what they are rather than for their 'portable property' and pocketbooks.

The central plot— with its secrets that Magwitch is responsible for Pip's fortune and that he is Estella's father—is obscured by surprisingly few digressions; the book's action is tight and well-knit, owing in part perhaps to its weekly as opposed to Dickens's usual monthly serial structure. Like its weekly-serialised brethren, *Hard Times* (1854) and *A Tale of* (1859), the 1861 novel has fewer characters and little sub plotting. Expectations and exploitation are its organizing and unifying motifs.

And, like its weekly-serialised brethren, *Great Expectations* lacks both the exuberance and melodrama of Dickens' s earlier, picaresque works. Rigorously maintaining the first-person point-of-view (rather than his avuncular, Fieldingesque point of view of so evident in earlier works such as *Martin Chuzzlewit*), Dickens deftly suggests a small boy's perspective in the childhood section by limiting himself strictly to what a child would see and feel. The opening is especially effective in this regard, as the convict turns both Pip and his small world of marshes and dykes upside-down.

The scene between the two fellow- victims (Magwitch, a victim of legal and social injustice, an escapee from the hulks; Pip, an orphan only temporarily free of the dictatorship of his sister when he visits his parents' grave) is sensational and dramatic because of the strongly-sensed undercurrent of violence and menace below the humourous, initially- tranquil surface. Magwitch presents Pip with a moral and physical dilemma. Joe, Mrs. Joe, and Biddy present him with a choice of adult characters to emulate. Uncle (in effect, stepfather) Joe and Mrs. Joe's Uncle Pumblechook, artisan and merchant, present Pip with value choices. Joe is animated by the doctrine of love, Miss Havisham by that of hate. Matthew and Herbert Pocket repeat the selfless kindness and companionship of Biddy and Joe. These characters constitute Pip's social environment: we note that, although an orphan, Pip has no shortage of step-fathers and step- mothers.

Through them Pip must learn how to achieve human happiness. Through them Dickens shows how from infancy the individual is oppressed, moulded, and channeled into his adult identity: "The Child is father of the Man" (Wordsworth). Satis House and London are a complementary microcosm and macrocosm. Dickens's symbols generally and of the world-as-prison metaphor in particular involve mud, dust, gardens, seeds, the courts, and the river.

He contrasts the purity of the Thames in the marsh country, at its mouth, with its pollution and corruption in the metropolis. Dickens' s ability to build suspense through adapting the devices of the late eighteenth-century's Gothic novel (the eerie setting, the child or young woman in danger, the evil and deformed monster, the plausive and villainous aristocrat, the nightmare, and so on) has served as a model for later novelists. Dickens uses the persecution and exploitation of children and the theatricality of funerals to build pathos.

However, Dickens is best remembered for his ability to create humour out of farce, nonsense, lampoon, slapstick, and satire, using such stock types as the drunk, the eccentric, the ham actor, the buffoon, the paltroon, the hypocrite, the mercenary physician and his accomplice, the undertaker, and such subjects as education, child abuse and neglect, and keeping up with the Joneses.

In "On Some Aspects of the Comic in *Great Expectations*" Henri Talon proposes that the style of humour in this novel differs from that of Dickens's earlier works in that here humour is an aspect of the first-person perspective:

The detachment that comic observation demands comes not only of the lapse of time but of the maturity and inner poise that the narrator has achieved at the time, he is writing. Because he has out-grown his past errors, he can speak about them. First and foremost, Pip's humorous self-portrait evinces his belated self-knowledge. He was ridiculous because of his illusions and comparative self-ignorance.

Chapter 2

Charles Dickens: Biography

Charles Dickens (1812-1870), English Victorian era author wrote numerous highly acclaimed novels including his most autobiographical *David Copperfield* (1848-1850).

"Whether I shall turn out to be the hero of my own life, or whether that station will be held by anybody else, these pages must show. To begin my life with the beginning of my life, I record that I was born (as I have been informed and believe) on a Friday, at twelve o'clock at night. It was remarked that the clock began to strike, and I began to cry, simultaneously."

As a prolific 19th Century author of short stories, plays, novellas, novels, fiction and non-fiction, Dickens was known all over the world for his remarkable characters, his mastery of prose in the telling of their lives, and his depictions of the social classes, mores and values of his times. Some considered him the spokesman for the poor, for he definitely brought much awareness to their plight, the downtrodden and the have-nots. He had his share of critics like Virginia Woolf and Henry James, but also many admirers, even into the 21st Century.

Gilbert Keith Chesterton wrote numerous introductions to his works, collected in his *Appreciations and Criticisms of the works of Charles Dickens* (1911) and in his highly acclaimed biography *Charles Dickens* (1906) he writes: *He was the voice in England of this humane intoxication and expansion, this encouraging of anybody to be anything.* Critic John Forster (1812-1876) became his best friend, editor of many of his serialisations, and official biographer after his death, publishing *The Life of Charles Dickens* in 1874. Scottish poet and author Andrew Lang (1844-1912) included a letter to Dickens in his *Letters to Dead Authors* (1886). Elbert Hubbard (1856-1915) in his *Little Journeys* (1916) series follows the footsteps of Dickens through his old haunts in London. George Gissing (1857-1903) also respected his works and wrote several introductions for them, as well as his *Charles Dickens: A Critical Study* (1898) in which he writes: *Humour is the soul of his work. Like the soul of man, it permeates a living fabric which, but for its creative breath, could never have existed.* While George Orwell (1903-1950) was at times a critic of Dickens, in his 1939 essay *Charles Dickens* he, like many others before, again brought to light the author still relevant today and worthy of continued study: Nearly everyone, whatever his actual conduct may be, responds emotionally to the idea of human brotherhood. Dickens voiced a code which was and on the whole still is believed in, even by people who violate it. It is difficult otherwise to explain why he could be both read by working people (a thing that has happened to no other novelist of his stature) and buried in Westminster Abbey.

Charles John Huffman Dickens was born on 7 February, 1812 in Portsmouth, Hampshire, England (now the Dickens Birthplace Museum) the son of Elizabeth née Barrow (1789-1863) and John Dickens (c.1785-1851) a clerk in the Navy Pay Office. John was a congenial man, hospitable and generous to a fault that caused him financial difficulties throughout his life. He inspired the character Mr. Micawber in *David Copperfield* (1849-1850). Charles had an older brother Frances, known as Fanny, and younger siblings Alfred Allen, Letitia Mary, Harriet, Frederick William known as Fred, Alfred Lamert, and Augustus Newnham.

When Dickens' father was transferred to Chatham in Kent County, the family settled into the genteel surroundings of a larger home with two live-in servants—one being Mary Weller who was young Charles' nursemaid. Dickens was a voracious reader of such authors as Henry Fielding, Daniel Defoe, and Oliver Goldsmith. When he was not attending the school of

William Giles where he was an apt pupil, he and his siblings played games of make-believe, gave recitations of poetry, sang songs, and created theatrical productions that would spark a lifelong love of the theatre in Dickens. But household expenses were rising and in 1824, John Dickens was imprisoned for debt in the Marshal sea Prison. All of the family went with him except for Charles who, at the age of twelve, was sent off to work at Warren's Shoe Blacking Factory to help support the family, pasting labels on boxes. He lived in a boarding house in Camden Town, walked to work everyday, and visited his father on Sundays.

It was one of the pivotal points in Dickens' education from the University of Hard Knocks and would stay with him forever. The idyllic days of his childhood were over and he was rudely introduced to the world of the working poor, where child labour was rampant and few if any adults spared a kind word for many abandoned or orphaned children. Many of his future characters like Oliver Twist, David Copperfield, and Philip Pirrip would be based on his own experiences.

The appalling working conditions, long hours and poor pay typical of the time were harsh, but the worst part of the experience was that when his father was released his mother insisted he continue to work there. While he felt betrayed by and resented her for many years to come, his father arranged for him to attend the Wellington House Academy in London as a day pupil from 1824-1827, perhaps saving him from a life of factory work and setting him on the road to becoming a writer.

In 1827 the Dickens were evicted from their home in Somers Town for unpaid rent dues and Charles had to leave school. He obtained a job as a clerk in the law firm of Ellis and Blackmore. He soon learned shorthand and became a court reporter for the Doctors Commons. He spent much of his spare time reading in the British Museum's library and studying acting. In 1830, he met and fell in love with Maria Beadnell, though her father sent her to finishing school in Paris a few years later. In 1833, his first story of many, "A Dinner at Poplar Walk" was published in the *Monthly Magazine*. He also had some sketches published in the *Morning Chronicl,e* which in 1834 he began reporting for and adopted the pseudonym 'Boz'. At this time Dickens moved out on his own to live as a bachelor at Furnival's Inn, Holborn. His father was arrested again for debts and Charles bailed him out, and for many years, later both his parents and some of his siblings turned to him for financial assistance.

Dickens' first book, a collection of stories titled *Sketches by Boz* was published in 1836, a fruitful year for him. He married Catherine Hogarth, daughter of the editor of the *Evening Chronicle* on 2 April, 1836, at St. Luke's in Chelsea. A year later, they moved into 48 Doughty Street, London, now a museum. The couple would have ten children: Charles Culliford Boz (b.1837), Mary (Mamie) (1838-1838), Kate Macready (b.1839), Walter Landor (b.1841), Francis (Frank) Jeffrey (b.1844), Alfred Tennyson (b.1845), Sydney Smith (b.1847), Henry Fielding (b.1849), Dora Annie (1850-1851), Edward Bulwer Lytton (b.1852). Also in the same year, 1836, Dickens became editor for *Bentley's Miscellany* of which *Pickwick Papers* (1836-1837) was first serialised.

Thus began a prolific and commercially successful period of Dickens' life as a writer. Most of his novels were first serialised in monthly magazines, as was a common practice of the time. *Oliver Twist* between 1837 and 1839 was followed by *Nicholas Nickleby* (1838-1839), *The Old Curiosity Shop* (1840-1841), and *Barnaby Rudge* (1841). Dickens' series of five Christmas Books were soon to follow; *A Christmas Carol* (1843), *The Chimes* (1844), *The Cricket on the Hearth* (1845), *The Battle of Life* (1846), and *The Haunted Man* (1848). Dickens had found a readership who eagerly anticipated his next installments.

After the death of Catherine's sister Mary in 1837, the couple holidayed in various parts of England. After Dickens resigned from *Bentley's* in 1839, they moved to 1 Devonshire Terrace, Regent's Park. Further travels to the United States and Canada in 1842 led to his controversial *American Notes* (1842). *Martin Chuzzlewit* was first serialised in 1843. The next year the Dickens traveled through Italy and settled in Genoa for a year of which his *Pictures From Italy* (1846) was written.

Dombey and Son (1846) was his next publication, followed by *David Copperfield* (1849). In 1850, he started his own weekly journal *Household Words* which would be in circulation for the next nine years. From 1851 to 1860 the Dickens lived at Tavistock House where Charles became heavily involved in amateur theatre. He wrote, directed, and acted in many productions at home with his children and friends, often donating the money raised from ticket sales to those in need.

He collaborated with Wilkie Collins on the drama *No Thoroughfare* (1867). Novels to follow were *Bleak House* (1852-1853), *Hard Times* (1854), and *Little Dorrit* (1855-1857). In 1856, Dickens purchased Gad's Hill, his last place of residence near Rochester in Kent County. He continued in the theatre as well, acting in Wilkie Collins' *The Frozen Deep* in 1857 with actress Ellen Ternan (1839-1914) playing opposite him. The two fell in love and Dickens would leave Catherine a year later.

By now, Dickens was widely read in Europe and in 1858, he set off on a tour of public readings. A year later he founded his second weekly journal *All the Year Round,* the same year *A Tale of Two Cities* (1859) was first serialised. *Great Expectations* (1860-1861) was followed by *Our Mutual Friend* (1864-1865). In 1865, traveling back from Paris with Ellen and her mother, they were involved in the disastrous Staplehurst train crash, of which Dickens sustained minor injuries, but never fully recovered from the post-traumatic shock of it.

Two years later, he traveled to America for a reading tour. His 'farewell readings' took place in London's St. James Hall. Charles Dickens died from a cerebral hemorrhage on 9 June 1870 at his home, Gad's Hill. He is buried in Poet's Corner of Westminster Abbey, London, his tomb inscribed thus: "He was a sympathiser to the poor, the suffering, and the oppressed; and by his death, one of England's greatest writers is lost to the world." Thomas Carlyle (1795-1881), Scottish historian and author, upon hearing of his death said: *The good, the gentle, high-gifted, ever friendly, noble Dickens—every inch of him an honest man.* Unfinished at his death, *The Mystery of Edwin Drood* was published in 1870.

My father had left a small collection of books in a little room upstairs, to which I had access (for it adjoined my own) and which nobody else in our house ever troubled. From that blessed little room, Roderick Random, Peregrine Pickle, Humphrey Clinker, Tom Jones, the Vicar of Wakefield, Don Quixote, Gil Blas, and Robinson Crusoe, came out, a glorious host, to keep me company. They kept alive my fancy, and my hope of something beyond that place and time, - they, and the Arabian Nights, and the Tales of the Genii, - and did me no harm; for whatever harm was in some of them was not there for me; I knew nothing of it. It is astonishing to me now, how I found time, in the midst of my porings and blunderings over heavier themes, to read those books as I did

Chapter 3

Timeline of Charles Dickens

1812 Born on February 7 to John and Elizabeth Dickens.

1824 John Dickens arrested and sent to the Marshal sea prison. Charles Dickens worked at the Warren's Blacking Factory.

1827 Rejoins the workforce as the clerk of an attorney.

1830 Dickens meets Maria Beadnell, his first love interest.

1833 The relationship with Maria Beadnell ends. *A Dinner at Poplar Walk* is published.

1834 Began using the pseudonym "Boz". Meets his future wife, Catherine Hogarth.

1835 Becomes engaged to Catherine.

1836 The first chapters of *The Pickwick Papers* are published. Marries Catherine Hogarth.

1837 The first of his 10 children, Charles Culliford Boz Dickens, is born. Mary Hogarth, Catherine's sister, dies. The publication of *Oliver Twist* begins.

1838 Dickens and Hablot Browne travel to Yorkshire to see the boarding schools. His daughter, Mary, is born. Publication of *Nicholas Nickleby* begins.

1839 His daughter, Kate, is born.

1840 Publication of *The Old Curiosity Shop* begins

1841 *Barnaby Rudge* is published. Charles and Catherine tour Scotland. Their son, Walter, is born.

1842 Charles and Catherine travel to America. Late in 1842 or early in the next year, Dickens begins work on *Martin Chuzzlewit*.

1843 *A Christmas Carol* is published.

1844 His son Francis Jeffrey (Frank) is born. Dickens and family travel to Italy. Treated Madame de la Rue with mesmerism.

1845 Another son, Alfred, is born.

1846 Dickens and his family travel to Switzerland. Publication of *Dombey and Son* begins.

1847 His son, Sydney, is born.

1848 Dickens' sister, Fanny, dies. *The Haunted Man*, his last Christmas book is published.

1849 His son, Henry Fielding Dickens, is born. The publication of *David Copperfield* begins.

1850 His daughter, Dora Annie Dickens, is born.

1851 Catherine Dickens suffers a nervous collapse. John Dickens, the father of Charles Dickens, dies. Dora Dickens dies when she is only eight months old. *What Shall we have for Dinner?*, a cookbook by Catherine Dickens is published.

1852 The publication of *Bleak House* begins. His son, Edward or "Plorn", is born.

1853 Dickens gives his first public reading of one of his works.

1854 *Hard Times* is published.

1855 Dickens has a disappointing reunion with Maria Winter (Maria Beadnell). Publication of *Little Dorrit* begins.

1856 Dickens works with Wilkie Collins on *The Frozen Deep*. Dickens purchases Gad's Hill Place.

1857 Hans Christian Anderson is entertained at Gad's Hill Place. Dickens meets Ellen Ternan.

1858 Dickens separates from Catherine, his wife.

1859 *A Tale of Two Cities* is published.

1860 Publication of *Great Expectations* begins in *All the Year Round*. His daughter, Katie, marries and ten days later his brother, Alfred, dies. Dickens burns his personal papers.

1863 Dickens' mother, Elizabeth, dies. Dickens begins work on *Our Mutual Friend*.

1864 His son, Walter, dies in India. The first installment of *Our Mutual Friend* is printed.

1865 Dickens is involved in the Staplehurst railway accident along with Ellen Ternan and her mother.

1867 Dickens tours America for the second time.

1868 He gives his first *Murder of Nancy* reading.

1869 Dickens is ordered by doctors to discontinue readings. Dickens begins writing *The Mystery of Edwin Drood.*

1870 Dickens gives his final public reading. Publication of *The Mystery of Edwin Drood* begins. Charles Dickens dies at Gad's Hill Place on June 9.

Chapter 4

The Author and His Times

"I seem to be sending some part of myself into the Shadowy World," Charles Dickens wrote in a letter just before he finished the final chapter of *David Copperfield*. Dickens, as a matter of course, became intensely involved with all his books while he was writing them. His daughter once recalled how her father would sit in his study, speaking the characters' speeches as he wrote them, making faces, giggling, or sighing with emotion. But in 1869, the year before he died, Dickens wrote that Copperfield was still his "favourite child." Why was he so attached to this novel, of all the masterpieces he had created?

Readers of his own time assumed, of course, that *David Copperfield* was thinly disguised autobiography. After all, it was the first novel Dickens had written in the first person. Like Dickens, David is a novelist who started out as a political reporter. David's initials are even Dickens' in reverse (though Dickens himself was surprised when that coincidence was pointed out to him). But now that more is known about Dickens' life, it is clear that he changed the facts a great deal to write *David Copperfield*, Let's compare the two stories.

Whereas David is a naive village boy and an orphan, Charles Dickens spent his childhood in the bustling seaside towns of Portsmouth and Chatham, on the southern coast of England, and was the second of eight children. His parents, John and Elizabeth Dickens, were charming and utterly irresponsible people, who lived far beyond Mr. Dickens' salary as a civil servant. When their financial situation grew desperate, they packed up and moved to London, to a cramped, grubby house, where bill-collectors were continually hammering at the door. Finally John Dickens was arrested for debt and sent to Marshal sea Prison. Most of the family moved in with him (a typical arrangement in debtors' prison, which was a fairly open place), but twelve-year-old Charles lived outside in rented rooms so he could work in a factory, pasting labels on bottles of boot blacking (a kind of shoe polish).

Although this experience lasted only four months, it scarred Charles so profoundly that he never spoke of it to anyone. We only know about it from a fragment of writing he once silently showed to his closest friend-and from his fictional treatment of it, when he sends David Copperfield to work in a similar sweatshop. Dickens never really forgave his parents-especially his mother, who had pushed the idea hardest for sending him to the factory.

Perhaps that is why he later identified so readily with the orphans in his novels, and wrote glowing descriptions of the "perfect" family he felt he'd never had. It's interesting, however, that John and Elizabeth Dickens' delightful personalities seem to have been the models for David's friends, the Micawbers, while Dickens created for David a wicked stepfather, Mr. Murdstone-a worthy target for the anger that still boiled deep in Dickens' heart.

A surprise inheritance from a distant relative freed the Dickens family from prison. Yet it took a bit of arguing for Charles to persuade his mother to let him quit working and go back to school. Unfortunately, he was finally sent to school, Wellington House that was run by a cruel headmaster who liked to beat boys, much like Mr. Creakle at Salem House, where David begins school. Whereas David later gets a good education from Dr. Strong, Charles had to make do with the little he learned at Wellington House. Again Charles was resentful, sensing that he had talent and feeling thwarted by his inferior education. He went to work first as a clerk in a lawyer's office and then, dissatisfied with law, learned shorthand so that he could get a job taking down the debates in Parliament for a newspaper that published transcripts of them. David Copperfield does this, too.

When he was seventeen, Dickens fell in love with Maria Beadnell, who by all accounts was as winsome and flirtatious as David Copperfield's sweetheart, Dora. Maria's father, a banker, apparently disapproved of Dickens, and after a couple of years, he sent his daughter abroad to separate them, just as Dora's father threatens to do in David Copperfield. Maria showed no interest in Charles after her return, and he felt crushed. In describing David Copperfield's courtship of Dora, Dickens may have been reliving his infatuation with Maria-and, in David's marriage to Dora, Dickens may have been speculating on what could have happened if he had married Maria. (Soon after publishing David Copperfield, Dickens would run into Maria Beadnell again and discover, with chagrin, that the living model for Dora had become a fat and extremely silly middle-aged matron.)

Hurt by Maria's rejection, Dickens threw himself into hard work. Then began another courtship, this time with Catherine Hogarth, the daughter of a fellow journalist. He was so desperate to settle down that he did not judge his prospective bride carefully, for they were not suited for each other in the long run. David's disappointment with his "child-wife" Dora may be realistically drawn from Charles' eventual discontent with the woman he did marry-dull, sweet Catherine.

But before he could get married, Dickens, like David, had to work furiously to set himself up in his career. He had won some fame as a journalist, and in 1836, just before his wedding, he published his first work of fiction-*Pickwick Papers,* a loosely connected series of comical sketches. This book appeared in serial installments, as all of his novels would. Month by month Dickens' fame mushroomed. Suddenly he was a celebrity. Even while Pickwick was still appearing, Dickens began a new book, *Oliver Twist,* which also was a best seller and he kept producing hits, year after year. By the time *David Copperfield,* his seventh novel, appeared in 1850, Charles Dickens was a British national institution.

To be a best-selling novelist in nineteenth-century England

was practically like being a pop star today. In those days before movies, radio, or television, people read novels as their main form of entertainment. They did not think of them as "literature." Dickens' books did a lot to make novels more respectable, because his novels were read by all levels of society. Intellectuals pored over them for their political satire and social commentary. Middle-class families in their cozy parlors looked forward to reading Dickens' latest book, admiring his sentimental scenes and moral messages. In poorer neighborhoods, people might gather in groups, breathlessly listening to it being read aloud; they laughed at the broad comedy and gasped at the thrilling suspense. Dickens had hit upon a formula for pleasing everybody: he spanned all levels of society with his multilayered plots and huge cast of characters, and he ended each serial installment with a thrilling climax, to make his readers rush out to buy the next month's.

Having begun his career as a political journalist, Dickens used his novels to examine problems he saw in society. In Oliver Twist, for example, he exposed the wretched living conditions of England's poorhouses and slums. In *Nicholas Nickleby* he attacked the cruel, negligent Yorkshire boarding schools. *In Bleak House* he went after the Court of Chancery. Thus, in *David Copperfield,* he protests against the sexual mores of his age that condemned "fallen" women-unmarried women (usually poor) who had affairs or gave birth to illegitimate children. He also shows the misery of child labour. (While his original readers probably assumed the warehouse scenes were invented for purposes of satire, we now know that Dickens was recording actual memories of his secret past.) Dickens criticizes the antiquated legal institution of Doctors' Commons in a few passages. He also devotes a chapter to satirizing prison reform.

Some of these bursts of satire are not really central to the book. It is almost as if Dickens felt he had to include satire, because that was what he was known for in that era. Much of Dickens' popularity was based on his reputation as a social critic. Many middle-class Victorians liked to think of themselves as concerned citizens, whose rational, humane efforts were creating the perfect society. Dickens was, like them, a reformer but not a radical. These reformers had already improved some of the conditions he criticized by the time he wrote about them. Dickens had no interest in tearing apart the framework of society-only in improving it to come closer to his ideals of justice and Christian charity. He was actually more of a conservative than many readers realise.

Some readers see the publication of David Copperfield as the turning point in Dickens' career. Until then, in novels such as Oliver Twist, Nicholas Nickleby, and Dombey and Son, he had written very much with his audience in mind. All the elements of comedy, melodrama, mystery, and social criticism appear in those books, for the author seems most concerned with entertaining his readers. But David Copperfield gave Dickens an opportunity to be more personal, to write about his own life and explore individual human nature rather than society as a whole. His later novels, such as Little Dorrit, Great Expectations, and Our Mutual Friend, move further into this psychological territory and leave satire further behind.

At the time, he wrote *David Copperfield*, Dickens was popular, admired, famous, and rich, just as David Copperfield is at the end of the novel. Yet Dickens' later years did not bring him the happy ending he had written for David. He found that the success he had driven so hard for only increased the demands upon his time and energies. He felt his ideal of domestic harmony falling to pieces. In 1858, he and his wife separated a scandalous action in those days. Though his ten children remained with him in his huge country house, he was bitterly disappointed by his sons' failures. Melancholy, restless, and irritable, he continued to write novels, but they became tinged with pessimism about human nature and society. He tried to stave off depression with more and more work, as well as with amateur theatricals, lecture tours, and dramatic readings from his own works. But this frenzied activity only hastened his death of a stroke in 1870.

Like most great artists, Dickens was a complex man, perhaps more complex than his character David Copperfield. His writer's instincts compelled him to shape the events of his life into a richer, more artistic form when he wrote about them in *David Copperfield*. If you want to read a biography of Dickens, there are plenty to choose from. But if you want to read a great work of literature, turn to *David Copperfield*.

From a very early age Charles Dickens knew he wanted to be gentleman. Unfortunately, the odds weren't in his favour.

His family was constantly on the edge of financial and social disaster. However, they did have some limited funds put aside to send one of their children to a university or academy. Mr. and Mrs. John Dickens considered the talents and qualifications of all their children. They wanted to use the money earmarked for education where it would do the most good. It was as if they were placing all their bets on one child.

Charles was not that child. His parents chose to send their daughter, Fanny, to school. She had a talent for music and was sent to an academy. Not long after that Charles was sent to work at the blacking factory.

It seemed as if everything was against him. However, he had talent, and more importantly he had desire, drive and a strong belief in himself. He worked hard to make his dream life into a reality.

Charles Dickens wasn't perfect. He was stubborn and sometimes quick tempered. He often blamed others for the problems that he himself caused. The force of will that enabled him to succeed prevented him from taking an honest look at his own life.

While he was unable to learn from the lessons of his own life perhaps we, his readers, can be more fortunate. A study of his life reveals that perfection is not a qualification for success and that no one really defines us but ourselves.

The Childhood of Charles Dickens

Charles Dickens was born on February 7, 1812 in Portsmouth. His parents were John and Elizabeth Dickens. Charles was the second of their eight children.

John was a clerk in a payroll office of the navy. He and Elizabeth were an outgoing, social couple. They loved parties, dinners and family functions. In fact, Elizabeth attended a ball on the night that she gave birth to Charles.

Finances were a constant concern for the family. The costs of entertaining along with the expenses of having a large family were too much for John's salary. In fact, when Charles was just four months old the family moved to a smaller home to cut expenses.

Mary Weller was an early influence on Charles. She was hired to care for the Dickens children. Her bedtime stories, stories she swore were quite true, featured people like Captain Murder who would make pies of out his wives.

The young woman who brought me acquainted with Captain Murderer had a fiendish enjoyment of my terrors, and used to begin, I remember - as a sort of introductory overture - by clawing the air with both hands, and uttering a long low hollow groan. So acutely did I suffer from this ceremony in combination with this infernal Captain, that I sometimes used to plead I thought I was hardly strong enough and old enough to hear the story again just yet. - *The Uncommercial Traveller - Nurse's Stories*

From a very young age, Charles dreamed of becoming a gentleman. He wanted an education. His parents did have some limited funds put aside to send one of their children to a university or academy. Mr. and Mrs. John Dickens considered the talents and qualifications of all their children. They wanted to use the money earmarked for education where it would do the most good. It was as if they were placing all their bets on one child. Charles was not that child.

His parents chose to send their daughter, Fanny, to school. She had a talent for music and was sent to an academy.

Then came the darkest hours in the life of Charles Dickens. When he was 12 it looked like his dreams would never come true. John Dickens was arrested and sent to jail for failure to pay a debt. At that time, the family sent Charles to work in a blacking or shoe-polish factory. (While employed there he met Bob Fagin. Charles later used the name in *Oliver Twist*.) Charles was deeply marked by these experiences. He rarely spoke of this time of his life.

Luckily, the situation improved within a year. Charles was

released from his duties at the factory and his father was released from jail.

Law Clerk to Journalist

The start of 1827 found Charles Dickens enrolled as a student at Wellington House Academy. In May, through connections made by his mother, he obtained a position at the law firm of Ellis and Blackmore.

Dickens was a law clerk. His duties included keeping the petty cash fund, delivering documents, running errands and other sundry tasks.

In November of 1828, Dickens took a similar position for the law firm of Charles Molley. However, Dickens remained with the firm for only a few months.

The law did not appeal to him as a career. He found the work of a law clerk tedious. Actually becoming a lawyer did not appeal to him either. So, he left to find another way to make a living.

His next job was as a court stenographer. To qualify for that position Dickens had to learn the Gurney system of shorthand writing. It took most people about three years to master the system. Dickens, no doubt aided by his excellent memory, learned it in about three months. Consequently, in 1829 he began work as a freelance court stenographer.

In 1831, he became a shorthand reporter with the *Mirror of Parliament*. The publication gave accounts of the activity in the House of Commons and the House of Lords. Dickens became known for his quick and accurate courtroom reporting.

During this time, he also considered becoming an actor. He was so serious about the matter that he arranged for an audition at the Lyceum Theater. However, he was ill on the day of his audition and could not go. He did have acting skills as proven later by his readings and performances in benefit productions. His life might have been dramatically different if it were not for his illness on that day.

In 1833, he began writing "sketches" or essays. His sketches continued to grow in popularity. They eventually led to the publication of the *The Pickwick Papers* in 1836.

"Vell," said Mr. Weller, "Now I s'pose he'll want to call

some witnesses to speak to his character, or p'raps to prove a alleybi. I've been a turnin' the bis'ness over in my mind, and he may make his-self easy, Sammy. I have some friends, as will do either for him, but my adwice 'ud be this here—never mind the character, and stick to the alleybi. Nothing like a alleybi, Sammy, nothing." - *The Pickwick Papers*.

I have tamed that savage stenographic mystery. I make a respectable income by it. I am in high repute for my accomplishment in all pertaining to the art, and am joined with eleven others in reporting the debates in Parliament for a Morning Newspaper. Night after night, I record predictions that never come to pass, professions that are never fulfilled, explanations that are only meant to mystify. I wallow in words. Britannia, that unfortunate female, is always before me, like a trussed fowl: skewered through and through with office-pens, and bound hand and foot with red tape. I am sufficiently behind the scenes to know the worth of political life. I am quite an Infidel about it, and shall never be converted. - *David Copperfield*

Maria Beadnell

Maria Beadnell was the first love of Charles Dickens. They met in 1830 and he fell madly in love with her. For Charles it was love at first sight. His mind was quickly filled with thoughts of ever-lasting romance and marriage.

However her parents did not approve of the relationship. Mr. Beadnell was a banker. He felt that Charles was too young and lacking in prospects to be considered a serious suitor.

During these years, Dickens worked as a court stenographer and shorthand reporter. His own dissatisfaction with his career and a desire to make a more favorable impression with the Beadnells lead him to consider becoming an actor. He even went so far as to schedule an audition. However he was sick on that day and missed his appointment.

The youthful Maria later inspired the character of Dora in *David Copperfield:*

I don't remember who was there, except Dora. I have not

the least idea what we had for dinner, besides Dora. My impression is, that I dined off Dora, entirely, and sent away half-a-dozen plates untouched. I sat next to her. I talked to her. She had the most delightful little voice, the gayest little laugh, the pleasantest and most fascinating little ways that ever led a lost youth into hopeless slavery. She was rather diminutive altogether. So much the more precious, I thought. - *David Copperfield*

We'll never know the nature of Maria's feelings for Charles. She sometimes treated him with indifference and sometimes seemed to encourage his affections. Later in life she claimed that she truly cared for him.

In early 1833, when Charles became twenty-one, he threw himself a coming-of-age party. The Beadnells were invited and accepted the invitation. During the evening Dickens was able to speak privately to Maria. He spoke of his feelings for her. She insulted him badly by referring to him as a "boy". Their relationship ended later that year. Maria Beadnell went on to become Mrs. Henry Winter.

After a twenty-four year separation, Maria contacted Dickens. They were both married and Dickens, the man who had been lacking in prospects, had become a famous author.

Dickens was thrilled upon receiving her letter. The letter from Maria brought back the memories of his intense love for her and perhaps fantasies of what might have been.

In 1855, they agreed to a secret meeting without their spouses. Maria warned Dickens that she was not the same young woman that he remembered. Despite her warnings, he apparently was surprised at the changes he saw in his first love. His feelings inspired him to base the character of of Flora Finching in *Little Dorrit* on Maria.

Flora, always tall, had grown to be very broad too, and short of breath; but that was not muchapter Flora, whom he had left a lily, had become a peony; but that was not muchapter Flora, who had seemed enchanting in all she said and thought, was diffuse and silly. That was muchapter Flora, who had been spoiled and artless long ago, was determined to be spoiled and artless now. That was a fatal blow. - *Little Dorrit*

They met once more for a dinner with their spouses. However after that, despite Maria's wishes for further contact, Dickens avoided her.

The Marriage of Charles Dickens

Catherine Hogarth was the eldest daughter of George and Georgina Hogarth. Catherine was born in Scotland. In 1834, she and her family moved to England where her father had taken a job as a music critic for the *Morning Chronicle.*

Charles Dickens, young and unattached, was also employed by the *Morning Chronicle.* His first romantic relationship, with Maria Beadnell, had ended badly. However, he was quite recovered and was quickly taken with Catherine.

They met in 1834, became engaged in 1835 and were married in April of 1836. In January of 1837 the first of their ten children was born.

The early years of their marriage were apparently quite happy. Dickens was in love with his young wife and she was very proud of her famous husband. In 1841, the couple traveled to Scotland. In 1842, they traveled to America together.

After the 1842 trip to America, Catherine's sister Georgina came to live with the couple. Catherine was becoming overwhelmed the duties of being the wife of a famous man and mother of ten children. Georgina stepped in to fill the gaps and eventually ran the Dickens household.

Dickens grew unhappy with Catherine and his marriage. He resented the fact that he had so many children to support. He did not approve of Catherine's lack of energy. He began to indicate that she was not nor had ever been his intellectual equal.

In 1855, his discontent leads him to accept an invitation to meet with his former girlfriend, Maria Beadnell. Maria had married and had become Mrs. Henry Winter. However, Mrs. Henry Winter did not live up to Dickens' romantic memories and nothing ever came of the reunion.

In 1857, Dickens met the woman who was to be his companion until his death, Ellen Ternan. Ellen, her mother and her sister were hired to act in a benefit presentation of *The Frozen Deep*. Their co-star, Charles Dickens, sponsored the event.

Dickens' life with Catherine seemed even more insufferable after meeting Ellen. Dickens wrote to his friend John Forster, "Poor Catherine and I are not made for each other, and there is no help for it. It is not only that she makes me uneasy and unhappy, but that I make her so too—and much more so."

In 1857, Charles and Catherine took separate bedrooms.

In the spring of 1858, a bracelet that Dickens bought as a present for Ellen was accidentally delivered to the Dickens household. Catherine discovered the bracelet and accused Dickens of having an affair. Dickens denied the accusation and said it was his custom to give small gifts to people that acted in his plays.

In June of 1858, Catherine and Charles were legally separated. Days later Dickens published a notice in the *London Times* and *Household Words* that tried to explain the separation to the public. In the notice he stated, "Some domestic trouble of mine, of long-standing, on which I will make no further remark than that it claims to be respected. As being of a sacredly private nature, has lately been brought to an arrangement, which involves no anger or ill-will of any kind, and the whole origin, progress, and surrounding circumstances of which have been, throughout, within the knowledge of my children. It is amicably composed, and its details have now to be forgotten by those concerned in it."

While an announcement of this sort seems extreme, Dickens was motivated to do so by some of the rumors circulating about the break-up. There was some gossip about an actress and some stories even suggested that Dickens was having an affair with his sister-in-law, Georgina. The second rumor was particularly upsetting because in those times such a relationship was incestuous.

Despite assurances that things were "amicably composed" Dickens and Catherine were never again on pleasant terms. Catherine was given a house. Their oldest son, Charley, moved in with her. Dickens retained custody of the rest of the children. While the children were not forbidden to visit their mother they were not encouraged to do so.

Catherine lived for another twenty years after the separation. Deprived of both the role of wife and mother, she never seemed to recover from the breakup of her marriage.

Gad's Hill Place

When he was a boy Charles Dickens and his father took a walk through Kent. On Gravesend Road they passed, a house called Gad's Hill Place. Young Charles was very impressed.

His family was plagued with financial problems. However, this imposing structure seemed to be part of a different world. His father noted his interest and told Charles that if he "were to be very persevering and work very hard" he might one day live there. He did, he bought the house in 1856 and lived there until his death in 1870.

Charles Dickens and Mesmerism

In 1849 John Leech, a friend of Charles Dickens, was injured. The accident left Leech with concussion-like symptoms that would not disappear despite all the work of his doctors. Leech was in a great deal of pain and unable to rest. Dickens heard of the incident and rushed to his friend's aid. Within a few days, Leech's condition had significantly improved. What could Dickens do that the doctors couldn't? Dickens helped his friend via the use of mesmerism.

Mesmerism was developed by Franz Anton Mesmer. It used hypnotic trances to heal people. In 1838, Dickens attended several lectures on the subject including some by John Elliotson. Elliotson was the professor of clinical medicine who introduced the stethoscope to England. He also had campaigned against corrupt medical practices. Despite his many accomplishments, Elliotson was forced to resign his teaching position in 1839 because of a scandal regarding mesmerism.

Despite the controversy, Dickens was a believer in mesmerism. Elliotson taught Dickens the technique and it quickly became apparent that Dickens was skilled in this area.

Initially he mesmerized family and friends just for fun or to help with minor illnesses. However, in late 1844 he took on a more serious case that of Madame de la Rue.

Augusta de la Rue suffered from extreme anxiety. It was so profound that it caused noticeable facial tics or spasms. Dickens was eager to help and during the next few months, he treated her frequently. The treatments were effective. After a month, Madame de la Rue showed much improvement. She was able to sleep and night and visibly looked more relaxed.

Once the physical symptoms of Madame de la Rue eased, Dickens became interested in their underlying causes. The sessions began to focus more on Madame de la Rue's dreams, hallucinations and thoughts. She spoke of being pursued by a"phantom". Their sessions became almost like those of a therapist and a patient.

How exactly did mesmerism work? Perhaps it acted as a tranquilizer and promoted rest. At this point, it is hard to say. However, the health of Leech and de la Rue did seem to improve after being treated by Dickens.

Bonfire at Gad's Hill Place

In September of 1860, behind his home at Gad's Hill Place, Charles Dickens tried to cover his tracks. He gathered "the accumulated letters and papers of twenty years" and set them ablaze in his backyard.

What moved him to such drastic action? There seem to be two factors in his life that drove him to make a bonfire of his correspondence.

The first is fear of the press. He was concerned that his personal letters would be published and details of his life would become public knowledge. What did he have to hide?

In 1858, he had a very public separation from his wife, but it was not widely known that he had a mistress. Ellen Ternan, his mistress, was an actress who was much younger than Dickens. If his relationship with Ellen were public knowledge, it would have created a scandal.

In 1843, he'd written about workhouses and prisons in *A Christmas Carol*. However very few people knew that

Dickens's father had been sent to Marshal sea prison for failure to pay a debt and that Charles Dickens, then only twelve years old, was sent to work in a shoe-polish factory. Dickens was deeply scarred by these incidents and rarely spoke of them.

A second inspiration for the bonfire at Gad's Hill Place could have been that Dickens was at a turning point in his life. The destruction of his private papers might have been his way of coming to terms with his past.

In 1860, he was still coming to terms with the separation from his wife and his relationship with Ellen. Also in July of that year his favourite daughter, Katie, married and left Gad's Hill Place. Ten days after the wedding Dickens's brother, Alfred, died. Additionally Dickens's mother had become senile and needed constant care. All of these items could have motivated Dickens, at least on a subconscious level, to try to free himself from the demons of his past.

Whatever his motivations we can only imagine the things we might have learned about the era, Dickens's life and the lives of famous Victorians. Burned on that day were letters from authors like Wilkie Collins, George Eliot and William Makepeace Thackeray.

Dickens's two youngest sons, Henry and Plorn, carried out baskets and baskets of letters to feed into the fire. His daughter Mamie begged him to reconsider and save some of the letters. However, Dickens was determined that the task must be completed. As they were finishing it began to rain. Dickens said, "... I suspect my correspondence of having overcast the face of the Heavens."

The Staplehurst Railway Accident

In June of 1865, Charles Dickens was involved in the Staplehurst railway accident. Dickens was returning from a trip to Paris. In the coach with him were Ellen Ternan and her mother.

The train track was being repaired near Staplehurst. Workers did not signal to oncoming trains that there was a gap, 42 feet long, in the tracks over a bridge. The train's engineer spotted the problem at the last minute, but it was too late. Momentum carried the engine and the first part of the train across the breachapter However, the coaches in the centre and the rear of the train fell into the riverbed below. All but one of the first-class coaches went into the ravine. That was the coach who carried Dickens, Ellen Ternan and Mrs. Ternan.

While their carriage did not fall into gap, it was hanging off the bridge at a steep angle. Dickens and Mrs. Ternan were uninjured. Ellen had only minor injuries. Others were not as lucky. Ten people were killed and about fifty were injured.

Once Dickens helped the Ternans from the coach, he went about the work of assisting his fellow passengers. He retrieved a flask of brandy from the train as well as his top hat. He filled the hat with water and then did what he could to aid and comfort the injured. Later, he said that the scene was unimaginable.

One poor man was visible to the rescuers, but there was no way to help him escape. The man later died, still pinned under the train. At one point Dickens gave an injured lady who was resting under a tree a sip of brandy. The next time he passed her she was dead. For three long hours, Dickens did what he could to lessen people's pain and suffering.

When help finally arrived and the accident scene was being evacuated Dickens remembered something. There was still something in his train compartment that he needed. He made his way back into the wrecked train one last time to retrieve the latest installment of *Our Mutual Friend*, the novel he was writing at the time.

For years afterward, Dickens would sometimes suffer from sudden feelings of anxiety when he was traveling by rail.

In the postscript for *Our Mutual Friend* Dickens wrote:

On Friday the Ninth of June in the present year, Mr. and Mrs. Boffin (in their manuscript dress of receiving Mr. and Mrs. Lammle at breakfast) were on the South Eastern Railway with me, in a terribly destructive accident. When I had done what I could to help others, I climbed back into my carriage—nearly turned over a viaduct, and caught aslant upon the turn—to extricate the worthy couple. They were much soiled, but otherwise unhurt. The same happy result attended Miss Bella

Wilfer on her wedding day, and Mr. Riderhood inspecting Bradley Headstone's red neckerchief as he lay asleep. I remember with devout thankfulness that I can never be much nearer parting company with my readers forever, than I was then, until there shall be written against my life, the two words with which I have this day closed this book:—THE END.

The Children of Charles Dickens

Charles and Catherine Dickens had ten children. There is circumstantial evidence that Dickens and Ellen Ternan had a child that died shortly after being born. However this has never been proven.

Charles Culliford Boz Dickens (1837-1896)

Charles was known as Charley within the family. Charley married Bessie Evans despite the fact that his father had disagreements with Bessie's father. Charley was involved in banking and business. In 1868 he went into bankruptcy and was then hired by his father to work at All The Year Round. He bought Gad's Hill Place after his father died, but later gave it up because of his own failing health.

Mary Dickens (1838-1896)

Mary was named after her mother's sister who died in 1837. After her father's death she lived with her aunt, Georgina. Mary went on to write *My Father as I Recall Him*.

Kate Macready Dickens (1839-1929)

When Dickens and Catherine separated Kate was the only child to stand up to Dickens and side with Catherine. That shouldn't have been a surprise to Dickens as Kate had been called "Lucifer Box" within the family because of her fiery temper. She married Charles Allston Collins and after his death she married Carlo Perugini.

Walter Landor Dickens (1841-1863)

Walter achieved the rank of lieutenant in the East India Company. It looked like he had a bright future, but sadly things started to fall apart for Walter. Like many of his family members he fell into debt. At about this time he also became ill. He passed away of an aortic aneurysm and left many unpaid bills to his father

Francis Jeffrey Dickens (1844-1886)

Francis considered many careers including medicine, farming and journalism. He ended up joining the Bengal Mounted Police. Later he joined Canada's Northwest Mounted Police. In 1886 he resigned his commission and passed away within the year.

Alfred D'Orsay Tennyson Dickens (1845-1912)

When he was 20 Alfred left England, as well as many unpaid bills, and went to Australia. There he married the "Belle of Melbourne", Jessie Devlin. Sadly she died in a carriage accident four years later leaving Alfred alone with their two girls. After his father's death Alfred gave lectures on his father's life and work.

Sydney Smith Haldimand Dickens (1847-1872)

Charles Dickens was very proud of Sydney's naval career. However later he was very displeased about Sydney's financial troubles. Sydney passed away when he was only twenty five. He died while trying to return home for sick leave.

Henry Fielding Dickens (1849-1933)

Henry was nicknamed Harry and is often called the most successful of Dickens' children. He was a sportsman and had a very successful career in law. In 1922 he was knighted. Henry was the grandfather of Monica Dickens who became an author like her great grandfather. Among her works is One Pair of Hands.

Dora Annie Dickens (1850-1851)

Dora was named after a character from one of her father's novels, Dora from David Copperfield. Dora was never a strong baby and died when she was only eight months old.

Edward Bulwer Lytton Dickens (1852-1902)

Edward was nicknamed Plorn. He left England to join his brother Alfred in Australia. Edward became a Member of Parliament in New South Wales.

Chapter 5

The Friends of Charles Dickens

Ellen Ternan

In 1857 Ellen, her mother and her sister were hired to act in a benefit presentation of *The Frozen Deep*. Their co-star, Charles Dickens, sponsored the event. This first meeting lead to an affair that would last until his death in 1870.

Wilkie Collins

Although twelve years younger than Dickens, Wilkie Collins became one of Dickens best friends. Collins was a popular novelist who helped to develop the mystery novel genre. *The Moonstone* is one of his best. He and Dickens wrote *The Frozen Deep*.

John Forster

John Forster was a biographer and historian. His close friendship with Dickens began when Forster critiqued his work. Later Forster wrote a book about his famous friend, *Life of Dickens*.

William Makepeace Thackeray

This author wrote *Vanity Fair*. He was also a friend of Charles Dickens.

Quotes by William Makepeace Thackeray

- "No, you are not worthy of the love which I have devoted to you. I knew all along that the prize I had set my life on was not worth the winning; that I was a fool, with fond fancies, too, bartering away my all of truth and ardour against your little feeble remnant of love. I will bargain no more: I withdraw."

- A woman with fair opportunities, and without an absolute hump, may marry whom she likes.
- The world is a looking glass, and gives back to every man the reflection of his own face. Frown at it, and it will in turn look sourly upon you; laugh at it and with it, and it is a jolly kind companion; and so let all young persons take their choice
- Mother is the name for God in the lips and hearts of little children.
- The true pleasure of life is to live with your inferiors
- The wicked are wicked, no doubt, they go astray, they fall, and they come by their deserts: but who can tell the mischief which the very virtuous do?
- "'Tis not the dying for a faith that's so hard, Master Harry—every man of every nation has done that—'tis the living up to it that is difficult... "
- 'Tis strange what a man may do, and a woman yet think him an angel
- 'Tis misfortune that awakens ingenuity, or fortitude, or endurance, in hearts where these qualities had never come to life but for the circumstance which gave them a being.
- He had placed himself at her feet so long that the poor little woman had been accustomed to trample upon him. She did not wish to marry him, but she wished to keep him. She wished to give him nothing, but that he should give her all. It is a bargain not infrequently levied in love.

Edgar Allan Poe

Poe was an American author best known for his poems and short fiction. *The Fall of the House of Usher* and *The Murders in the Rue Morgue* are two of his most popular works.

Dickens met Edgar Allan Poe in Philadelphia while Dickens was on his first tour of the United States. They talked about literature and seemed to enjoy one another's company. However two years later Poe broke off the relationship because he was angry about an article on American poetry. The article was written by Thackarey, but Poe believed that Dickens was behind the article.

Quotes by Edgar Allan Poe

- The best chess-player in Christendom may be little more than the best player of chess; but proficiency in whist implies capacity for success in all those more important undertakings where mind struggles with mind
- By undue profundity, we perplex and enfeeble thought; and it is possible to make even Venus herself vanish from the firmament by a scrutiny too sustained, too concentrated, or too direct.
- A valet, of stealthy step, thence conducted me, in silence, through many dark and intricate passages in my progress to the studio of his master.
- I have, indeed, no abhorrence of danger, except in its absolute effect - in terror.
- Deep into that darkness peering, long I stood there wondering, fearing,
  Doubting, dreaming dreams no mortals ever dared to dream before;
- Deep into that darkness peering, long I stood there wondering, fearing,

Doubting, dreaming dreams no mortals ever dared to dream before;

- Once upon a midnight dreary, while I pondered, weak and weary,
  Over many a quaint and curious volume of forgotten lore—

Chapter 6

Dicken's Satire

SATIRIC PORTRAITURE

Not only does Dickens give poetic shape to the better characteristics of English life; he is also England's satirist. Often directed against abuses in their temporary nature, his satire has in some part lost its edge, and would have only historic interest but for the great preservative, humour, mingled with all his books. Much of it, however, is of enduring significance, and reminds us that the graver faults of Englishmen are not to be overcome by a few years of popular education, by general increase of comfort and refinement, by the spread of a democratic spirit. Some of these blemishes, it is true, belong more or less to all mankind; but in Dickens's England they were peculiarly disfiguring, and the worst of them seem inseparable from the national character.

Much as they loved and glorified him, his countrymen did not fail to make protest when wounded by the force of his satiric portraiture. The cry was "exaggeration". Naturally, this protest was very loud during the publication of *Martin Chuzzlewit*, in which book a vice supposed to be peculiarly English was vigorously dealt with. Dickens used the opportunity of a preface to answer his critics; he remarked that peculiarities of character often escape observation until they are directly pointed out, and asked whether the charge of exaggeration brought against him might not simply mean that he, a professed student of life, saw more than ordinary people. There was undoubted truth in the plea; Browning has put the same thought — as an apology for art — into the mouth of Fra Lippo Lippi. Dickens assuredly saw a great deal more in every day of his life than his average readers in threescore years and ten. But it remained a question whether, in his desire to stigmatize an objectionable peculiarity, the satirist had not erred by making this peculiarity the whole man. Exaggeration there was, beyond dispute, in such a picture as that of Pecksniff, inasmuch as no man can be so consistently illustrative of an evil habit of mind. There was lack of proportion; the figure failed in human symmetry. Just as, in the same book, the pictures of American life erred through one-sidedness. Dickens had written satire, and satire as pointed, as effective, as any in literature. Let the galled jade wince; there was an outcry of many voices, appealing to common judgment. It might be noted that these same sensitive critics had never objected to "exaggeration" when the point at issue was merely one of art; they became aware of their favourite author's defect only when it involved a question of morals or of national character.

Merely as satirist, however, Dickens never for a moment endangered his popularity. The fact, already noticed, that *Martin Chuzzlewit* found fewer admirers than the books preceding it, had nothing to do with its moral theme. But must be traced to causes, generally more or less vague, such as from time to time affect the reception of every author's work; not long after its completion, this book became one of the most widely read. There is the satire, which leaves cold, or alienates, the ordinary man, because it passes above his head, or conflicts with his cherished prejudices. There is the satire, which, by appealing to his better self, — that is, to a standard of morality which he theoretically, or in very deed, accepts, — commands his sympathy as soon as he sees its drift. What is called the "popular conscience" was on Dickens's side; and he had the immense advantage of being able to raise a hearty laugh even whilst pointing his lesson. Among the rarest of things is this thorough understanding between author and public, permitting a man of genius to say aloud with impunity that which all his hearers say within themselves dumbly, inarticulately. Dickens never went too far; never struck at a genuine conviction of the multitude. Let us imagine him, in some moment of aberration, suggesting criticism of the popular idea of sexual morality! Would it have availed him that he had done the state some service? Would argument or authority have helped for one moment to win him a patient hearing? We know that he never desired to provoke such antagonism. Broadly speaking, he was one with his readers, and therein lay his strength for reform.

As for the charge of exaggeration, the truth is that Dickens exaggerated no whit more in his satire than in his sympathetic portraiture. It is an idle objection. Of course, he exaggerated, in all but every page. In the last chapter I pointed to exceptional instances of literal or subdued truthfulness; not by these did he achieve his triumphs; they lurk for discovery by the curious. Granting his idealistic method, such censure falls wide of the mark. We are struck more forcibly when a character is exhibited as compact of knavery or grotesque cruelty, than when it presents incarnate goodness; that is all. The one question we are justified in urging is, whether his characterization is consistent with itself. In the great majority of cases, I believe the answer must be affirmative. Were it not so, Dickens's reputation would by this time linger only among the untaught; among those who are content to laugh, no matter how the mirth be raised.

His satire covers a great part of English life, public and private. Education, charity, religion, social morality in its broadest sense, society in its narrowest; legal procedure, the machinery of politics, and the forms of government. Licensed to speak his mind, he aims laughingly or sternly, but always in the same admirable spirit, at every glaring abuse of the day. He devotes a whole book, a prodigy of skilful labour, to that crowning example of the law's delay, which had wrought ruin in innumerable homes; he throws off a brilliant little sketch, in a Christmas number, and makes everybody laugh at the absurd defects of railway refreshment-rooms. We marvel at such breadth of untiring observation in the service of human welfare. Impossible to follow him through all the achievements of his satire; I can but select examples in each field, proceeding in the order just indicated.

It is natural that he should turn, at the beginning of his career, to abuses evident in the parish, the school, the place of worship. These were nearest at hand; they stared at him in his observant childhood, and during his life as a journalist. Consequently, we soon meet with Mr. Bumble, with Mr. Squeers, with the Rev. Mr. Stiggins. Of these three figures, the one most open to the charge of exaggeration is the Yorkshire schoolmaster; yet who shall declare with assurance that Squeers's brutality outdoes the probable in his place and generation. There is crude workmanship in the portrait, and still more in the picture of Dotheboys, where overcharging defeats its own end. The extraordinary feature of this bit of work is the inextricable blending of horror and jocosity. Later, when Dickens had fuller command of his resources, he would have made Dotheboys very much more impressive; it remains an illustration of superabundant spirits in a man of genius. We can hardly help an amiable feeling towards the Squeers family, seeing the hearty gusto with which they pursue their monstrous business.

The children who suffer under them are so shadowy that we cannot feel the wrong as we ought; such a spectacle should lay waste the heart, and yet we continue smiling. Dickens, of course, did not intend that this gathering of martyred children should have the effect of reality. Enough if he called attention to the existence of a monstrous state of things; reflection shall come afterwards; his immediate business is story telling, that is to say, amusement. Wonderfully did he adapt means to ends; we find, in fact, that nothing could have been practically more effectual than this exhibition of strange gaiety. Mr. Bumble, though he comes earlier, is, in truth, better work than Squeers. Read carefully chapter iv of *Oliver Twist*, and you will discover, probably to your surprise, that the "porochial" functionary is, after all, human: in one line — in a delicate touch — we are shown Bumble softened, to the point of a brief silence, by Oliver's pleading for kind usage. No such moment occurs in the history of Squeers. And we see why not. The master of

Dotheboys is not meant for a conscientious study of a human being; he is merely the representative of a vile institution. Admit a lurking humanity, and we have suggestion of possible reform. Now the parochial system, bad as it was, seemed a necessity, and only needed a thorough overhauling, — observe the perfectly human behaviour of certain of the guardians before whom Oliver appears; but with the Yorkshire schools, it was root and branch, they must be swept from the earth. I do not think this is refining overmuch; Dickens's genius declared itself so consistently in his adaptation of literary means to ends of various kinds; and, however immature the details of his performance, he shows from the first this marvellous precision in effect.

Dotheboys was of course, even in these bad times, an exceptional method for the rearing of youth. It is not cold-blooded cruelty, but block-headed ignorance, against which Dickens has to fight over the whole ground of education. We have noticed his attitude towards the system of classical training; the genteel private schools of his day invited satire, and supplied him with some of his most entertaining chapters. Dr. Blimber's establishment is a favourable specimen of the kind of thing that satisfied well-to-do parents; genial ridicule suffices for its condemnation. But Dickens went deeper and laid stress upon the initial stages of the absurd system. Mrs. Pipchin, however distinct a personality, was not singular in her mode of dealing with children fresh from the nursery.

Always profoundly interested in these little people, Dickens, without reaching any very clear conception of reform, well understood the evil consequences of such gross neglect or mistaken zeal as were common in households of every class. He knew that the vices of society could for the most part be traced to these bad beginnings A leader in this as in so many other directions, he taught his readers to think much of children just at the time when England had especial need of an educational awakening. Not his satire alone, but his so-called sentimentality, served a great purpose, and the death-bed of Paul Dombey, no less than the sufferings of Mr. Creakle's little victim, helped on the better day.

Though it has been "proved to demonstration" — by persons who care for such proof — that tenderness of heart led him astray in his bitterness against the new Poor Law, we see, of course, that herein he pursued his humane task, seeking in all possible ways to mitigate the harshness of institutions which pressed hardly upon the poor and weak. He could not away with those who held — or spoke as if they held — that a man had no duty to his fellows beyond the strict letter of the law. In this respect that very poor book, *Hard Times*, has noteworthy significance; but the figures of Gradgrind and Bounderby show how completely he could fail when he dispensed (or all but dispensed) with the aid of humour. Oliver Twist's "old gentleman in the white waistcoat" is decidedly better as portraiture, and as satire more effective. Apologists, or rampant glorifiers, of the workhouse, such as appear in the Christmas Books, need not be viewed too seriously; they stood forth at a season of none too refined joviality, and were in keeping with barons of beef, tons of plum-pudding, and other such heavy extravagances. They do not live in one's mind; nor, I think, does any one of Dickens's persons who are meant to satirize poor-law abuses. In this matter, his spirit did its work, his art not greatly assisting.

But when we come to his lashings of religious hypocrisy, the figures castigated are substantial enough. Always delighted to present a humbug, Dickens can scarce restrain himself when he gets hold of a religious humbug, especially of the coarse type. Brother Stiggins shines immortal in the same pages with Mr. Pickwick and the Wellers. Compare with him the Reverend Mr. Chadband. They are the same men, but one lived in 1837, the other in 1853. Brother Stiggins is, in plain English, a drunkard; Mr. Chadband would think shame of himself to be even once overtaken: he is a consumer of tea and muffins. It suited the author's mood, and the day in which he was writing, to have Mr. Stiggins soundly beaten in a pugilistic encounter with Tony Weller, to say nothing of other undignified positions in which the reverend gentleman finds himself. But Mr. Chadband may discourse upon "Terewth" in Mr. Snagsby's parlour to any length that pleases him with no fear of such outrage. These same discourses are among the most mirth-provoking things in all Dickens: impossible to regard with nothing but contempt or dislike the man who has so shaken our sides. It might be well for the world if the race of Chadband should disappear (a consummation still far out of sight); but the satirist frankly glories in him, and to us he is a joy forever. This is the best of the full-length pictures; but we have many a glimpse of kindred personages, always shown us with infinite gusto. The Rev.

Melchisedech Howler, for instance. With what extravagance of humour, with what a rapture of robust mirth, are his characteristics touched off in a short passage of *Dombey and Son*! I must give myself the pleasure of copying it. "The Rev. Melchisedech Howler, who, having been one day discharged from the West India Docks on a false suspicion (got up expressly against him by the general enemy) of screwing gimlets into puncheons, and applying his lips to the orifice. He had announced the destruction of the world for that day two years, at ten in the morning, and opened a front parlour for the reception of ladies and gentlemen, of the ranting persuasion, upon whom, on the first occasion of their assemblage, the admonition of the Rev.

Melchisedech had produced so powerful effect, that, in their rapturous performance of a sacred jig, which closed the service, the whole flock broke through into a kitchen below and disabled a mangle belonging to one of the fold" (chap. xv). There is a sheer boyishness in this irresistible glee; yet the passage was written more than ten years after *Pickwick*. It is the same all but to the end. Dickens treats a thoroughgoing humbug as though he loved him. Reverent of all true religion, and inclined to bitterness against respectable shortcomings in the high places of the Church, he goes wild with merriment over back-parlour proselytism and the braying of Little Bethel. Perhaps in this respect alone did he give grave and lasting offence to numbers of people who would otherwise have been amongst his admirers. Later, he could draw, or attempt, a sympathetic portrait of a clergyman of the Established Church, in *Our Mutual Friend*, and, in his last book, could speak respectfully of Canons; but with Dissent, he never reconciled himself. To this day, I believe, his books are excluded, on religious grounds, from certain families holding austere views. Remembering the England he sets before us, it is perhaps the highest testimony to his power that such hostility did not make itself more felt when he was mocking so light-heartedly at Stiggins and Chadband and the Rev. Melchisedechapter

Connected with hypocrisy in religion, but very skilfully kept apart from it, is his finest satiric portrait, that of Mr. Pecksniff. Think of all that is suggested in this representative of an odious vice, and marvel at the adroitness with which a hundred pitfalls of the incautious satirist are successfully avoided. A moral hypocrite, an incarnation of middle-class respectability in the worst sense of the word, in the sense so loathed by Carlyle, and by every other man of brains then living; yet never a hint at subjects forbidden in the family circle, never a word to which that relative of Mr. Pecksniff, the famous Podsnap, could possibly object. The thing would seem impossible, but that it is done. Let the understanding read between the lines; as in all great art, much is implied that finds no direct expression. Mr. Pecksniff walks and talks before us, a cause of hilarity to old and young, yet the type of as ugly a failing as any class or people can be afflicted withal.

The book in which he figures is directed against self-interest in all its forms. We see the sagacious swindler, and the greedy dupe whose unscrupulousness ends in murder. We see the flocking of the Chuzzlewit family, like birds of prey, about the sickbed of their wealthy relative. Among them the courteous architect of unctuous phrase, who, hearing himself called a hypocrite, signalizes his pre-eminence in an immortal remark: "Charity, my dear, when I take my chamber-candlestick to-night, remind me to be more than usually particular in praying for Mr. Anthony Chuzzlewit, who has done me an injustice". This man is another than Tartufe; he belongs to a different age, and different country. His religion is not an end in itself; he does not desire to be thought a saint; his prayers are inseparable from the chamber-candlestick, a mere item in the character of British respectability. A like subordination appears in the piety of all Dickens's religious pretenders; their language never becomes offensive to the ordinary reader, simply because it avoids the use of sacred names and phrases, and is seen to have a purely temporal application. Mr. Chadband is a tradesman, dealing in a species of exhortation, which his hearers have agreed to call spiritual, and to rate at a certain value in coin of the realm; religion in its true sense never comes into question.

Mr. Pecksniff, of course, might have become a shining light in some great conventicle, but destiny has made him a layman; he published his habit of praying, because to pray (over the chamber-candlestick) was incumbent upon an Englishman who had a position to support, who had a stake in the country. A reputation for piety, however, would not suffice to his self-respect, and to the needs of his business; he adds an all-embracing benevolence, his smile falls like the blessed sunshine on all who meet him in his daily walk. This it is which so impresses the simple-minded Tom Pinchapter Tom, a thorough Englishman for all his virtues, would not be attracted by a show of merely religious exaltation; faith must be translated into works. Pecksniff must seem to him good, kind, generous, a great man at his profession, sound and trustworthy in all he undertakes.

In other words, the Pecksniff whom Tom believes in is the type of English excellence, and evidently no bad type to be set before a nation. Such men existed, and do, and will; we talk little about them, and it is their last desire that we should; they live, mostly in silence, for the honour of their race and of humankind. But, since the Puritan revolution, it has unhappily seemed necessary to our countrymen in general to profess in a peculiar way certain peculiar forms of godliness, and this habit, gradually associated with social prejudices arising from high prosperity, results in the respectable man. Analysing this person down to his elements, Carlyle found it an essential, if not *the* essential, that he should "keep a gig". Mr. Pecksniff's gig, one remembers, was no very imposing vehicle; it looked "like a gig with a tumours". "Let us be moral", says the great man (happening at that moment to be drunk); and here we get to the honest root of the matter. Though the Englishman may dispense with a gig and remain respectable, he must not be suspected of immorality. "Let us contemplate existence", pursues the inebriate sage. We do so, we English, and find that the term morality (more decidedly than religion) includes all that, in our souls, we rate most highly. According to his recognized morality (sexual first and foremost), do we put trust in a man. We are a practical people; we point to our wealth in evidence; and our experience has set it beyond doubt that chastity of thought and act is a nation's prime safeguard.

Could we but be satisfied with the conviction, and simply act upon it! It is not enough. We must hold it as an article of faith that respectability not only does not err, but knows not temptation. A poet who never asked to be thought respectable has put into words we shall not easily forget his thought about immorality:

"I waive the quantum o' the sin,
The hazard of concealing;
But och! it hardens a' within,
And petrifies the feeling!"

The quantum of the sin is so grave, the hazard of concealing so momentous, in English eyes, that we form a national conspiracy to exhibit English nature as distinct, in several points, from the merely human. Hence, a characteristic delicacy, a singular refinement, is resulting at its best in very sweet and noble lives. Hence, also, that counter balancing vice which would fain atone for vice in the more usual sense of the word. Though, all within may be hopelessly hardened, the feeling petrified into a little idol of egoism, outwardly there shall be a show of everything we respect. "Homage to virtue", quota? Well and good, were it nothing more. But Mr. Pecksniff takes up his parable, his innumerable kindred hold forth in the marketplace. Respectability cannot hold its tongue, in fact; and the language it affects is wont to be nauseous.

Lower than Pecksniff, but of obvious brotherhood with him, stands Uriah Heep. This example of a low-born man, who, chancing to have brains, deems it most expedient to use them for dishonest purposes, will not yield in the essentials of respectability to the best in the land. He is poor, he is 'umble, but his morals must not for a moment be doubted. The undisguisable fact of poverty is accepted and made the most of; it becomes his tower of strength. Mr. Pecksniff, conscious of a well-filled purse, assumes a certain modesty of demeanour — a foretaste, by the by, of that affectation in rich people which promises such an opportunity for satire in our own day.

Uriah Heep wallows in perpetual humility; he grovels before his social superiors, that he may prove to them his equality in soul. With regard to this slimy personage, we note at once that he is a victim of circumstances, the outcome of a bad education and of a society affected with disease. His like abounded at the time; nowadays they will not so easily be discovered. The doctrine that "A man's a man for a' that" has taken solid shape, and our triumphant democracy will soon be ashamed of a motto so disparaging. But Heep saw no prospect when he stood upright; only when he crawled did a chance of issue from that too humble life present itself. "Remember your place!" — from his earliest years this admonition had sounded for him.

This prime duty is ever present to his mind; it prompts him to avow, in and out of season, that he belongs to a very 'umble family, that he is himself the 'umblest of mortals. Meanwhile the man's vitals are consumed with envy, hatred, and malice. He cannot respect himself; his training has made the thing impossible; and all men are his enemies. When he is detected in criminal proceedings, we are hard upon him, very hard. Dickens cannot relent to this victim of all that is worst in the society he criticises. Had Uriah stopped short of crime, something might have been said for him, but the fellow is fatally logical. Logic of that kind we cannot hear of for a moment; in our own logic of the police court and the assizes, we will take remarkably good care that there is no flaw.

Pecksniff and Uriah have a certain amount of intellect. In his last book Dickens presents us with the monumental humbug who is at the same time an egregious fool. Mr. Sapsea very honestly worships himself; he is respectability weighing a good many stone, with heavy watch-guard and expensive tailoring. By incessant lauding of his own virtues to a world always more or less attentive when such a speaker carries social weight, Sapsea has developed a mania of self-importance. His thickness of hide, his stolidity, are well displayed, but it seems to me that in this case Dickens has been guilty of a piece of exaggeration altogether exceeding the limits of art; perhaps the one instance where his illusion fails to make us accept an extravagance even for a moment. I refer to Sapsea's inscription for his wife's tomb (*Edwin Drood*, chap. iv). Contrasting this with anything to be found in Pecksniff or Uriah Heep, we perceive the limits of his satire, strictly imposed by art, even where he is commonly held to have been most fantastic.

Dickens applied with extraordinary skill the only method that, granted all his genius, could have ensured him so vast a sway over the public of that time. His art, especially as satirist, lies in the judicious use of emphasis and iteration. Emphasis alone would not have answered his purpose; the striking thing must be said over and over again until the most stupid hearer has it by heart. We of to-day sometimes congratulate ourselves on an improvement in the public taste and intelligence, and it is true that some popular authors conciliate their admirers by an appeal in a comparatively subdued note. But — who has a popularity like to that of Dickens? Should there again rise an author to be compared with him in sincerity and universality of acceptance, once more will be heard that unmistakable voice of summons to Goodman Dull.

We are educated, we are cultured; be it so; but, to say the least, some few millions of us turn with weariness from pages of concentrated art. Fifty years ago, the people who did *not* might have been gathered from the English-speaking world into a London hall, without uncomfortable crowding. Dickens well understood that he must cry aloud and spare not; he did it naturally, as a man of his generation; he, and his fellow reformers, educators, popular entertainers, were perforce vociferous to the half-awakened multitudes. Carlyle was even more emphatic, and reiterated throughout a much longer life. Education notwithstanding, these will again be the characteristics of any writer for whom fate reserves a gigantic popularity in the century just beginning.

Yes, it is quite true that Mr. Micawber, Mr. Pecksniff, Uriah Heep, and all Dickens's prominent creations say the same thing in the same way, over and over again. The literary exquisite is disgusted, the man of letters shakes his head with a smile. Remember: for twenty months did these characters of favourite fiction make a periodical appearance, and not the most stupid man in England forgot them between one month and the next. The method is at the disposal of all and sundry; who will use it to this effect?

In his satires on "high life", Dickens was less successful than with the middle class. I have spoken of Sir Leicester Dedlock and Cousin Feenix, both well done, the latter especially, and characterizations worthy of the author, but they hold no place in the general memory. His earliest attempt at this kind of thing was unfortunate; Lord Frederick Verisopht and Sir Mulberry Hawk are on a par with the literary lady in *Pickwick,* who wrote the ode to an Expiring Frog — an exercise of fancy which has no relation whatever to the facts of life. Possibly the young author of *Nicholas Nickleby* fancied he had drawn a typical baronet and a lord; more likely he worked with conscious reference to the theatre. In *Little Dorrit* we are introduced to certain high-born or highly-connected people, who make themselves deliberately offensive, but their names cannot be recalled. Much better is the study of an ancient worldling in Edith Dombey's mother, Mrs. Skewton. Her paralytic seizure, her death in life, is fine and grisly realism; but we do not accept Mrs. Skewton as a typical figure.

Too obvious is the comparison with Thackeray's work; Dickens is here at a grave disadvantage, and would have done better not to touch that ground at all. Perhaps the same must be said of his incursions into political satire; and yet, one would be lot to lose the Circumlocution Office. Though, by the choice of such a name he seems to forbid our expecting any picture of reality, there seems reason to believe that those pages of *Little Dorrit* are not much less true than amusing; at all events they are admirably written. Of the Barnacle family we accept readily enough the one who is described as bright and young; indeed, this youngster is a good deal of a gentleman, and represents the surviving element of that day's Civil Service; under a competitive system, he alone would have a chance. His relatives have significance enough, but very little life. Dickens wrote of them in anger, which was never the case in his satiric masterpieces. Anger abundantly justified, no doubt; but at the same time another critic of the English government was making heard his wrathful voice (it came from Chelsea), and with more of the true prophetic vehemence. Dickens did not feel at home in this Barnacle atmosphere; something of personal feeling entered into his description of its stifling properties. He could write brilliantly on the subject, but not with the calmness necessary for the creation of lasting characters.

The upstarts of commerce and speculation came more within his scope. Montague Tigg keeps a place in one's recollection, but chiefly, I think, as the impecunious braggart rather than as the successful knave. There is an impressiveness about Mr. Merdle, but perhaps rather in the description of his surroundings than in the figure of the man himself; readers in general know nothing of him, his name never points a paragraph. The Veneerings, in *Our Mutual Friend*, seem better on a re-reading than in a memory of the acquaintance with them long ago. This is often the case with Dickens, and speaks strongly in his favour. They smell of furniture polish; their newness in society is a positive distress to the nerves; to read of them is to revive a sensation one has occasionally experienced in fact. Being but sketches, they are of necessity (in Dickens's method) *all* emphasis; we never lose sight of their satiric meaning; their very name (like that of the Circumlocution Office) signals caricature.

At this point, Dickens connects himself once more with literary traditions; we are reminded of the nomenclature of English drama; of Justice Greedy, of Anthony Absolute, Mrs. Malaprop, and the rest. It is only in his subordinate figures, and rarely then, that he falls into this bad habit, so destructive of illusion. For the most part, his names are aptly selected, or invented with great skill — skill, of course, different from that of Balzac, who aims at another kind of effectiveness. Gamp, Micawber, Bumble, Pipchin — to be sure they are so familiar to us that we associate them inevitably with certain characters, but one recognizes their exquisite rightness. Pecksniff is more daring, and touches the limit of fine discretion. In a very few cases he drew upon that list of grotesque names which anyone can compile from a directory, names which are generally valueless in fiction just because they really exist; Venus, for example.

Anything but a caricature, though as significant a figure as any among these minor groups, is Mr. Casby in *Little Dorrit*, the venerable grandsire, of snowy locks and childlike visage; the Patriarch, as he is called, who walks in a light of contemplative benevolence. Mr. Casby is a humbug of a peculiarly dangerous kind; under various disguises, he is constantly met with in the England of to-day. This sweetly philosophic being owns houses, and those of the kind, which we now call slums. Of course, he knows nothing about their evil condition; of course he employs an agent to collect his rents, and is naturally surprised when this agent falls short in the expected receipts. It pains him that human nature should be so dishonest; for the sake of his tenants themselves it behoves him to insist on full and regular payment. When, in the end, Mr. Casby has his impressive locks ruthlessly shorn by the agent risen in revolt against such a mass of lies and cruelty and unclean selfishness, we feel that the punishment is inadequate. Dickens should have treated the question of landlordism on a larger scale; it remains one of the curses of English life, and is likely to do so until the victims of house-owners see their way to cut, not the hair, but the throats, of a few selected specimens.

Mr. Casby, nowadays, does not take the trouble to assume a sweet or reverend aspect; if he lives in the neighbourhood of his property, he is frankly a brute; if, as is so often the case, he resides in a very different part of the town, his associates are persons who would smile indeed at any affectation of sanctity. In this, and some other directions, hypocrisy has declined among us. Our people of all classes have advanced in the understanding of business, a word that will justify most atrocities, and excuse all but every form of shamelessness.

That rich little book, *Great Expectations*, contains a humbug less offensive than Casby, and on the surface greatly amusing, but illustrative of a contemptible quality closely allied with the commercial spirit. Seen at a distance Mr. Pumblechook is a source of inextinguishable laughter; near at hand he is seen to be a very sordid creature. A time-server to his marrow, he adds the preposterous self-esteem which always gave Dickens so congenial an opportunity. Here we have a form of moral dishonesty peculiar to no one people. Mr. Pumblechook's barefaced pretence that he is the maker of Pip's fortune, his heavy patronage whilst that fortune endures, and his sour desertion of the young man when circumstances alter, is mere overfed humanity discoverable all the world over. He has English traits, and we are constrained to own the man as a relative. We meet him as often as we do the tailor who grovels before the customer unexpectedly become richapter Compare him with the other embodiments of dishonesty, and it is seen, not only what inexhaustible material of this kind lay at Dickens's command, but with what excellent art he differentiates his characters.

Less successful are the last pieces of satiric drawing I can find space to mention. In this chapter, rather than in the next, is the place for Mrs. Jellyby, who loses all distinction of sex, and comes near to losing all humanity, in her special craze. Women have gone far towards such a consummation, and one dare not refuse to admit her possibility; but the extravagance of the thing rather repels, and we are never so assured of Mrs. Jellyby as of Mr. Pecksniff.

Unacceptable in the same way is that fiercely charitable lady who goes about with her tracts and her insolence among the cottages of the poor. One knows how such persons nowadays demean themselves, and we can readily believe that they behaved more outrageously half a century ago; but being meant as a type, this religious female dragoon misses the mark; we refuse credence and turn away.

Caricature in general is a word of depreciatory meaning. I have already made it clear how far I am from agreeing with the critics who think that to call Dickens a caricaturist, and to praise his humour, is to dismiss him once for all. It seems to me that in all his very best work he pursues an ideal widely apart from that of caricature in any sense; and that in other instances he permits himself an emphasis, like in kind to that of the caricaturist, but by its excellence of art, its fine sincerity of purpose, removed from every inferior association. To call Mrs. Gamp a caricature is an obvious abuse of language; not less so, I think, to apply the word to Mr. Pecksniff or to Uriah Heep. Occasionally, missing the effect he intended, Dickens produced work that invites this definition; at times, again, he deliberately drew a figure with that literary overcharging that corresponds to the exaggeration, small or great, of professed caricaturists with the pencil.

His finest humour, his most successful satire, belongs to a different order of art. To be convinced of this one need but think of the multiplicity of detail, all exquisitely finished, which goes to make his best-known portraits. Full justice has never been done to this abounding richness of invention, this untiring felicity of touch in minutiæ innumerable. Caricature proceeds by a broad and simple method. It is no more the name for Dickens's full fervour of creation, than for Shakespeare's in his prose comedy. Each is a supreme idealist.

Chapter 7

Women and Children in Dickens' Novel

Women and Children

With female readers, Dickens was never a prime favourite. One feels very sure that they contributed little or nothing to the success of *Pickwick*. In the angelic Oliver they began, no doubt, to find matter of interest, and thence onward they might "take to" the triumphant novelist for the pathos of his child-life and to some extent because of his note of domesticity. But on the whole it was for men that Dickens wrote. To-day the women must be very few who by deliberate choice open a volume of his works.

The humorist never strongly appeals to that audience. Moreover, it is natural enough that a writer so often boisterous, who deals so largely with the coarser aspects of life, who gives us very little of what is conventionally called tenderness, and a good deal of bloodthirsty violence, should yield to many others in women's choice. For certain of them, Dickens is simply "vulgar" — and there an end of it; they can no more read him with pleasure than they can his forerunners of the eighteenth century. In a class where this might not be honestly felt as an objection, he is practically unknown to mothers and daughters who devote abundant leisure to fiction of other kinds; and representatives of this public have been known to speak of him with frank dislike. One reason, it seems, for such coldness in presumably gentle hearts goes deeper than those, which first suggest themselves. If George Eliot was of opinion that Shakespeare shows himself unjust to women, and on that account could not wholly revere him, we need not be surprised that average members of her sex should see in Dickens something like a personal enemy, a confirmed libeller of all who speak the feminine tongue.

For, setting aside his would-be tragic figures, the Lady Dedlocks and Edith Dombeys of whom enough has been said; neglecting also for the moment his exemplars in the life of home (doubtfully sympathetic to female readers of our day); it is obvious that Dickens wrote of women in his liveliest spirit of satire. Wonderful as fact, and admirable as art, are the numberless pictures of more or less detestable widows, wives, and spinsters which appear throughout his books. Beyond dispute, they must be held among his finest work; this portraiture alone would establish his claim to greatness. And I think it might be forcibly argued that, for incontestable proof of Dickens's fidelity in reproducing the life he knew, one should turn in the first place to his gallery of foolish, ridiculous, or offensive women.

These remarkable creatures belong for the most part to one rank of life, that which we vaguely designate as the lower middle class. In general, their circumstances are comfortable; they suffer no hardship — save that of birth, which they do not perceive as such; nothing is asked of them but a quiet and amiable discharge of household duties; their male kindred with great, often with extraordinary, consideration, treat them. Yet their characteristic is acidity of temper and boundless license of querulous or insulting talk. The real business of their lives is to make all about them as uncomfortable as they can. Invariably, they are unintelligent and untaught; very often they are flagrantly imbecile. Their very virtues (if such persons can be said to have any) become a scourge. In the highways and by-ways of life, by the fireside, and in the bedchamber, their voices shrill upon the terrified ear. It is difficult to believe that death can stifle them; one imagines them upon the threshold of some other world, sounding confusion among unhappy spirits who hoped to have found peace.

The historical investigation is not necessary to ascertain the truthfulness of these presentments. Among the poorer folk, especially in London, such women may be observed to-day by any inquirer sufficiently courageous, they are a multitude that no man can number; every other house in the cheap suburbs will be found to contain at least one specimen — very often two, for the advantage of quarrelling when men are not at hand. Education has done little as yet to improve the tempers and the intellects of women in this rank. A humorist of our time suggests that sheer dullness and monotony of existence explains their unamiable habits that they quarrel because they can get no other form of excitement.

I believe there is some truth in this, but it does not cover the whole ground. Many a woman who frequents theatres and music halls, goes shopping and lives in comparative luxury, has brought the arts of ill-temper to high perfection. Indeed, I am not sure that increase of liberty is not tending to exasperate these evil characteristics in women vulgarly bred; if Dickens were now writing, I believe he would have to add to his representative women the well-dressed shrew who proceeds on the slightest provocation from fury of language to violence of act. Mrs. Varden does not dream of assaulting her husband, for in truth she loves him; Mrs. Snagsby is in genuine terror at the thought that the deferential law-stationer may come to harm. Nowadays these ladies would enjoy a very much larger life, would systematically neglect their children (if they chose to have any); and would soothe their nerves, in moments carefully chosen, by flinging at the remonstrant husband any domestic object to which they attached no special value.

Through his early life, Dickens must have been in constant observation of these social pests. In every lodging-house he entered, such a voice would surely be sounding. His women use utterance such as no male genius could have invented; from the beginning he knew it perfectly, the vocabulary, the syntax, the figurative flights of this appalling language. "God's great gift of speech abused" was the commonplace of his world. Another man, obtaining his release from those depths, would have turned away in loathing; Dickens found therein matter for his mirth, material for his art. When one thinks of it, how strange it is that such an unutterable curse should become, in the artist hands, an incitement to joyous laughter! As a matter of fact, these women produced more misery than can be calculated. That he does not exhibit this side of the picture is the peculiarity of Dickens's method; a defect, of course, from one point of view, but inseparable from his humorous treatment of life. Women, who might well have wrecked homes, are shown as laughable foils for the infinite goodness and patience of men about them. Justly, it became a matter of complaint to the female critic.

Weller, and Varden, and Snagsby, and Joe Gargery are too favourable specimens of the average husband; in such situations, one or other of them would certainly have lost his patience, and either have fled the country, or have turned wife-beater. Varden is a trifle vexed now and then, but he clinks it off at his cheery anvil, and restores his jovial mood with a draught from Toby. Mr. Snagsby coughs behind his hand, is nervously perturbed, and heartily wishes things were otherwise, but never allows himself a harsh word to his "little woman". As for Joe Gargery, what could be expected of the sweetest and humanest temper man was ever blest withal? No, it is decidedly unfair. Not even Jonas Chuzzlewit (who, of course, has a martyr of a wife) can outbalance such a partial record of long-suffering in husbands.

It is worthwhile to consider with some attention these promoters of public mirth. *Pickwick* would have been incomplete without this element of joviality, and we are not likely to forget the thorn in the flesh of Mr. Weller, senior. Sam's father is responsible, I suppose, for that jesting on the subject of widows, which even to-day will serve its turn on the stage or in the comic paper; it is vulgar, to be sure, but vulgarity in *Pickwick* becomes a fine art; we cannot lose a word of the old coaching hero. Mrs. Weller it is hard to describe in moderate terms; taking the matter prosaically, she has all the minor vices that can inhere in woman; but the mere mention of her moves to chuckling. On her deathbed, we are given to understand, she saw the error of her ways. Such persons occasionally do, but her conversion comes a trifle late. Enough for Dickens that we are touched by the old man's spirit of forgiveness. It is the bit of light in a picture felt, after all, to be grimy enough; the bit of sweet and clean humanity which our author always desires to show after he has made his fun out of sorry circumstance. In *Oliver Twist*, the feminine note grows shriller; we have Mrs. Sowerberry, sordid tyrant and scold, and the woman who becomes Mrs. Bumble. We are meant to reflect, of course, that the "porochial" dignitary gets only his deserts; he who marries with his eye upon a pair of silver sugar-tongs, and is a blustering jackass to boot, can hardly be too severely dealt with.

So Mrs. Bumble exhibits her true self for her husband's benefit, and, so far as we know, does not repent of her triumphs as an obese virago. *Barnaby Rudge* is enriched with Mrs. Varden and her handmaid Miggs. Now of Mrs. Varden it can be said that she typifies a large class of most respectable wives. She is not coarse, she is not malignant, she is not incapable of good-humour; but so much value does she attach to the gleams of that bright quality, that not one is suffered to escape her until her household has been brought to the verge of despair by her persistent sourness and sulkiness. No reason whatever can be assigned for it; when she takes offence, it pleases her to do so. She has in perfection all the illogicality of thought, all the maddening tricks of senseless language, which, doubtless for many thousands of years, have served her like for weapons. It is an odd thing that evolution has allowed the persistence of this art, for we may be quite sure that many a primitive woman paid for it with a broken skull.

Here it is, however, flourishing, and like to flourish. The generations do not improve upon it; this art of irritation has long ago been brought to its highest possible point. Who knows? A future civilization may discover lapses of common sense and a finesse of fatuous language unknown to Mrs. Varden. For the present, she points a limit of possibility in these directions. Her talk is marvelously reported; never a note of exaggeration, and nothing essential ever forgotten. The same is always to be noted in Dickens's idiotic women; their phrases might have been taken down by a phonograph for reproduction in literature. Such accuracy is a very great thing indeed; few novelists can compare in it with Dickens. His men he may permit to luxuriate in periods obviously artificial; their peculiarities are sometimes overdone, their talk becomes a fantasia of the author's elaboration, but with his women (of the class we are reviewing), it is never so. Partly, no doubt, because one cannot exaggerate what is already exaggerated to the n'th power; but it was very possible to miss the right in such a maze of imbecilities, and I believe that Dickens does it never.

Mrs. Varden repents, Mrs. Varden is stricken with remorse, Mrs. Varden becomes a model wife. Let the Jew believe it! Not even on her deathbed did it happen, but simply because she had a fright in the Gordon riots. Yes; for one week, or perchance for two, she might have affected (even felt) penitence; after that, Heaven pity poor Gabriel for having taken her at her word! The thing is plainly impossible. Such women, at her age, are incapable of change; they will but grow worse, till the pangs of death shake them. Mrs. Varden would have lingered to her ninetieth year, mopping and mowing her ill humour when language failed, and grinning illogicality with toothless gums. She is converted, to make things pleasant for us. We thank the author's goodness, and say, 'tis but a story.

Miggs, the admirer of Sam Tappertit, is idiocy and malice combined. To tell the truth, one does not much like to read of Miggs: we feel it is all a little hard upon women soured by celibacy. Dickens's time *was* hard indeed on the unwilling spinster, and we do not think it an amiable trait.

Nowadays things are so different; it is common to find spinsters who are such by choice, and not a few of them are doing good work in the world. Sixty years ago, every unmarried woman of a certain age was a subject of open or covert mockery: she had failed in her chase of men, and must be presumed full of rancour against both sexes. As for Miggs, of course, the detestable Mrs. Varden was largely answerable for her evil qualities; when the handmaid was turned out of doors, the mistress should by rights have gone with her. She amuses a certain class of readers, but has not much value either as humour or satire or plain fact.

There looms upon us the lachrymose countenance of Mrs. Gummidge. This superannuated nuisance serves primarily, of course, to illustrate the fine qualities of the Peggotty household; that she is borne with for one day says indeed much for their conscientious kindness. The boatman, delicately sympathetic, explains her fits of depression by saying that she has "been thinking of the old 'un". Possibly so, and the result of her mournful reflection is that she behaves with monstrous ingratitude to the people who keep her out of the workhouse. "I'm a lone lorn creature, and everything goes contrary with me." This vice of querulousness is one of the most intolerable beheld by the sun. Dickens merely smiles; and it is large-hearted in him to do so: he would have us forbearing with such poor creatures, would have us understand that they suffer as well as cause suffering to others.

One acknowledges the justice of the lesson. But we have not done with Mrs. Gummidge; together with the Yarmouth family, she emigrated to Australia, and there — became a bright, happy, serviceable woman! Converted, she, by the great grief that had befallen her friends; made ashamed of whining over megrims when death and shame were making havoc in the little home. Well, it may have been so; but Mrs. Gummidge was very old for such a ray of reason to pierce her skull. In any case, we do not think of her in Australia. She sits forever in the house on Yarmouth sands (sands not yet polluted by her kin from Whitechapel), and shakes her head and pipes her eye, a monument of selfish misery.

Behold Mrs. Snagsby. To all Mrs. Varden's vices this woman adds one that may be strongly recommended for the ruin of domestic peace when the others have failed — if fail they can. She is jealous of the little law-stationer; she imagines for him all manner of licentious intrigues. That such imagination is inconsistent with the plainest facts of life in no way invalidates its hold upon Mrs. Snagsby's mind. She will make things as unpleasant as possible in the grimy house in Cook's Court; the little man shall have rest neither day nor night; his life shall become a burden to him. And goodness knows that the house, at the best of times, falls a good deal short of cheerfulness. There is Guster. Who shall restrain a laugh, hearing of Guster? Plainly described, this girl is an underpaid, underfed, and overworked slavey, without a friend in the world, — unless it be Mr. Snagsby, — and subject to frequent epileptic fits. And we roar with laughter as often as she is named! It is Dickens's pleasure that we shall do so, and, if it comes to defence of so strange a subject of humour, one can only say that, from a certain point of view, everything in this world is laughable.

Look broadly enough, and it is undoubtedly amusing that such a woman as Mrs. Snagsby should coarsely tyrannize over a poor diseased creature, who toils hard and lives on a pittance. But, in strictness, the humour here perceivable is not of the kind we usually attribute to Dickens; it has something either of philosophic sublimity or of mortal bitterness. For my own part, I think Dickens points, in such situations as this, to larger significances than were consciously in his mind. I may return to the matter in speaking expressly of his humour; here we are specially concerned with the exhibition of Mrs. Snagsby's personality. Happily, she undergoes no moral palingenesis; by the date of *Bleak House* her creator had outgrown the inclination for that kind of thing. We are sure that she made the deferential little man miserable to the end of his days. When she had buried him, she held forth for many years more on the martyrdom of her married life She is decidedly more hateful than Mrs. Varden, by virtue of her cruelty to the girl, and more of a force for ill by virtue of her animal jealousy. In short — a most amusing figure.

It certainly is a troublesome fact for sensitive female readers that this, a great English novelist of the Victorian age, so abounds in women who are the curse of their husbands' lives. A complete list of them would, I imagine, occupy nearly a page of this book. Mrs. Jellyby I have already discussed. I have spoken of the much more lifelike Mrs. Pocket, a capital portrait. I have alluded to the uncommon realism of Dr. Marigold's wife. A mention must at least be made of Mrs.

Macstinger, who, as Mrs. Bunsby, enters upon such a promising field of fresh activity. But there remains one full-length picture which we may by no means neglect, its name Mrs. Joe Gargery.

Mrs. Gargery belongs to Dickens's later manner. In such work as this, his hand was still inimitably true, and his artistic conscience no longer allowed him to play with circumstance as in the days of Mrs. Varden. The blacksmith's wife is a shrew of the most highly developed order. If ever she is good-tempered in the common sense of the word, she never lets it be suspected; without any assignable cause, she is invariably acrid, and ready at a moment's notice to break into fury of abuse. It gratifies her immensely to have married the softest-hearted man that ever lived, and also that he happens to be physically one of the strongest; the joy of trampling upon him, knowing that he who could kill her with a backhand blow will never even answer the bitterest insult with an unkind word! It delights her, too, that she has a little brother, a mere baby still, whom she can ill-use at her leisure, remembering always that every harshness to the child is felt still worse by the big good fellow, her husband. Do you urge that Dickens should give a cause for this evil temper? Cause there is none — save of that scientific kind which has no place in English novels. It is the peculiarity of these women that no one can conjecture why they behave so ill. The nature of the animals — nothing more can be said.

Notice, now, that in Mrs. Gargery, though he still disguises the worst of the situation with his unfailing humour, Dickens gives us more of the harsh truth than in any previous book. That is a fine scene where the woman, by a malicious lie, causes a fight between Joe and Orlick; a true illustration of character, and well brought out. Again, Mrs. Joe's punishment. Here we are very far from the early novels. Mrs. Gargery shall be brought to quietness; but how? By a half-murderous blow on the back of her head, from which she will never recover. Dickens understood by this time that there is no other efficacious way with these ornaments of their sex. A felling and stunning and all but killing blow, followed by paralysis and slow death. A sharp remedy, but no whit sharper than the evil it cures. Mrs. Gargery, under such treatment, learns patience and the rights of other people. We are half sorry she cannot rise and put her learning into practice, but there is always a doubt. As likely as not she would take to drinking, and enter on a new phase of ferocity.

Of higher social standing, not perhaps better educated but certainly better bred, are the women who acknowledge their great exemplar in Mrs. Nickleby. This lady — all things considered, the term may be applied without abuse — has passed the greater part of her life in a rural district, and morally she belongs, I think, rather to the country than the town; there is a freshness about her, a *naïveté* not — up to a certain point — disagreeable; her manners and conversation are suggestive of long afternoons, and evenings of infinite leisure. Mrs. Nickleby is, above all, well meaning; according to her lights she is gracious and tolerant; she has natural affections, and would be sincerely distressed by a charge of selfishness. Unhappily, the poor woman has been born with the intellectual equipment of a Somerset ewe. It would be a delicate question of psychology to distinguish her from the harmless, smiling idiot whom we think it unnecessary and cruel to put under restraint. One may say, indeed, that this defect is radical in all Dickens's female characters; the better hearted succeed in keeping it out of sight — in the others it becomes flagrant and a terror. Sixty years ago there was practically no provision in England for the mental training of women.

Sent early to a good school, and kept there till the age, say, of one-and-twenty, Mrs. Nickleby would have grown into a quite endurable gentlewoman, aware of her natural weakness, and a modest participant in general conversation. Allowed to develop in her own way, and married to a man only less unintelligent than herself she puts forth a wonderful luxuriance of amiable fatuity. Thoughts, in the strict sense of the word, she has none; her brain is a mere blind mechanism for setting in motion an irresponsible tongue; together they express in human language the sentiments of the ewe aforesaid. Mr. Nickleby died in the prime of life; what else could be the fate of a man doomed to listen to this talk morning, noon, and night? With Mrs. Nickleby, one cannot converse; she understands the meaning of nothing that is said to her; she is incapable of answering a question, or of seeing the logical bearings of any statement whatsoever. One conviction is impressed upon her (pardon the word) mind: that throughout life she has invariably said and done the right thing, and that other persons, in their relations with her, have been as invariably wrong. Let events turn how they may, they do but serve to confirm her complacent position.

Having exerted herself to the utmost in urging a particular line of conduct, which, on trial, proves to have been the worst that could have been followed, Mrs. Nickleby blandly reminds her victims that she had known from the first, and repeatedly declared, what would be the result of such manifest imprudence. Should this lead to an outbreak of masculine impatience, not to say anger, the good lady receives a nervous shock, under which she pales, and pants, and falters as the domestic martyr, the victim of surprising unreason and brutality. As it happens, she does not bring her children to the gutter and herself to the workhouse; we acknowledge the providence that watches over exemplary fools. And after all, as men must laugh at something, it is as well that they should find in Mrs. Nickleby matter for mirth. She is ubiquitous, and doubtless always will be. She cannot be chained and muzzled, or forbidden to propagate her kind. We must endure her, as we endure the caprices of the sky. An ultimate fact of nature, and a great argument for those who decline to take life too seriously.

This was early work of Dickens, but not to be improved upon by any increase of experience or of skill. A good many years later, he produced a companion portrait, that of Flora Finching in *Little Dorrit* — the neglected book which contains several of his best things. We are told that the picture is from life (as was that of Mrs. Nickleby), and that the exuberant Flora, in the bloom of her youth, had been to Dickens himself even what Dora was to David Copperfield — a piece of biography in which one is very willing to put faith. I am disposed to credit

Flora Finching with mental power superior to Mrs. Nickleby's; the preference may provoke a charge of subtlety, but I adhere to it after a long acquaintance with both ladies. Indeed, one rather likes Flora. Of course she has killed her husband; but one chooses to forget all that. Flora, to tell the truth, has some imagination, a touch of poetry; in her heart she is convinced that as Mrs. Clennam she would have been a happier woman. Yet she has sense enough and fantasy enough only to play with the thought; it becomes something graceful in her commonplace life; a little lacking in delicacy, she causes her old lover some embarrassment, but never seriously hopes to win him back. When Clennam marries little Dorrit, Flora behaves admirably — the all-sufficient proof of what I have just said. Her character is in truth a very strong plea for the fair education of women. Flora needed but that; it would have made her, I really think, rather a charming person.

Nowadays one will rarely meet any one suggestive of her; for she was at all times an exception in the vulgar world, and her like have since been schooled into the self-restraint, of which, under favourable conditions, they are perfectly capable. The species of sentimentality seen in Flora was at that time fed upon songs and verses congenial to the feeble mind; born thirty years later, Flora would have been led to a much better taste in that direction, with the result of greater self-command in all. She is a kind soul, and doubtless became a very pleasant, even useful, friend of little Mrs. Clennam. Such a woman is only dangerous when she feels that the law has surrendered to her a real live man — has given him, bound hand and foot, to her care and her mercy. As a maid, as a widow, she will do no harm, nor wish to do any, beyond distressing the tympanum and tasking the patience of anyone with whom she genially converses.

One does not venture to begin praising work such as this. Eulogy would lose itself in enthusiasm. Pass, rather, to the gallery of women who are neither married shrews nor well-meaning pests, yet each peculiar for her mental and moral vice. We glance at Miss Squeers. Fanny, it is plain, has relatives in the pages of Smollett; one seems to remember a damsel in

Roderick Random of whom, perhaps, the less said the better; the intercourse between Miss Squeers and Nicholas brings this chapter to mind, and points a change alike in national manners and in literature. As a wife, Fanny would pass into that other category with which we have done. Her London parallel is perhaps Sophy Wackles, from whom Mr. Swiveller had so narrow and so fortunate an escape. Such maidens as these, Dickens must have had many opportunities of observing; his social canvas would have been imperfect without them. Though it seems unjust to put her in this place, I must mention Susan Nipper, the nurse of Florence Dombey.

Susan begins well on the pattern of her class; she is snappy, and brief-tempered, fond of giving smacks and pulling hair; one sees no reason why with favouring circumstances she should not develop into a nagger of distinction. But something is observable in her which imposes caution on prophecy; we see that Susan, though a mere domestic, has a very unusual endowment of wit; she is sharp in retort, but also in perception; in any case she cannot become a mere mouthing idiot. In course of time we see that she has a good heart. Therefore, it comes to pass that, in spite of origin and evil example, the girl grows in grace. She is fortunately situated; her sweet young mistress does her every kind of good; and when she marries Mr. Toots we have no misgivings whatever as to that eccentric gentleman's happiness.

Then, typical of a very large class indeed, comes Mrs. Crupp, who "does for" David Copperfield in his chambers. It is unnecessary to use the short words, which would adequately describe Mrs. Crupp; enough to say that she stands for the baser kind of London landlady — a phrase which speaks volumes. Some day it will cause laughter, indeed, and something else, to think that young men beginning life as students, and what not, should have fallen, as a matter of course, into the hand of Mrs. Crupp. Her name smells of strong liquor; it includes all dishonesty and uncleanliness. The monstrosity of her pretensions touches the highest point of the ludicrous. What, then, is one to say of Sarah Gamp, of Betsy Prig, considered as women? Of Mrs. Gamp in another aspect

I have spoken at some length; she is one of those figures in Dickens to which one necessarily returns, again and again; as art, the very quintessence of his genius; as social fact, worthy of repeated contemplation. After all, women they are, these sister hags of the birth and death chamber. Mrs. Gamp has her own ideas of tender emotion; she is touched by the sight of an undertaker's children "playing at berryings down in the shop, and follerin' the order-book to its long home in the iron safe!" Be it remarked that there is an appreciable difference between Mrs. Gamp's nature and that of Mrs. Prig; we are clearly shown that Betsy is the harder, coarser, more mercenary of the twain. If well plied with spirits and pickled cucumber, Sarah Gamp might be capable of an elementary generosity; it is our perception of this which helps to keep the creature amusing, where she might so easily sink below everything but our contemptuous disgust.

Betsy Prig is of a lower order, even socially; one may be sure that she had much less to do with the better class of clients. There is in her a spitefulness, a greedy malignancy, not found in the nurse of Kingsgate Street; where Mrs. Gamp would exhibit hostility in astounding contortions of thick-throated phrase, irresistibly laughable, Betsy Prig would fall into the mere language of the gutter. Their quarrel (one of the great things in literature) makes proof of this, though Dickens's most adroit idealism avoids the offensiveness of the real dialogue. As a girl — try to imagine Sarah Gamp as a young girl! We know where and how she lived, what examples she had. It was practically Hogarth's London which saw her birth and breeding; but the London of to-day is well able to produce such women; one catches a glimpse of her life in the market streets, and the public-houses.

Well, as a girl she must have been very plump and good-humoured, with quaint turns of speech, foretelling the eloquence of her prime. Mr. Ruskin has well pointed out the broad distinction between this London jargon and anything worthy of being called a dialect. He adds that the speech of Mrs. Gamp is pure vulgarity, its insurpassable illustration. And the woman herself (one lingers over her affectionately) may be dismissed as vulgarity incarnate. Her profession, her time, even her sex, may, from this point of view, be called accidents. Desiring to study the essential meaning of the *vulgar*, one turns from every living instance, every acute disquisition, and muses over Sarah Gamp.

When we speak of the working-class, we understand something quite distinct from, though not of necessity inferior to, the classes represented by all these women; though Mrs. Gargery, no doubt, belongs to that social order. With the working-class household, Dickens, I think, is never entirely successful; one reason among others being that he shrinks from criticising the very poor. In the homes of toilers his great heart has its way, and he can only in general show us such people at their best. But one recalls two working-class women, who, however gently drawn, are living characters: Polly Toodle and Mrs. Plornish. Paul Dombey's nurse, who would have it considered in the wages if she is to be called "out of her name", and who as the mother of Rob the Grinder suffers so many anxieties, may fairly stand for a good woman of the proletary; and how very favourably she compares with ordinary women in the class (for reasons of money) just above her! She is not vulgar, and, as a typical good wife in that rank, need not be so; for it is easier to escape such taint in the house of the engine-driver Toodle than in Mr. Snagsby's upstairs parlour.

Mrs. Plornish, the plasterer's wife, is likewise an excellent creature marked by more peculiarity; her firm belief that she makes herself intelligible to a foreigner by grotesque distortion of the English tongue is one of the truest and most amusing things in Dickens. Many a Mrs. Plornish honestly supposes that in order to speak foreign languages, it is only necessary — as I once heard one of them remark — to "learn how to twist the mouth". This is an innocent conviction, which disturbs nobody's peace. We like Mrs. Plornish, too, for her tenderness to the old father from the workhouse, and her sincere admiration when he pipes his thin little song. These women are blessed with a good temper, the source of everything enjoyable in life. However poor and ignorant, they shed about them the light of home. It is a type that does not change much and one thinks with misgivings of the day when that increased comfort which is their due, shall open to such women the dreadful possibilities of half-knowledge.

Come the eccentrics; of all classes, of all tempers; the signal for mirth. Here, I suppose, must be introduced the sister of Sampson Brass; though one finds it difficult to think of Miss Sally as feminine. She has the courage of her opinions, and shows something like heroism in scoundreldom, when brought face to face with the criminal law. One never met Miss Brass, but it is very possible that Dickens did. Later, he omits the ferocity from his grotesques. Miss Mowcher, we are told, was meant originally to play a very ugly part in the story of Emily and Steerforth, but an odd incident, nothing less than the reception of a letter from Miss Mowcher herself, led Dickens to use the character in quite another way, making it point a lesson of charity.

Mr. Dombey's friend Miss Tox is a first-rate toady, if the word may be used of one so respectable and kind-hearted; she represents, with abundance of oddity, the army of genteel old maids, as the term was in that day understood. Miss Tox is out of date, or very nearly so; to-day she finds much better occupation than in prostrating herself before Mr. Dombey, or jealously watching the Major, or looking after her canaries; her goodness is reinforced by knowledge, and her presence is a blessing in many of the dark places of our vast city. Eccentric, indeed, but on a fine basis of sense and character, is the immortal Betsy Trotwood. Chapter 15Wasted in her time, or nearly so; no scope for her beyond the care of Mr. Dick, varied by assaults upon seaside donkeys (the quadrupeds). To be sure, she is the making of David, but that came accidentally. But Miss Trotwood is in advance of her age; victim of a bad marriage, she does not see in this an all-sufficient destiny; where others would have passed their life in tears and tracts, Miss Betsy sets about making for herself a rational existence. We all know her — in various disguises, and should not be sorry to meet her more frequently. For the woman of sense and character is the salt of the earth; with however flagrant peculiarities, may she increase and multiply!

One remembers Miss La Creevy, in her way no less admirably independent. That she got her living by the travesty of art was a misfortune which neither she nor any of her contemporaries (half a dozen perhaps excepted) saw in that light, for she is of the Earliest Victorian. Rememberable, too, is the little doll's dressmaker in *Our Mutual Friend*, whose "bad child", her boneless drunkard of a father, keeps her leisure so fully occupied. But they are too numerous for several mention, these quaint examples of more or less distorted womankind — distorted by evil circumstances, and then ridiculed by the world responsible for their abnormalities. Dickens looked on them with tenderness, and makes us like, or respect, them, even whilst we laugh. He saw, too, the larger questions involved in their existence; but on these it was no part of his mission as a story-teller to insist. Had he uttered his whole thought it would hardly have satisfied us for whom a new century has begun. His view of the possibilities of womanhood becomes tolerably clear when we turn to his normal types of marriageable maiden.

In *Pickwick*, there are several of them, and we think them vulgar. They must be called young ladies; they are in an easy position, and find it occupation enough to amuse themselves. Speaking plainly, Dickens as a young man could hardly have a just criterion of refinement; the damsels of Dingley Dell were probably as like ladies as anything he had seen. Does he mean them to be delicate in thought and speech and behaviour? Or is he designedly showing us the decent girl of an unrefined class? Their little screams — their shrill laughter — their amorous facetiousness — you will not find that kind of thing now at Dingley Dell; and even then, I fancy, it was rather out of place in the home of a country gentleman. Put these girls at Pentonville, and the picture excites no uneasiness.

Mrs. Varden, we know, had a daughter, and the blushing, laughing, petulant Dolly has always been a favourite. Has she not even given her name to millinery? For my own part, I see in Dolly her mother restored to youth, and notwithstanding the Gordon riots, notwithstanding Joe Willet's loss of an arm in "the Salwanners, in America where the war is", I feel an unpleasant certainty as to Dolly's conduct when she becomes a matron. It was (and is) precisely because so many men admire the foolish in girlhood that at least an equal number deplore the intolerable in wives. Dolly is a sort of kitten. This comparison is used by George Eliot of Hetty Sorrel, and George Eliot used it advisedly; she knew very well indeed what comes of human kittenishness. The reader perhaps interposes, smilingly protests, that this is considering altogether too curiously; would hint, with civility, at a defect in appreciation of humour. But no; Dickens's humour and delightfulness are as much to me as to any man living. For the moment, I write of him as the social historian of his day, and endeavour to disclose his real thoughts concerning woman.

To Dickens, Dolly Varden was an ideal maiden; one, to be sure, of several ideals which haunt the young man's brain. It is nothing to him that Dolly is totally without education, and that her mother's failings are traceable first and foremost to that very source. Instruction was needless for sweet seventeen; it tended, if anything, to blue-stockingism. Dolly's business in graver hours is to look after stockings of a more common hue. For relaxation, she may smirk and simper and tell little fibs, and smile treacherous little smiles, and on occasion drop a little tear, which means nothing but pique or selfish annoyance. This is the very truth of Dolly. But she wore a delicious hat, and had a dainty little mouth, and was altogether so very kittenish; and to the end of time poor Gabriel Varden, poor Joe Willet, will find these things irresistible.

Passing to a book written nearly a quarter of a century after *Barnaby Rudge,* I discover Dolly in a new incarnation; she has learnt somewhat, she obeys a stricter rule of decorum, and her name is now Bella Wilfer. I admit that Miss Wilfer belongs to a slightly, very slightly, higher grade of society, but in those five-and-twenty years all things had advanced. Of Bella one easily grants the charm, and one admires her for not being more spoilt by good fortune; we perceive, however, the old traits; we tremble, now and then, at lurking kittenishness. It is permitted us to behold Bella as wife and mother, and we see her doing well in both relations; but the peril is not past. There will come a day when her husband is less fascinated by pretty ways, when he wants a little intellectual companionship by his fireside, and that moment must test Bella's mettle. Dolly would have made hopeless failure, reproducing Mrs. Vardon in the sourest particulars. Bella, perchance, had her self-respect strengthened by the example of her time, and fought down the worst of the feminine.

Between *Barnaby* and *Our Mutual Friend*, Dickens had portrayed many girls. Early come the daughters of Mr. Pecksniff, Charity and Mercy, "not unholy names, I hope". They are masterpieces, finished to the nail. Here — I cannot remind the reader too often of this fact in regard to Dickens's women — one discerns absolutely nothing of "exaggeration"; not a word, not a gesture, goes beyond the very truth. Here the master would have nothing to learn from later art; he is the realist's exemplar. How admirably are these sisters likened and contrasted! That Jonas Chuzzlewit's wife becomes broken in spirit, meek, morally hopeful, is no instance of such literary optimism as one has noticed elsewhere, but a strict development of character. Her sister's rancorous appetency, with its train of consequences, belongs no less to nature. The artist must glory in these figures, so representative, so finely individualized. Public merriment has, of course, done them only the scantiest justice; their value cannot be appraised in laughter. They are among the most precious things left to us by Victorian literature.

Together with them, let me speak of Fanny Dorrit. In the London of to-day, there is a very familiar female type, known as the shop-girl. Her sphere of action is extensive, for we meet her not only in shops, strictly speaking, but at liquor-bars, in workrooms, and, unfortunately, sometimes in the post-office, to say nothing of fifty other forms of employment open to the underbred, and more or less aggressive, young woman. Dickens saw nothing like so much of her, but he has drawn her portrait, with unerring hand, in Fanny Dorrit. Her first characteristic is a paltry and ignorant ambition, of course allied with vanity; she is crudely selfish, and has only the elementary scruples of her sex. Withal, there glimmers in her, under favouring circumstance, a vulgar good nature; if she has much too spare she will bestow it upon those she likes, and at all times she prefers to see cheerfulness around her. In a time of social transition, when the womankind of labourer and office-man tend to intermingle, and together gall the kibes of the daughters of quick-growing capital, Fanny becomes a *question*. It is not easy to get her taught, either in literature or good manners; it is not easy to recompense her services, such as they are, on a scale which makes her free of the temptation ever present to this class. When she marries, her knowledge of domestic duties is found to be on a par, say, with that of a newspaper-boy; her ideas as to expenditure resemble those of a prima donna. Miss Dorrit, we know, had an unhappy training; but not worse in degree, though different in kind, from that of her modern parallel. Dickens did not know how significant was the picture when working at its details in the year of the Crimean War. Before his death he must have had many opportunities of recalling, and reflecting upon, the features of that young person.

It occurs to one how little love-making there is in all his books. This results, in part, from the fact of his dealing with a class which is anything but sentimental, and as little endowed with imagination as any order of civilized beings discoverable throughout the world; partly, again, from his own practical nature. Little Dorrit has her love story, and at one moment it is well told; the chapter describing her travel in Italy deserves high praise. But, on the whole, Amy Dorrit is not a success in characterization. Florence Dombey is, no doubt, in love, but we never think of it as more than the affection of a child; one forms no image whatever of her married life with Walter Gay. Then there is the shadowy betrothed of Richard Carstone, a good girl, to be sure, but remarkably placid. Esther Summerson cannot count, she has no existence. A favourite with readers of her own sex is Lizzie Hexam, and, putting aside her impossibility, Dickens has perhaps made her his most sympathetic love-heroine. One credits her with loyalty, with ardour; she is more nearly a poetical figure than that of any other girl in his books. Of Little Emily I find it difficult to say more than had its place in a previous chapter. She belongs to the stage, where such a story as hers is necessarily presented in the falsest possible light. Let us note one thing, however. Out of regard for what we call propriety, is it not obvious that this girl is shown to us as acting with something like cold-blooded deliberation, the simplest form of true immorality? We have no hint of her temptation, and it really looks very much as if she had calculated the probable advantages of flight with Steerforth. I have always felt the same with regard to the central incident of *Adam Bede;* it comes upon one, at the first reading, as a moral shock.

So determined are these novelists not to offend our precious delicacy that in the upshot they offend it beyond endurance, springing upon us, so to speak, the results of uncontrollable passion, without ever allowing us to suspect that such a motive was in play. The effect of this is a sort of grossness, which dishonours our heroine. So far as we are permitted to judge, there is much reason in the insults hurled at Emily by the frantic Rosa Dartle — a pretty result, indeed, of all our author's delicate gliding over slippery places.

The Emperor Augustus, we are told, objected to the presence of women at the public games when athletes appeared unclad; but he saw nothing improper in their watching the death combats of gladiators. May we not find a parallel to this in the English censorship? To exhibit the actual course of things in a story of lawless (nay, or of lawful) love is utterly forbidden; on the other hand, a novelist may indulge in ghastly bloodshed to any extent of which his stomach is capable. Dickens, the great writer, even appears on a public platform and recites with terrible power the murder of a prostitute by a burglar, yet hardly a voice is raised in protest. Gore is perfectly decent; but the secrets of an impassioned heart are too shameful to come before us even in a whisper.

On this account I do not think it worth while to speak of Nancy, or of other lost creatures appearing in Dickens. But read, I beg, that passage of *Little Dorrit* where Amy herself and her idiot friend Maggy, wandering about the streets at night, are addressed by a woman of the town (Book i, chap. 14). Read that passage, and wonder that the same man who penned this shocking rubbish could have written in the same volume pages of truthfulness beyond all eulogy.

Little Em'ly has, after all, but a subordinate part in *David Copperfield*. The leading lady is Dora. Dora is wooed, Dora is wed — the wooing and wedding of a butterfly. Yet it is Dickens's prettiest bit of love, and I shall scarce find it in my heart to criticise the "little Blossom", the gauze-winged fairy of that "insubstantial, happy, foolish time". Dora is Dolly Varden volatilized; every fault is there, prevented from becoming vice only by utter lack of purpose. The featherbrained little creature has no responsibility; as reasonably would one begin to argue with her toy dog, Jip, when he takes his stand on the cookery book. I have said that we cannot look in *Copperfield* for any true picture of an author's daily life; but, worse than that, we have very comical misrepresentation. Think only of David at his desk and Dora holding the pens! Pray, how much work was our friend likely to get through with that charming assistance? But it is all a fantasy and defies the test of common daylight. Take Dora seriously, and at once you are compelled to ask by what right an author demands your sympathy for such a brainless, nerveless, profitless simpleton. Enter into the spirit of the chapter, and you are held by one of the sweetest dreams of humour and tenderness ever translated into language.

There is no better illustration of Dickens's progress with the time than a comparison of his heroine in *Edwin Drood* with those of the early books. I think it is a great misfortune that we so abruptly lost sight of Rosa Bud; if; as seemed likely, the development of her character was to go on throughout the story, she would have been by far the best of Dickens's intelligent and sympathetic women. At first we have misgivings; Dolly Varden and Dora and others of our old acquaintances seem blended in Miss Twinkleton's pupil; a tricksy and provoking little person, whose reason for not knowing her own mind is probably the old one — that she has no mind to know. But presently we understand; the girl — little more than a child — is in a false position, and suffers under it very consciously. A few pages more, and we see her behaving with rational force of character, the silly prettiness is thrown aside; Rosa declares herself as sensible and just and kind a girl as one could wish to meet. In the days of *Copperfield,* Dickens could not have managed this characterization; in the days of *Barnaby Rudge* he could as soon have created Rosalind. Change of times, growth of experience, widening of artistic consciousness and power — all are evident in this study, which was never to be completed.

He laughs at Miss Twinkleton and her establishment, but we have an assurance that Rosa Bud was receiving a much better education than fell to the lot of girls thirty years before; even as we feel convinced that Mr. Crisparkle's tuition was a vast improvement upon that of Dr. Blimber. It is possible, of course, that Edwin Drood's paltry "mystery", with its blood and opium, would have ousted Rosa from the scene; perhaps we had seen the best of her. Nonetheless, she remains a real and interesting little woman, and we should much have liked to watch the course of her affection for Tartar.

A "little woman". The phrase is inevitable in speaking of Dickens's pets. A Lady Dedlock might have stature; a Betsy Trotwood even might be of average height; but Em'ly and Amy and Ruth, Dolly and Dora and Esther, must all be tiny vessels for their great virtues. Shakespeare took another view of this matter; but Shakespeare was not concerned with the lower middle-class of the nineteenth century. There is agreement, I am told, among trustworthy observers that the stature of English women has notably increased during the last two or three decades; a natural consequence of improvement in the conditions of their life. In Dickens's day, when girls took no sort of exercise, fed badly, and (amid London streets) never breathed fresh air, of course, they were generally diminutive. And among all the little women he presents to us, who exhibits more concentrated charm of littleness than Ruth Pinch?

I have left her to the last, because she will serve us as the type of all that Dickens really admired in woman. Truth to tell, it was no bad ideal. Granted that the world must go on very much in the old way, that children must be born and looked after, that dinners must be cooked, that houses must be kept sweet, it is hard to see how Ruth Pinch can ever be supplanted. Ruth is no imbecile — your thoroughly kind-hearted and home-loving woman never will be; with opportunities, she would learn much, even beyond domestic limits, and still would delight in her dainty little aprons, her pastry-board and roller. Ruth would be an excellent mother; when, in the latter days, she sat grey-haired and spectacled, surely would her children arise and call her blessed. A very homely little woman, to be sure. She could not be quite comfortable with domestics at her command; a little house, a little garden, the cooking her own peculiar care, a little maid for the little babies — this is her dream. But never, within those walls, a sound of complaining or of strife, never a wry face, acidly discontented with the husband's doings or sayings. Upon my word — is it a bad ideal?

There are who surmise that in the far-off time when girls are universally well-taught, when it is the exception to meet, in any class, with the maiden or the wife who deems herself a natural inferior of brother, lover, husband, the homely virtues of Ruth Pinch will be even more highly rated than in the stupid old world. There are who suspect that our *servant-question* foretells a radical change in ways of thinking about the life of home. That the lady of a hundred years hence will be much more competent and active in cares domestic than the average shopkeeper's wife today; that it may not be found impossible to turn from a page of Sophocles to the boiling of a potato, or even the scrubbing of a floor.

When every spendthrift idiot of a mistress, and every lying lazybones of a kitchen-wench, is swept into Time's dust-bin, it may come to pass that a race of brave and intelligent women will smile sister-like at this portrait of little Ruth. They will prize Dickens, instead of turning from him in disgust or weariness; for in his pages they will see that ancient deformity of their sex, and will recognize how justly he pointed out the way of safe reform. No startling innovation, no extravagant idealism, but a gentle insistence on the facts of human nature, a kindly glorifying of one humble little woman, who saw her duty, and did it singing the while.

A word or two about the children whom he loved to bring into his books, and to make pathetic or amusing. First, of course, we see little Nell; we see her, because she is the mid-figure in a delightful romance; but her face is not very plain to us. She is innocence walking among grotesque forms of suffering and wrong; simplicity set amid quaint contortions. Her death is not the dying of a little girl, but the vanishing of a beautiful dream. Oliver Twist is no more real, and certainly less interesting. Into what sort of man did this astonishing lad develop? The children of Dotheboys are writhing ghosts; perhaps they had lived in some other world, and were bad boys, and afterwards came into Squeers' hands for purification. Sally Brass's poor little slavey is, on the other hand, well realised; a good study of childhood brought to the verge of idiocy by evil treatment. Tiny Tim serves his admirable purpose in a book, which no one can bear to criticise; we know that he *did* die, but in his little lifetime he has softened many a heart. Next rises the son and heir of "our friend Dombey". Dickens believed that little Paul was one of the best things he had ever done; contemporary readers were much excited about the child, whose "old-fashioned" ways became a by-word.

I do not find it difficult to accept Paul's enquiry about what the waves were saying (in spite of a most dreadful song, made of that passage, which sounds in my ears from long ago), and of a surety I give more credit to Paul's death-bed speeches than to those of the child in *Our Mutual Friend*, who bequeathed a kiss to "the boofer lady"; but on the whole, Mr. Dombey's hope has only a little more of substance than little Nell. His sister Florence is prettiness and gentleness; an abstraction, which affects us not. Passing to young David Copperfield, it is a different matter. Here we have the author's vision of his own childhood, and he makes it abundantly convincing.

This part of *Copperfield* is one of the narratives which every reader illustrates for himself; the poor little lad stands plain before us, as we read, and in our memory. The picture, I should say, suggests very faithfully an artist's early years, his susceptibility, his abnormal faculty of observation, the vivid workings of his mind and heart. Dickens told Forster that this bit of autobiography might be worthy to stand on the shelf together with the corresponding part of that written by Holcroft. Holcroft is forgotten, I suppose; if the mention of him leads a stray reader to his book, that reader's time will not be wasted.

Of Dickens's true and deep sympathy with childhood there can be no doubt; it becomes passionate in the case of little ones doomed to suffering by a cruel or careless world. In all his excellent public speeches, perhaps the best and most moving passage is that which describes a poor baby he saw in Scotland, a wasting little mortal, whose cradle was an old egg-box; where, he says, it lay dumb and pitiful, its eyes seeming to wonder "why, in the name of an All-merciful God, such things should be". In his novels, we like those children best, of whom we obtain only a passing glimpse, the reason, again, being that remorseless necessity of drama which spoils so many of his older people.

But in one case he has written a whole story about children, and these toddlers the most lifelike to be found in his pages. It is the story put into the mouth of Boots at the Holly Tree. Accept the fantasy, and these little actors are well shown; their talk is true, their behaviour — down to the crossness of the bride-elect when she gets tired — as truly observed as it is mirth provoking. No wonder that Boots at the Holly Tree was one of the "readings" most acceptable to Dickens s audience. If he must needs read in public, he could not have chosen a piece more likely to keep sweet his personal memory with those who heard him.

Chapter 8

Humour and Pathos

To write of Dickens at all, is to presuppose his humour. The plan of my essay has necessitated a separate consideration of the various features of his work, and at moments it may have appeared that I found fault without regard to a vast counterbalance; but it was never possible for me to lose sight of that supreme quality of his genius which must be now dwelt upon with undivided attention. It was as a humorist that Dickens made his name; and in a retrospect of his life's activity one perceives that his most earnest purposes depended for their furtherance upon this genial power, which he shares with nearly all the greatest of English writers.

Holding, as he did, that the first duty of an author is to influence his reader for good, Dickens necessarily esteemed as the most precious of his gifts that by virtue of which he commanded so great an audience. Without his humour, he might have been a vigorous advocate of social reform, but as a novelist, assuredly, he would have failed; and as to the advocacy of far-reaching reforms by men who have only earnestness and eloquence to work with, English history tells its tale. Only because they laughed with him so heartily, did multitudes of people turn to discussing the question his page suggested. As a storyteller pure and simple, the powers that remain to him, if humour were subtracted, would never have ensured popularity.

Nor, on the other hand, would they have availed him in the struggle for artistic perfection, which is a better thing. Humour is the soul of his work. Like the soul of man, it permeates a living fabric which, but for its creative breath, could never have existed.

In his earliest writing, we discover only the suggestion of this quality. The *Sketches* have a touch of true humour, but (apart from the merits of acute observation and great descriptive power) there is much more of merely youthful high spirits, tending to the farcical. Such a piece as *The Tuggs's at Ramsgate* is distinct farce, and not remarkably good of its kind. This vein Dickens continued to work throughout his career, and often with great success. One must distinguish between the parts of his writing which stir to mere hilarity, and his humour in the strict sense of the word. It is none of my business to define that term, which has long ago been adequately expounded; enough that the humorist has by no means invariably a chuckle in his throat; at moments of his supreme success, he will hardly move us to more of merriment than appears in a thoughtful smile.

But there is a perfectly legitimate, and tolerably wide, range for the capers of a laughing spirit, and as a writer of true farce I suppose Dickens has never been surpassed *Pickwick* abounds in it, now quite distinct from, and now all but blending with, the higher characteristic. One can imagine that the public approval of his *Sketches* had given the author an impetus, which carried him of a sudden into regions of extravagant buoyancy and mirthfulness. The first few pages are farce of the frankest. Winkle, Snodgrass, and Tupman remain throughout farcical characters, but not so Mr. Pickwick himself. Farce is the election at Eatanswill, and the quarrel of the rival Editors, and many another well-remembered passage. Only a man of genius has the privilege of being so emphatically young. "Though the merriment was rather boisterous, still it came from the heart and not from the lips; and this is the right sort of merriment after all."

How could one better describe, than in these words from the book itself, that overflowing cheeriness which conquered Dickens's first public! Or take the description of old Wardle coming through the early sunshine to bid Mr. Pickwick good morning, — "out of breath with his own anticipations of pleasure". Alas old gentlemen, however jolly, do not get breathless in this fashion; but the young may, and Dickens, a mere boy himself, was writing for the breathless boyhood of many an age to come.

The farce in his younger work always results from this exuberance of spirits; later, he introduces it deliberately; with conscious art — save perhaps at those moments when the impulse of satire is too much for him. One easily recalls his best efforts in this direction. The wild absurdity of the Muffin Company at the beginning of *Nickleby* shows him still in his boyish mood, and the first chapter of *Chuzzlewit* finds him unluckily reverting to it at the moment when he was about to produce a masterpiece of genuine humour. Mr. Mantalini is capital fun; he never quite loses his hold upon one, and to the end we shall laugh over the "demnition egg" and the "demnition bow-wows". At this stage Dickens was capable of a facetiousness of descriptive phrase which hints the peril involved in a reputation such as he had won. "Madame Mantalini wrung her hands for grief and rung the bell for her husband; which done, she fell into a chair and a fainting fit simultaneously."

When he had written that passage, and allowed it to stand, his genius warned him; I remember nothing so dangerous in after-time. Quilp, at his best, is rich entertainment; in Dick Swiveller we touch higher things. The scene between little David Copperfield and the waiter (chapter v) seems to me farce, though very good; country innkeepers were never in the habit of setting a dish-load of cutlets before a little boy who wanted dinner, and not even the shrewdest of waiters, having devoured them all, could make people believe that it was the little boy's achievement; but the comic vigour of the thing is irresistible. Better still is the forced marriage of Jack Bunsby to the great MacStinger.

Here, I think, Dickens reaches his highest point. We cannot call it "screaming" farce; it appeals not only to the groundlings. Laughter holding both his sides was never more delightfully justified; gall and the megrims were never more effectually dispelled. It is the ludicrous in its purest form, tainted by no sort of unkindliness, and leaving behind it nothing but the wholesome aftertaste of self-forgetful mirth.

We may notice how Dickens makes use of farcical extravagance to soften the bitterness of truth. When Sally Brass goes down into the grimy cellar-kitchen to give the little slavey her food, we are told that she cut from the joint "two square inches of cold mutton", and bade her victim never say that she had not had meat in *that* house. This makes one laugh; who can refrain? If he had avoided exaggeration, and shown us the ragged, starving child swallowing the kind of meal which was really set before her, who could have endured it? The point is vastly important for an understanding of Dickens's genius and his popularity. That "two square inches" makes all the difference between painful realism and fiction universally acceptable; it is the secret of Dickens's power for good. Beside it may be set another instance.

Judy Smallweed, in *Bleak House,* likewise has her little slavey over whom she tyrannizes; a child, too, who has won our sympathy in a high degree, and whom we could not bear to see brutally used. She *is* brutally used; but then Judy Smallweed is a comical figure; so comical that no one takes her doings with seriousness. Harsh words and broken meats are again provocative of laughter, when in very truth we should sob. With Dickens's end in view, how wise his method! After merriment comes the thought: "But what a shame!" And henceforth the reader thinks sympathetically of poor little girls, whether ruled by vicious trollops or working under easier conditions. Omit the jest — and the story becomes too unpleasant to remember.

Between Dickens's farce and his scenes of humour, the difference is obvious. In Mantalini or Jack Bunsby we have nothing illuminative; they amuse, and there the matter ends. But true humour always suggests a thought, always throws light on human nature. The humorist may not be fully conscious of his own meaning; he always, indeed, implies more than he can possibly have thought out; and therefore it is that we find the best humour inexhaustible, ever fresh when we return to it, ever; as our knowledge of life increases, more suggestive of wisdom.

Both the Wellers are creations strictly humorous. For one thing, each is socially representative; each, moreover, is a human type, forever recognizable beneath time's disguises. Be it noticed that neither the old coachman nor his son is ever shown in a grotesque, or improbable, situation; there is no cutting of capers, even when they make us laugh the loudest. The fantastic is here needless; nature has wrought with roguish intention, and we are aware of it at every moment of their common life. No one takes Mantalini to his heart; but Tony and Sam become in very truth our friends, and for knowing them, improbable as it might seem, we know ourselves the better. They are surprising incarnations of the spirit of man, which is doomed to inhabit so variously.

The joke consists in perceiving how this spirit adjusts itself to an odd situation, reconciles itself with queerest circumstance. In old Weller, it is a matter of stress; his difficulties, never too severe, bring out the quaint philosophy of the man, and set us smiling in fellowship. Sam, at ease in the world, makes life his jest, and we ask nothing better than to laugh with one who sees so shrewdly, feels so honestly. Sam cannot away with a humbug — in this respect, Dickens's own child. Put him face to face with Job Trotter, and how his countenance shines, how his tongue is loosed! It is a great part of Sam's business in life to come into genial conflict with Job Trotter; his weapon of mockery is in the end irresistible, and a Cockney serving-man strikes many a stroke for the good of humankind. Of course he does not know it; that is our part, as we look on, and feel in our hearts the warmth of kindly merriment, and give thanks to the great humorist who teaches us so muchapter

To survey all his humorous characters would be to repeat, in substance, the same remarks again and again. I have no space for a discussion, from this point of view, of the figures that have already passed before us. But of Mrs. Gamp one word. She sometimes comes into my thought together with Falstaff, and I am tempted to say that there is a certain propriety in the association. Where else since Shakespeare shall we find such force in the humorous presentment of gross humanity? The two figures, of course, stand on different planes. In Falstaff, intellect and breeding are at issue with the flesh, however sorely worsted; in Sarah Gamp, little intellect and less breeding are to be looked for, and the flesh has its way; but I discover some likeness of character. If Betsy Prig's awful assertion regarding Mrs. Harris must be held as proved is there not a hint of resemblance between the mood that elaborated this delicious fiction and the temper native to the hero of Gadshill? A fancy; let it pass. But to my imagination the thick-tongued, leering, yet half-genial woman walks as palpably in Kingsgate Street as yon mountain of a man in Eastcheap. The literary power exhibited in one and the other portrait is of the same kind; the same perfect method of idealism is put to use in converting to a source of pleasure things that in life repel or nauseate; and in both cases the sublimation of character, of circumstance, is effected by a humour which seems unsurpassable.

From a mention of Mrs. Harris, one passes very naturally to Spenlow and Jorkins — an only less happy bit of humour. Of course it was taken straight from life; we know that without any authority; at this moment, be sure of it, more than one Mr. Spenlow is excusing his necessity or his meanness with the plea of Mr. Jorkins's inflexibility. But only the man of genius notes such a thing, and records it forever among human traits.

Very rich is Dickens's humour in those passages, which serve rather as illustrations of manners than of individual character. Take the scene at Mrs. Kenwigs's confinement — a shining chapter in the often weak and crude pages of *Nickleby*. So quietly it is done, yet so vividly; never a note of the extravagant; every detail of the scene set before us as it must have been shown in fact, but invested with such mirthful significance. Or, again, the servants' hall at Mr. Dombey's; so much better, because done with so much more geniality, than the life that went on upstairs. Or Mr. Guppy giving his friend Jobling a dinner at the chop-house; where we hear the chink of plates and glasses, and feel hungry at Jobling's acceptance of each new succulent suggestion, and see the law-clerk's wink as he reckons up with Polly the waitress. Among things supreme stands "Todgers's". Whenever I chance to come within sight of the Monument, it is not of the fire of London that I think, but of Todgers's. One feels that the house must still exist, discoverable by sufficiently earnest searchapter. It is inconceivable that any age which has not outgrown our language should forget this priceless description: every line close-packed with humorous truth.

And how generous the scale! Here is no "hitting off" in a page or so; a broad canvas filled with detail that never tires, and no touch ever superfluous. Not only are the inhabitants of Todgers's made real to us, collectively and individually, by the minutest portraiture; but the very building and its furniture fix themselves in the mind, so described that each room, each table, becomes symbolic, instinct with a meaning which the ordinary observer would never have suspected. The grim old city of London has of a sudden revealed to us a bit of its very self, and we see in it a museum of human peculiarities, foibles, and vices. There this little group of people lives squeezed amid the brick-and-mortar labyrinth; each so vastly important to himself, so infinitesimal in the general view. They remind us of busy ants, running about with what seems such ridiculous earnestness; yet we know that their concerns are ours, and turn from laughing at them — to go and do likewise.

The subtlest bit of humour in all Dickens's books is, to my mind, that scene I have already mentioned as a triumph of characterization, the Father of the Marshal sea entertaining his old pensioner Nandy. But public favour turns to pictures of life that have more familiarity. Dickens was always happy when dealing with that common object of his time — nothing like so common nowadays — the travelling show: were it dramatic or equestrian, waxworks or Punch and Judy. From Mr. Crummles and his troupe in *Nickleby* down to Chops the Dwarf in a story written for *All the Year Round*, he never failed in such humorous picturing. Codlin and Short are typical instances. These figures never become farcical; they are always profoundly true, and amuse by pure virtue of their humanity. Akin to this order of beings is another with which he had remarkable acquaintance — the inn waiter. Read again (or only too possibly read for the first time) the waiter's autobiography in *Somebody's Luggage*. Here is no satire, but very fact made vocal; made, at the same time, such a delightful example of unconscious self-disclosure that we cannot sufficiently wonder at the author's sympathetic knowledge.

No one has equalled him in bringing out the humours of stupidity. One of his masterpieces is old Willet, the landlord of the Maypole. Willet is all but a born idiot, in the proper sense of the word; and that "all but" becomes in Dickens's hand the opportunity for elaborate portraiture. You may compare the man with the weakest-minded of Dickens's lower-class women (whichever that may be), and find in the parallel a rich subject of speculation.

Being masculine, Willet is sparing of his words; his great resource is a blank stare of imbecile resentment, implying an estimate of his own importance at which the very gods might stand fixed between amaze and laughter. Inimitable the skill with which this asserter of human dignity is shown at last suffering from mental shock — a shock so severe that it almost reduces him to the condition of a deaf-mute. We had thought it impossible that he could fall intellectually lower; when it comes, we can only acknowledge the author's reserve of power. There he sits, amid the wreck of his fine old inn, staring at his old-time companion, the kitchen boiler. Seeing him thus, we have it brought to mind that he really was, in his way, a capable landlord, and had kept the Maypole spick and span for many a long year; which possibly suggests an aspect of English character, and English conservatism, not out of keeping with some of Dickens's views on such subjects.

I must not omit mention of those sketches of genuine grotesques — not Quilp-like extravagances — which now and then flash upon us at some odd moment of the story: wonders of swift character-drawing, and instinct with humour. The finest examples I can remember are the figure of Mr. Nadgett, in *Chuzzlewit* (chap. xxvii), and that of the old woman called Tamaroo, in the same book (chap. xxxii). Language cannot do more in the calling up of a vivid image before the mind; and this result is mainly traceable to the writer's humorous insight. There could be no better illustration of the difference between Dickens's grasp and presentment of a bit of human nature, a bit of observable fact, and that method, which the critics of to-day, inaccurately but intelligibly, call photographic. Nadgett, the tracker of sordid mysteries, and Tamaroo, successor of young Bailey at Todgers's, acquire an imaginative importance like in kind (however different in degree) to that of the grandest figures in fiction. Every stroke of such outlines is a manifestation of genius.

Inseparable from the gift of humour is that of pathos. It was Dickens's misfortune that, owing to habits of his mind already sufficiently discussed; he sometimes elaborated pathetic *scenes*, in the theatrical sense of the word. I do not attribute to him the cold insincerity so common in the work of playwrights; but at times, he lost self-restraint and unconsciously responded to the crude ideals of a popular audience. Emphasis and iteration, however necessary for such hearers, were out of place in pathetic narrative. Thus, it comes about that he is charged with mawkishness, and we hear of some who greatly enjoy his humour rapidly turning the pages meant to draw a tear. Chiefly; I suppose, it is the death of Paul Dombey that such critics have in mind; they would point also to the death of Jo, the crossing-sweeper, and to that of little Nell. On a re-perusal of these chapters, I feel that nothing can be said in defence of Jo; on his deathbed he is an impossible creature, and here for once moral purpose has been undeniably fatal to every quality of art. Regarding the other narratives, it strikes me that they have been too hastily condemned. The one line, which describes the death of Paul's mother is better, no doubt, than the hundreds through which we follow the fading of Paul himself; but these pages I cannot call mawkish, for I do not feel that they are flagrantly untrue. The tear may rise or not — that depends upon how we are constituted — but we are really standing by the bed of a gentle little child, precociously gifted and cruelly overwrought, and, if the situation is to be presented at all, it might be much worse done. Such pathos is called "cheap". I can only repeat that in

Dickens's day, the lives, the happiness of children were very cheap indeed, and that he had his purpose in insisting on their claims to attention. As for the heroine of *The Old Curiosity Shop*, distaste for her as a pathetic figure seems to me unintelligent. She is a child of romance; her death is purely symbolical, signifying the premature close of any sweet, innocent, and delicate life. Heaven forbid that I should attribute to Dickens a deliberate allegory. But, having in mind those hapless children who were then being tortured in England's mines and factories, I like to see in Little Nell a type of their sufferings; she, the victim of avarice, dragged with bleeding feet along the hard roads, ever pursued by heartless self-interest, and finding her one safe refuge in the grave. Look back upon the close of that delightful novel, and who can deny its charm? Something I shall have to say presently about the literary style; but as a story of peaceful death it is beautifully imagined and touchingly told.

Of true pathos Dickens has abundance. The earliest instance I can call to mind is the death of the Chancery prisoner in *Pickwick*, described at no great length, but very powerful over the emotions. It worthily holds a place amid the scenes of humour enriching that part of the book. We feel intensely the contrast between the prisoner's life and that which was going on in the free world only a few yards away; we see in his death a pitifulness beyond words. A scene in another book, — *Bleak House*, — this, too, connected with that accursed system of imprisonment for debt, shows Dickens at his best in bringing out the pathos of child-life. The man known to Mr. Skimpole as "Coavinses" has died, and Coavinses' children, viewed askance by neighbours because of their father's calling, are living alone in a garret. They are presented as simply as possible — nothing here of stage emphasis — yet the eyes dazzle as we look. I must quote a line or two. "We were looking at one another," says Esther Summerson, "and at these two children, when there came into the room a very little girl, childish in figure but shrewd and older-looking in the face — pretty faced too — wearing a womanly sort of bonnet much too large for her, and drying her bare arms on a womanly sort of apron. Her fingers were white and wrinkled with washing, and the soapsuds were yet smoking which she wiped oft her arms. But for this, she might have been a child playing at washing and imitating a poor working-woman with a quick observation of the truth." It is Charley, of course, who had found a way to support herself and the younger ones. We see how closely the true pathetic and a "quick observation" are allied. Another picture shown us in Esther's narrative that of the baby's death in the starved labourer's cottage, moves by legitimate art. Still more of it is felt in the story of Doctor Marigold, the Cheap-Jack, whose child is dying in his arms, whilst for daily bread he plays buffoon before the crowd. This is a noble piece of work, and defies criticism. The tale is told by the man himself as simply as possible; he never insists upon the pitifulness of his position. We hear his whispers to the child, between his hoarse professional shoutings and the guffaws in front; then he finds his word of tenderness brings no response — he looks closer — he turns from the platform. A piece of work that might atone for literary sins far worse than Dickens ever committed.

Little Dorrit is strong in pathos, as in humour. Dickens's memories of childhood made his touch very sure whenever he dealt with the squalid prison-world, and life there was for him no less fertile in pathos than death. Very often it is inextricably blended with his humour; in the details of the Marshal sea picture, who shall say which element of his genius prevails? Vet, comparing it with the corresponding scenes in *Pickwick*, we perceive a subdual of tone, which comes not only of advancing years, but of riper art; and as we watch the Dorrits step forth from the prison door, it is another mood than that which accompanied the release of Mr. Pickwick. Pathos of this graver and subtler kind is the distinguishing note of *Great Expectations*, a book which Dickens meant, and rightly meant, to end in the minor key. The old convict, Magwitch, if he cannot be called a tragical personality, has feeling enough to move the reader's deeper interest, and in the very end acquires through suffering a dignity which makes him very impressive. Rightly seen, is there not much pathos in the story of Pip's foolishness? It would be more manifest if we could forget Lytton's imbecile suggestion, and restore the original close of the story.

To the majority of readers it seemed — and perhaps still seems — that Dickens achieved his best pathos in the Christmas books. Two of those stories answered their purpose admirably; the other two showed a flagging spirit; but not even in the *Carol* can we look for anything to be seriously compared with the finer features of his novels. The true value of these little books lies in their deliberate illustration of a theme which occupied Dickens's mind from first to last. Writing for the season of peace, good-will, and jollity, he sets himself to exhibit these virtues in an idealization of the English home. The type of domestic beauty he finds, as a matter of course, beneath a humble roof. And we have but to glance in memory through the many volumes of his life's work to recognize that his gentlest, brightest humour, his simplest pathos, occur in those unexciting pages which depict the everyday life of poor and homely English folk. This is Dickens's most delightful aspect, and I believe it is the most certainly enduring portion of what he has left us.

His genius plays like a warm light on the characteristic aspects of homely England. No man ever loved England more; and the proof of it remains in picture after picture of her plain, old-fashioned life — in wayside inns and cottages, in little dwellings hidden amid the city's vastness and tumult, in queer musty shops, in booths and caravans. Finding comfort or jollity, he enjoys it beyond measure, he rubs his hands, he sparkles, he makes us laugh with him from the very heart. Coming upon hardship and woe, he is moved as nowhere else, holds out the hand of true brotherhood, tells to the world his indignation and his grief. There would be no end of selecting passages in illustration, but we must recall a few for the mere pleasure of the thing. Try to imagine the warmest welcome of a cosy little inn, at the end of a long lonely road, on a night of foul weather; you must needs have recourse to the Jolly Sandboys, where Nell and her grandfather and the wandering showmen all found shelter. "There was a deep ruddy blush upon the room, and when the landlord stirred the fire, sending the flames skipping and leaping up. When he took off the lid of the iron pot, and there rushed out a savoury smell, while the bubbling sound grew deeper and more rich, and an unctuous steam came floating out, hanging in a delicious mist above their heads — when he did this, Mr. Codlin's heart was touched" (*Old Curiosity Shop*, chap. xxviii). And whose is not? What dyspeptic exquisite but must laugh with appetite over such a description?

As good is the picture of Ruth Pinch at the butcher's. "To see him slap the steak before he laid it on the block, and give his knife a sharpening, was to forget breakfast instantly. It was agreeable, too, — it really was — to see him cut it off, so smooth and juicy. There was nothing savage in the act. Although the knife was large and keen, it was a piece of high art.... Perhaps the greenest cabbage-leaf ever grown in a garden was wrapped about this steak before it was delivered over to Tom. But the butcher had a sentiment for his business, and knew how to refine upon it. When he saw Tom putting the cabbage-leaf into his pocket awkwardly, he begged to be allowed to do it for him; 'for meat', he said with some emotion, 'must be humoured and not drove'!" (*Chuzzlewit*, chap. xxxix). Reading this, how does one regret that Dickens should have filled with melodrama many a page which might have been given to the commonest doings of the humble street!

There is a great chapter of *The Old Curiosity Shop* (chap. xxxix), where Kit and Barbara, with their respective mothers, with little Jacob, too, and the Baby, go to spend the evening at Astley's. It would have seemed impossible to get so much kindly fun out of a group of the London poor. Dickens does it by dint of his profound, his overflowing sympathy with them. He glows with delight when *they* are delighted; he understands precisely what they enjoy, and why; it does his very soul good to hear Kit's guffaws and the screaming laugh of little Jacob. Where else in literature is there such infinite good-feeling expressed with such wondrous whimsicality? After the circus, Kit takes all his companions to have an oyster supper (by the way, in those days, as Sam Weller assures us, poverty and oysters always went together). And not one of them enjoyed the meal more than he who gaily described it. How the London poor should love Dickens! But — with his books always obtainable — they can scarce be said to read him at all.

Remember that such a scene as this was *new* in literature, a bold innovation. Dickens had no model to imitate when he sat down to tell of the joys of servant-lads and servant-girls with their washerwomen and sempstress mothers, But in spirit he continues the work of two writers whom he always held dear, Goldsmith and Sterne. Goldsmith's sweetness and compassion, Sterne's sensitive humanity, necessarily had their part, and that no small one, in forming Dickens. There is a foretaste of his humour in Moses ("Boz", as we know), the son of the Vicar of Wakefield, and in the would-be fine company; there is a palpable hint to him in the Vicar preaching among poor prisoners. Turning to Uncle Toby, to Corporal Trim, we are perforce reminded of those examples of grotesque goodness, of sweet humility under the oddest exteriors, upon which Dickens lavished his humour and his love.

Captain Cuttle is well known an\mong all of them. In what terms of literary criticism shall one describe that scene (*Dombey*, chap. xlix) where the Captain sits in Solomon Gills's parlour and Florence mixes his grog for him? It is a sort of fairy tale of modern life. No one can for a moment believe that two such persons ever were in such relations; but so irrelevant an objection never occurs to us. All we know is, that a spell is laid upon us; that we pass from smiles to laughter, and from laughter to smiles again. Who ever paused to think that the old coasting Captain, Mrs. MacStinger's lodger, must have been in person and manners and speech not a little repulsive to a young lady straight from a great house in the west of London? It is not germane to the matter. These are actors in the world of humour and imagination, raised above the inessentials of life. Dickens's thought. was to make a picture delightful to every heart which can enjoy fun, respect innocence, and sympathize with kindness. Moreover, he wished to point a contrast between the stately house, inhabited by wealth and pride, the atmosphere of which had grown poisonous from the evil passions nurtured in it; and the little back parlour of a shop somewhere amid the City's noisiest streets, where the homeliest — and therefore the most precious — virtues have a secure abode. Fleeing from the home that is none, the mansion where her womanly instincts have been outraged, Florence betakes herself to this poor haven of refuge, and lives there guarded and honoured as any queen in her palace. What could make stronger appeal to the sensibilities of English readers? No national foible is here concerned: we respond with the very best that is in us. We feel that these are the ideals of English life. We are proud of the possibility underlying a fancy of such irresistible charm.

For his own fame, Dickens, I think, never puts his genius to better use than in the idealization of English life and character. Whatever in his work may be of doubtful interest to future time, here is its enduring feature. To be truly and profoundly national is great strength in the maker of literature. What a vast difference from all but every point of view between Dickens and Tennyson; yet it is likely enough that these two may survive together as chosen writers of the Victorian age. They are at one in their English sentiment They excite the same emotion whenever they speak of the English home; none, I think, of their contemporaries touches so powerfully that island note. In Tennyson's glorious range, humour is not lacking; it exercises itself on a theme of the most intimately national significance, and his Northern Farmer will live as long as the poet's memory. Of humour the very incarnation, Dickens cannot think of his country without a sunny smile. In our hearts we love him for it, and so, surely, will the island people for many an age to come.

STYLE

Dickens is one of the masters of prose, but in a sense that carries qualification. He cannot be compared with Thackeray for flow of pure idiom, for command of subtle melodies. He is often mannered to the last point of endurance; he has one fault which offends the prime law of prose composition. For all that, he made unique use of the English language, and his style must be examined as one of the justifications of his place in literature.

In the beginning, it had excellent qualities; his *Sketches* are phrased with vigour, with variety, and with a soundness of construction which he owed to his eighteenth-century studies. Dealing for the most part with vulgarity, his first book is very free from vulgarisms. In one of the earliest letters to Forster, he speaks of "your invite"; but no such abomination deforms his printed pages. Facetiousness is now and then to blame for an affected sentence, and this fault once or twice crops up in later books. Someone in *Pickwick* wears "a grin which agitated his countenance from one auricular organ to the other"; and in *Bleak House*, when grandfather Smallweed threw his cushion at the old woman, we are told that "the effect of this act of jaculation was twofold". Without much effort Dickens kept clear of such pitfalls; what *might* have befallen him but for his fine models and his good sense, we may surmise from the style of certain of his more or less conscious imitators, Slovenly English he never wrote; the nature of the man made it impossible. And in this respect he contrasts remarkably with all save the greatest of his day.

As an illustration of what a generally sound writer could permit himself in the hurry of writing a "mere novel", I remember a passage in Henry Kingsley's *Ravenshoe* (chap. xxviii), where a dog is trying to attract his master's attention; we read, with a little shock of surprise, that "the dog wagged his tail and pawed his waistcoat". But Dickens respected both himself and his public — never a common virtue in the everyday English novelist.

The gravest of his faults, from *Oliver Twist* onwards — and he never wholly overcame it — is the habit of writing metrically. He is not alone in this vice. Charles Kingsley illustrates it very badly in some of his prose; especially, I remember, in the *Heroes*. Should any one wish to see how far the trick (unconsciously, of course) can be carried, let him open Richard Jefferies' paper "The Open Air", where he will find several pages written, with very few breaks, precisely in a metre made familiar by Longfellow. As thus: "All the devious brooklet's sweetness / where the iris stays the sunlight; / all the wild woods hold of beauty: / all the broad hills' thyme and freedom: / thrice a hundred years repeated". This, of course, betrays an ear untrained in the harmonies of prose; the worst of it is, that many readers would discover it with delight, and point to it as admirable. A good many years since, I came upon a magazine article entitled "Dickens as a Poet", the absurd aim whereof was to show admiringly how many passages from the novels could be written and read as blank verse. The fact unfortunately cannot be disputed. Dickens wrote thus under the influence of strong emotion. He observed the tendency, speaks of it as something he cannot help, and is not disturbed by it. The habit overcame him in his moods of softness; and therefore is particularly noticeable towards the end of the *Old Curiosity Shop*.

When his emotion is indignant, on the other hand, he is not thus tempted; simply as a bit of prose, the paragraph giving a general description of the children at Dotheboys, is good, well-balanced, with no out-of-place rhythm. But turn to a passage quoted by Forster (Book iii, chap. 8) from the *American Notes*; quoted as a fine expression of Dickens's sympathy with the poor. It is nobly felt, most admirably worded; yet the five-foot cadence is flagrant here and there. "But bring him here, upon this crowded deck. / Strip from his fair young wife her silken dress /... pinch her pale cheek with care and much privation" — and so on. One is half inclined to think that Dickens did it deliberately, regarding it as an improvement on plain prose.

For a style simple, direct, and forcible, one may turn to *Barnaby Rudge*. Taking it all in all, this is perhaps the best written of his novels; best, that is to say, in the sense of presenting the smoothest and closest strain of narrative. There are no irruptions of metre; the periods are flowing, the language is full of subdued energy. Among the first few books it is very noticeable for this peculiar excellence. One reason, possibly, is its comparative shortness. *Nickleby*, on the other hand, has faults of style plainly due to the necessity of writing more than the author wished to say. One of its best-knit chapters is that describing Nicholas's walk from London through Surrey, with Smike. We breathe the very air of the downs, and smell the sweetness of wayside hedges. This power of suggesting a country atmosphere is remarkable in Dickens. He hardly ever mentions a tree or flower by its name; he never elaborates — perhaps never even sketches — a landscape; yet we see and feel the open-air surroundings. The secret is his own delight in the road and the meadow, and his infinite power of suggestion in seemingly unconsidered words.

In narrative, he is always excellent when describing rapid journeys. The best coach-drive ever put into words is that of the Muggleton coach, in *Pickwick*. It surpasses the much longer description in *Chuzzlewit*, which comes near to being monotonous after many paragraphs beginning with the same words. It is incredibly exhilarating, and would put a healthy glow, as of a fine frosty morning, into the veins of a man languishing in the tropics. We are asked to believe that the story (in *Bleak House*) of the posting journey conducted by Inspector Bucket, came from the pen of Miss Esther Summerson; the brain, at all events, was Dickens's, and working with its most characteristic vigour.

He knew every stage covered by the travellers; he saw the gleam of the lamps, the faces they illumined but for a moment; the very horses brought out fresh were his old acquaintances. Such writing is no mere question of selecting and collocating words; there must first be vision, and that of extraordinary clearness. Dickens tells us that in times of worry or of grave trouble he could still write; he had but to sit down at his desk, and straightway he *saw*. Where — as would happen — he saw untruly, a mere fantasm thrown forward by the mind, his hand at once had lost its cunning. When vision was but a subtly enhanced memory, he never lacked the skill to make it seen by others.

Think of the easy graphic power that Dickens possessed, and compare it for a moment with the results of such laborious effort to the same ends as was put forth by the French novelist Flaubert. On the one hand, here is a man who works hard indeed, and methodically, but whose work is ever a joy to him, and not seldom a rapture. On the other, we have growls and groans; toil advancing at snail's pace, whilst sweat drips from the toiler's brow; little or no satisfaction to him in the end from all his suffering. And not one page of Flaubert gives proof of sight and grasp equal to that evinced in a thousand of Dickens. This thing cometh not by prayer and fasting, nor by any amount of thinking about art. You have it or you have it not. As a boy or youth, Dickens was occupied in *seeing*; as a young man, he took his pen and began to write of what he had seen. And the world saw with him — much better than with its own poor, purblind eyes.

In the story of David Copperfield's journey on the Dover road, we have as good a piece of narrative prose as can be found in English. Equally as good, in another way, are those passages of rapid retrospect, in which David tells us of his later boyhood; a concentration of memory perfumed with the sweetest humour. It is not an easy thing to relate with perfect proportion of detail, with interest that never for a moment drops, the course of a year or two of wholly uneventful marriage; but read the chapter entitled "Our Domestic Life" and try to award adequate praise to the great artist who composed it. One can readily suggest how the chapter might have been spoiled; ever so little undue satire, ever so little excess of sentiment; but who can point to a line in which it might be bettered? It is perfect writing; one can say no more and no less.

Another kind of descriptive writing appears in the nineteenth chapter of *Chuzzlewit*: the funeral of old Anthony conducted by Mr. Mould. What of the scope declared in a contrast of this chapter with the one in *Copperfield* just mentioned? I should not like to say that one excels the other; I should find it impossible to decide between their merits. Where is the "extravagance" which, we are told, has pronounced Dickens's doom? Mr. Mould and his retainers, the whole funeral from house to grave, seems to me realism of the finest; it is clearest vision and narrative, without a hint of effort; and there stands the thing forever.

A fine piece of the grimly picturesque is Quilp's death. Better, because more human, is the narrative in *Barnaby Rudge* of the day and night before the gaol-delivery when the rioters are to be hung. It has the effect of rapidity, but contains an immense amount of detail, actual and imaginative. Dennis, Hugh, and Barnaby, together in their cell, are seen by us as the swift hours pass, and at the same time we know what is going on without. Of all the broad and the delicate touches in which these pages abound, not one could be omitted as superfluous; and the impression aimed at is obtained with absolute success.

Narrative, of course, includes description; but in description by itself and in elaborate picturing, as distinguished from the hints that so often serve his purpose, Dickens is very strong. Before speaking of the familiar instances let me mention that chapter at the beginning of *Little Dorrit,* which opens with a picture of London as seen on a gloomy Sunday — if the phrase be not tautological. It is very curious reading. For once we have Dickens quite divested of his humour, and beholding the great city in something like a splenetic mood. As conveying an impression, the passage could not be better; it makes us feel precisely what one has felt times innumerable amid the black lifeless houses, under a sky that crushes the spirit. But seldom indeed can Dickens have seen and felt thus. Compare with it his picture of the fog — Mr. Guppy's "London particular" — at the opening of *Bleak House*. This darkness visible makes one rather cheerful than otherwise, for we are spectators in the company of a man who allows nothing to balk his enjoyment of life, and who can jest unaffectedly even in such circumstances. Those few pages of *Little Dorrit,* admirable as art, suggest the kind of novels Dickens might have written without his humour. But in that case he would not have written them at all.

His normal manner is seen in the description of the Fleet, in *Pickwick*. It would appear difficult to make a vivid picture of such a place, a picture which convinces, and yet to omit things vile or intolerable to the feelings; but here it is done. The same art manifests itself as in his masterpieces of characterization; something is obscured, nothing falsified. At times, he could make a sketch in what is known as the impressionist manner; rapid, strong, and in the broadest lines suggesting a vast amount of detail; as in the description of the Gordon rioters seen, passing in their drunken fury along the street, from an upper window (*Barnaby*, chapter L). Dickens was rather proud of this passage; he calls attention to it in a letter written at the time. Innumerable the aspects of London presented in his books; what a wonderful little volume might be made by collecting such passages! Of the West-end we have glimpses only; one remembers, however, that very genteel but stuffy corner inhabited by the house of Barnacle, and the similar locality where dwelt Miss Tox.

Stately and wealthy London he does not show us; his artistic preference is for the quaint, out-of-the-way quarters, or for the grim and the lurid, out of which he made a picturesque of his own. Writing once from Naples (where he was merely disappointed and disgusted, we can see why), he says, "I am afraid the conventional idea of the picturesque is associated with such misery and degradation that a new picturesque will have to be established as the world goes onward". Conventional his own ideas and presentments certainly were not, but for the most part they *are* closely connected with misery and degradation. Jacob's Island and Tom-all-alone's have the affect of fine, wild etchings lighted only just sufficiently to show broad features and suggest details one does not desire to pry into. Krook's house and its surroundings make an essential part of the world shadowed by Chancery; unutterably foul and stifling, yet so shown as to hold the imagination in no painful way. Dickens views such scenes in a romantic light. It is the property of his genius to perceive romance in the commonplace and the squalid, no less than in clean and comfortable homeliness.

What he can make out of a wretched little room a few feet square, in a close-packed, sordid neighbourhood, is shown in chapter xlvi of *Chuzzlewit*. Jonas, become a murderer, is lurking in his own house, and chooses a corner of it where he is not likely to be observed. "The room in which he had shut himself up was on the ground-floor, at the back of the house. It was lighted by a dirty sky-light, and had a door in the wall, opening into a narrow, covered passage or blind alley.... It was a blotched, stained, mouldering room, like a vault; and there were water-pipes running through it, which, at unexpected times in the night, when other things were quiet, clicked and gurgled suddenly, as if they were choking." Nothing could be more insignificant, and at the same time more grim. An out-of-doors companion to it may be found in *Great Expectations*. I came into Smithfield; the shameful place, being all filth and fat and blood and foam, seemed to stick to me. So I rubbed it off with all possible speed by turning into a street where I saw the great black dome of St. Paul's bulging at me from behind a grim stone building which a bystander said was Newgate Prison. Following the wall of the jail, I found the roadway covered with straw to deaden the sound of passing vehicles; and from the quantity of people standing about, smelling strongly of spirits and beer, I inferred that the trials were on" (chap. xx). This is "locality" as good as the bit of human portraiture which follows (Mr. Jaggers walking through the throng of his clients); and higher praise could not be bestowed.

I suppose there is no English writer, perhaps no writer in any literature, who so often gives proof of wonderfully minute observation. It is an important source of his strength; it helps him to put people and things before us more clearly than, as a rule, we should ourselves see them. Two examples only can I find room for; but they will suffice. Peggotty's purse, given to little David on his departure from Yarmouth, was found to contain "three bright shillings, which Peggotty had evidently polished up with whiting for my greater delight". And again, little Pip, after being washed by his sister, is led to make the remark: "I suppose myself to be better acquainted than any living authority with the ridgy effect of a wedding-ring, passing unsympathetically over the human countenance". You will come across no such instances as these in any other novelist, of observation, memory, and imaginative force, all evinced in a touch of detail so indescribably trivial; its very triviality being the proof of power in one who could so choose for his purposes among the neglected incidents of life.

When Dickens writes in his pleasantest mood of things either pleasant in themselves, or especially suggestive of humorous reflection, his style is faultless; perfectly suited, that is to say, to the author's aim and to the matter in hand. His Christmas number called *The Holly Tree* begins with a chapter on Inns; we rise from it feeling that on that subject the last word has been said, and said in the best possible way. His book of collected papers, *The Uncommercial Traveller*, consists almost wholly of such writing. Whether its theme is City of London Churches, or Shy Neighbourhoods, Tramps, or Night-walks, or London Chambers, he is invariably happy in phrase, and in flow of language which, always easy, never falls below the level of literature. In such work he must be put beside the eighteenth-century essayists, whom he always had in mind. His English is not less idiomatic than theirs, and his views of life find no less complete expression through the medium of a style so lightly and deftly handled.

Chapter 9

Dickens and Society

Throughout his career, Dickens protested the abuse of children and the corruption of individual feelings. His portrayal of the destructiveness of society's institutions and values becomes more insistent and savage in his later novels. In his early, hopeful novels, the problems of his protagonists, who are often orphaned or abandoned as children, are solved by the benevolence of good men; the charitable nature of the Cheeryble Brothers in *Nicholas Nickl by* is indicated by their name, and David Copperfield is rescued from the Murdstones' clutches by Aunt Betsey. But Dickens lost faith in the ability of individuals to remedy the unjust treatment of individuals; he perceived that injustice, indifference, and cruelty were pervasive and incorporated into society's institutions.

Because of Dickens's moral outrage and his attacks on society's institutions and values, later critics, who were often Marxists, hailed him variously as subversive, rebellious, and even revolutionary. They did not necessarily claim that Dickens was aware of the subversion or revolutionary thrust of his novels. George Bernard Shaw compared Marx and Dickens thus: "The difference between Marx and Dickens was that Marx knew he was a revolutionist whilst Dickens had not the faintest suspicion of that part of his calling." There was good reason for contrasting the two men; Marx fled to London in 1849, died there in 1883, and was a writer. Thus, the two men were observing the same society and class structure; both were subject to similar social conditions and pressures. Furthermore, *Barnaby Rudge* and *A Tale of Two Cities* both are set in revolutionary times, identify some of the abuses that sparked the outbreaks, and describe the violent, chaotic behaviour of the mobs.

George Orwell, in 1946, viewed Dickens's "rebelliousness" from a different perspective:

In *Oliver Twist, Hard Times, Bleak House, Little Dorrit,* Dickens attacked English institutions with a ferocity that has never since been approached. Yet he managed to do it without making himself hated, and, more than this, the very people he attacked have welcomed him so completely that he has become a national institution himself.

It is true that Dickens's readership remained loyal to him; despite his savage attacks on society and his forcing his wife of twenty-some years to leave their marriage and their home (remember that Dickens was perceived as the upholder of the sacred domestic hearth and the family). One reason that he retained his popularity may be that Dickens had no agenda or systematic programme, as Marx did, to tear down society and replace it with a new structure. Some critics have wondered whether Dickens was really attacking human nature and not society. Granted, Dickens did repeatedly reject the assumptions that class was more important than common humanity or that rank was superior to virtue:

I believe that virtue shows quite as well in rags and palaces as she does in purple and fine linen.... I believe that she goes barefoot as well as shod. I believe that she dwells rather oftener in alleys and by-ways than she does in courts and palaces...

Nonetheless, Dickens still accepted the existing class structure and distinctions: "Differences of wealth, of rank, of intellect, we know there must be, and we respect them."

His attacks on society were based on traditional moral beliefs and humanism rather than on social or political theories and programmes. He urged a secular ideal of human brotherhood. *Fraser's Magazine,* in its obituary of Dickens, noted this aspect of Dickens's beliefs: "He spent no thought on religious doctrines or religious reforms, but regarded the Sermon on the Mount as good teaching, had a regard for the village church and churchyard, and quarrelled with nothing but intolerance." Writing of Dickens's belief in domestic life as the source of happiness and the alternative to social evil, Angus Wilson added, "Even more vital to Dickens was the idea of pure love as the means of redemption of flawed, weak, or sinful men. Neither of these beliefs can properly take the weight that he imposed on them..." Moreover, his contemporaries saw him as a member of and the spokesman for a particular class; a reviewer for *Blackwood's* in 1855 noted:

We cannot but express our conviction that it is to the fact that he represents a class that he owes his speedy elevation to the top of the wave of popular favour. He is a man of very liberal sentiments–an assailer of constituted wrongs and authorities–one of the advocates in the plea of Poor versus Rich, to the progress of which he has lent no small aid in his day. But he is, notwithstanding, perhaps more distinctly than any other author of his time, a class writer, the historian and representative of one circle in the many ranks in our social scale. Despite their descents into the lowest class, and their occasional flights into the less familiar ground of fashion, it is the air and breath of middle-class respectability which fills the books of Mr. Dickens.

Unlike Thackeray, Dickens was not seen as quite or fully a gentleman. Thackeray's province was, as W.C. Roscoe described it, "the debatableble land between the aristocracy and the middle classes"; Dickens showed the efforts of the lower strata of the middle class to rise from being tradesmen and upper servants into the respectable middle classes. Thackeray wrote that "an English gentleman knows as much about the people of Lapland or California as he does of the aborigines of the Seven Dials or the natives of Wapping." Dickens, of course, knew, and wrote with sympathy and understanding, about the classes who lived in such neighborhoods as Seven Dials and Wapping. Furthermore, Dickens was accused of being unable to describe a gentleman. G. K. Chesterton explained that this accusation really meant that Dickens could not describe a gentleman as gentlemen feel a gentleman. They mean that he could not take that atmosphere easily, accept it as the normal atmosphere, or describe that world from the inside... Dickens did not describe gentleman in the way that gentlemen describe gentlemen... He described them... from the outside, as he described any other oddity or special trade.

Chapter 10

Dickens and the Victorian Serial Novel

The nineteenth-century Victorian serial novel was a way for readers and writers to make a novel last years and be talked about endlessly like the daily soap opera of this century. The serial is an ongoing story that is told over time through installments with interruptions or stops. Its history will give great understanding to just how important Charles Dickens was to serial publication and how important serial publication was to nineteenth-century readers. The nineteenth-century serial novel was something readers looked forward to. Whether published alone or in a magazine, each monthly or weekly installment contained text readers could not wait to feast their eyes upon.

The continuing story of a serial is a literary example of the lengthened vision of nineteenth-century life. Most readers of the serial were part of the working middle class. They were looking for a better way of life, for hopes and for dreams, and the serial offered this to them. The serial is a whole novel that is printed a part at a time, each installment being about ten pages. It became a popular format for fiction, poetry, and prose. With each installment, the literary work grew from simple to more complex, from single character and plot to multiple characters and plot lines. Some serials were published alone but most were published in magazines. For serials that were published in magazines, the installments contained the serials along with advertisements of almost anything from a to z. Even when poetry was being issued serially, it, too, was not alone. Surrounding it were other works of history, science, and politics. All forms of serials were put together nicely with illustrations to entice and amuse the reader even more.

However, the serial was not just a piece of writing for mere entertainment. It was more involved in the lifestyle of the nineteenth-century people than it was thought to be. The images of life in the nineteenth-century were focused on expansion, length, and richness, and the serial illustrated this. Because the serial was a vision and an angle on stories about life in the Victorian times and culture, it enlightened people of all social classes, but especially the middle class. These people, like the characters in the novels, were looking for betterment. The reviews of serial novels depended on how well the stories depicted and envisioned the life that existed in the Victorian times.

The serial initially began as a way to avoid an English tax. Newspapers were expected to pay a higher tax than they were initially paying on the paper they used to publish their work; they avoided the extra tax by using bigger sheets of paper and calling their newspapers pamphlets. However, these bigger sheets had more space for text, and serialization filled up this empty space. The "London Spy," the first serial, was issued in 1698. When the paper tax was finally repealed, serialization continued because readers enjoyed it so muchapter Newspapers and magazines alike included serials in their publication in order to gain more customers; "a popular serial could double readership".

Publications of all types, including serials, were reduced due to the higher paper taxes. Serial novels made a comeback in the Victorian era with Charles Dickens and his *Pickwick Papers* in 1836. It was publishers Chapman and Hall who gave Dickens the chance to show his talent as a serial writer. They decided to release a series of sporting illustrations in installments with text narrating each picture. Robert Seymour was hired by Chapman and Hall to illustrate and Dickens to write the text. Due to Seymour's death, Dickens took control of the project with a new illustrator, Hablot Brown. The work they produced became known as the *Pickwick Papers*, each issue increasing in popularity.

Linda K. Hughes and Michael Lund point out that beginning with Dickens, serial novels gave readers a taste of the Victorian philosophy on life. Victorians were almost obsessed with becoming better people and building a better life for themselves, and serials mirrored these beliefs that progress was slow but sure to come. Through serials, readers could see the type of changes and developments characters went through. Readers could also see that there was progress to be had, even if it was slow. Victorians thought of society as capable of achieving great things; serials were the main reason that readers had hope. Victorians felt a close connection to the serial, as if they were part of the making and outcome of the story, partly because in serial reading there is a definite investment. In order to learn the outcome of a single story, readers had to invest their time and feelings in the story line. Installments allowed those feelings to grow and strengthen as readers committed themselves to years of waiting for the novel to end.

There are different views of why exactly people read serials. Some people read them as "serious entertainment" while others thought of them simply as "comical". Not everyone thought they were the literary expression of Victorian ideas about progress and personal achievement. Norman Feltes, who has studied the production of serial novels, says that the Victorian serial was just a "cheap-luxury" form of entertainment for the middle class. Thus, the entertainment was in analyzing the installments of the novel and then discussing them. Readers enjoyed gathering to converse about their own assumptions of people, places, and events and particularly the outcome of the novel as it neared. We cannot comprehend how the amount of time it took to complete one novel greatly affected how the nineteenth-century readers viewed the serial. Thus, it is understood why serials were interpreted and viewed differently.

Despite the fact that some people liked them and some people did not, serials were in great demand during the Victorian era, so writers had to adjust their talents to accommodate serial readers. There was great pressure for writers at this time. Authors of serials had to capture and keep the reader's attention from the first installment to the last. Writers who could not keep up were susceptible to losing the security and contracts serials could promise. With publication came deadlines. Most authors did their best to stay a few installments ahead, some keeping right up with the deadlines, other falling behind, and the very rare finishing the book all at once. Charles Dickens himself would complain about upcoming deadlines and would write in his own notebooks and in a letter to friend, "I MUST WRITE" (Thus, his ambition to always write and to construct better things was part of his great success.

Ambition was not the only reason for Dickens' success with the serial. To begin with, he could turn out almost seventeen pages of text a week. What made him a real writer was the fact that he traveled to the places he had planned to write about in his works. Also, his training in writing at the newspaper as well as his experience in writing character sketches gave him advantages. Dickens also took the time to plot and carefully organize all of his writing. He became such a sensation to the Victorians because he became a part of the "Victorian rage for progress".

He did this through his characters. Victorian writers expected Dickens to enlighten them with a character that "changed and improved, a character who embodied the promise of a betterment and a self-fulfillment" in each novel What happened to the wonderful serial form and Dickens? In the nineteenth-century more serials came and went, but as full novels became more popular people were interested in them more and more. They allowed the readers to read at their own pace as well as re-read or look ahead. But in essence, serials never died, they just changed. We still see serials in episodic television, and juvenile serials were popular during the first half of the twentieth century. The serials of today are predictable and have a loss of characterization. "Gone were the rising stars in literature. In their place unspectacular writers took up the slack". Through it all Dickens' novels are still read, although not in serial form. He will be remembered for the serial writing that Victorians encountered.

Chapter 11

Great Expectations: List of Characters

Pip

The narrator as well as the protagonist of the story. Pip is an orphan being raised by his sister, Mrs. Joe Gargery and her husband, Mr. Joe Gargery, a blacksmith.

Mrs. Joe Gargery

A bitter, angry woman who brings up Pip "by hand." That is, she whips him whenever she can and complains about what a burden he is while she does it.

Mr. Joe Gargery

A kind, if browbeaten, blacksmith. Though he is theoretically Pip's adoptive father, Pip sees him as an equal and a friend. Joe is uneducated and perhaps a little slow but he understands the important things in life.

Mr. Wopsle

The village church clerk whose dream it is to get on the pulpit and preach as he considers himself an excellent speaker. As it is, he becomes an actor.

Mr. and Mrs. Hubble

Simple, silly folks from Pip's village. Mr. Hubble is a wheelwright.

Uncle Pumblechook

Joe's uncle, a well-to-do corn-chandler in the village. He considers himself upper class and is actually a bombastic fool.

Mr. Wopsle's Great Aunt

Runs the so-called school in town out of a cottage. A "ridiculous old lady."

Biddy

A kind, intelligent girl Pip's age who works for Mr. Wopsle's great aunt at the school. Later, she comes to work for Joe taking care of Mrs. Joe Gargery.

Miss Havisham

A strange, wrinkled up lady who never sees the sunlight and never gets out of her bridal gown. She's actually a very cold hearted, yet wealthy, lady who lives just outside the village in a the Satis House.

Estella

Miss Havisham's adopted daughter. Cold and very proud but very beautiful. She's about Pip's age and is the love of Pip's life.

Geogiana

Aging relatives of Miss Havisham who don't have an inch of love for the woman but are greedy for her money. They buzz around Miss Havisham like flies.

Sarah Pocket

Aging relatives of Miss Havisham who don't have an inch of love for the woman but are greedy for her money. They buzz around Miss Havisham like flies.

Cousin Raymond

Aging relatives of Miss Havisham who don't have an inch of love for the woman but are greedy for her money. They buzz around Miss Havisham like flies.

Camilla

Aging relatives of Miss Havisham who don't have an inch of love for the woman but are greedy for her money. They buzz around Miss Havisham like flies.

Orlick

A gruff evil man that Joe employs around the forge. He seems to hate just about everybody, but has a crush on Biddy.

Matthew Pocket

Miss Havisham's cousin, but not one of her relatives that is greedy. Matthew Pocket has charge of nine children, two nurses, and a pretty but useless wife. He also tutors young gentlemen, including Pip.

Herbert Pocket

Matthew's son. An extremely cheerful and honest boy about Pip's age. He become Pip's best friend in London.

Jaggers

Rational and seemingly emotionless lawyer for Miss Havisham and for Pip. He is an excellent speaker and logician, however, and specializes in getting criminals light sentences.

Wemmick

Jaggers' stiff clerk by day, esoteric and generous man in private. Wemmick lives in a cottage he fashioned into a castle and fights to divide his public and private life. Wemmick becomes a good friend of Pip's (in private).

The "Aged"

Wemmick's elderly, and quite deaf, relative (of unknown relations). The Aged lives with Wemmick in his castle and is quite happy when you nod at him.

The "Avenger"

Pip's servant boy who Pip finds more of a nuisance than a help. Pip never has enough for him to do, so the Avenger always seems to be standing around.

Drummle

Another student and boarder of Matthew Pocket. He is a moody, disgruntled "spider" but comes from an upper-class family.

Startop

Another student and boarder of Matthew Pocket. He is a good friend of Pip's.

Miss Skiffins

Wemmick's sweetheart.

Clara

Herbert secret sweetheart. She is secret because Herbert knows his mother would say she is below his "station." She's actually a sweet, fairy-like girl who takes care of her dying drunk of a father.

Magwitch

The convict that Pip helps at the beginning of the movie. He later returns as Pip's benefactor under the name of Provis. He is a rough ex-con, but seems to have a good heart.

Compeyson

Magwitch's mortal enemy and the other convict Pip saw in the marshes fighting with Magwitchapter Compeyson is a gentlemanly swindler who was the fiancé that swindled Miss Havisham out of her heart.

Chapter 12

Plot Summary

Great Expectations is the story of Pip, an orphan boy adopted by a blacksmith's family, who has good luck and great expectations, and then loses both his luck and his expectations. Through this rise and fall, however, Pip learns how to find happiness. He learns the meaning of friendship and the meaning of love and, of course, becomes a better person for it.

The story opens with the narrator, Pip, who introduces himself and describes a much younger Pip staring at the gravestones of his parents. This tiny, shivering bundle of a boy is suddenly terrified by a man dressed in a prison uniform. The man tells Pip that if he wants to live, he'll go down to his house and bring him back some food and a file for the shackle on his leg.

Pip runs home to his sister, Mrs. Joe Gragery, and his adoptive father, Joe Gragery. Mrs. Joe is a loud, angry, nagging woman who constantly reminds Pip and her husband Joe of the difficulties she has gone through to raise Pip and take care of the house. Pip finds solace from these rages in Joe, who is more his equal than a paternal figure, and they are united under a common oppression.

Pip steals food and a pork pie from the pantry shelf and a file from Joe's forge and brings them back to the escaped convict the next morning. Soon thereafter, Pip watches the man get caught by soldiers and the whole event soon disappears from his young mind.

Mrs. Joe comes home one evening, quite excited, and proclaims that Pip is going to "play" for Miss Havisham, "a rich and grim lady who lived in a large and dismal house."

Pip is brought to Miss Havisham's place, a mansion called the "Satis House," where sunshine never enters. He meets a girl about his age, Estella, "who was very pretty and seemed very proud." Pip instantly falls in love with her and will love her the rest of the story. He then meets Miss Havisham, a willowy, yellowed old woman dressed in an old wedding gown. Miss Havisham seems most happy when Estella insults Pip's coarse hands and his thick boots as they play.

Pip is insulted, but thinks there is something wrong with him. He vows to change, to become uncommon, and to become a gentleman.

Pip continues to visit Estella and Miss Havisham for eight months and learns more about their strange life. Miss Havisham brings him into a great banquet hall where a table is set with food and large wedding cake. But the food and the cake are years old, untouched except by a vast array of rats, beetles and spiders which crawl freely through the room. Her relatives all come to see her on the same day of the year: her birthday and wedding day, the day when the cake was set out and the clocks were stopped many years before; i.e. the day Miss Havisham stopped living.

Pip begins to dream what life would be like if he were a gentleman and wealthy. This dream ends when Miss Havisham asks Pip to bring Joe to visit her, in order that he may start his indenture as a blacksmith. Miss Havisham gives Joe twenty five pounds for Pip's service to her and says good-bye.

Pip explains his misery to his readers: he is ashamed of his home, ashamed of his trade. He wants to be uncommon, he wants to be a gentleman. He wants to be a part of the environment that he had a small taste of at the Manor House.

Early in his indenture, Mrs. Joe is found lying unconscious, knocked senseless by some unknown assailant. She has suffered some serious brain damage, having lost much of voice, her hearing, and her memory. Furthermore, her "temper was greatly improved, and she was patient." To help with the housework and to take care of Mrs. Joe, Biddy, a young orphan friend of Pip's, moves into the house.

The years pass quickly. It is the fourth year of Pip's apprenticeship and he is sitting with Joe at the pub when they are approached by a stranger. Pip recognizes him, and his "smell of soap," as a man he had once run into at Miss Havisham's house years before.

Back at the house, the man, Jaggers, explains that Pip now has "great expectations." He is to be given a large monthly stipend, administered by Jaggers who is a lawyer. The benefactor, however, does not want to be known and is to remain a mystery.

Pip spends an uncomfortable evening with Biddy and Joe, then retires to bed. There, despite having all his dreams come true, he finds himself feeling very lonely. Pip visits Miss Havisham who hints subtly that she is his unknown sponsor.

Pip goes to live in London and meets Wemmick, Jagger's square-mouth clerk. Wemmick brings Pip to Bernard's Inn, where Pip will live for the next five years with Matthew Pocket's son Herbert, a cheerful young gentleman that becomes one of Pip's best friends. From Herbert, Pips finds out that Miss Havisham adopted Estella and raised her to wreak revenge on the male gender by making them fall in love with her, and then breaking their hearts.

Pip is invited to dinner at Wemmick's whose slogan seems to be "Office is one thing, private life is another." Indeed, Wemmick has a fantastical private life. Although he lives in a small cottage, the cottage has been modified to look a bit like a castle, complete with moat, drawbridge, and a firing cannon.

The next day, Jaggers himself invites Pip and friends to dinner. Pip, on Wemmick's suggestion, looks carefully at Jagger's servant woman — a "tigress" according to Wemmick. She is about forty, and seems to regard Jaggers with a mix of fear and duty.

Pip journeys back to the Satis House to see Miss Havisham and Estella, who is now older and so much more beautiful that he does not recognize her at first. Facing her now, he slips back "into the coarse and common voice" of his youth and she, in return, treats him like the boy he used to be. Pip sees something strikingly familiar in Estella's face. He cannot quite place the look, but an expression on her face reminds him of someone.

Pip stays away from Joe and Biddy's house and the forge, but walks around town, enjoying the admiring looks he gets from his past neighbours.

Soon thereafter, a letter for Pip announces the death of Mrs. Joe Gragery. Pip returns home again to attend the funeral. Later, Joe and Pip sit comfortably by the fire like times of old. Biddy insinuates that Pip will not be returning soon as he promises and he leaves insulted. Back in London, Pip asks Wemmick for advice on how to give Herbert some of his yearly stipend anonymously.

Narrator Pip describes his relationship to Estella while she lived in the city: "I suffered every kind and degree of torture that Estella could cause me," he says. Pip finds out that Drummle, the most repulsive of his acquaintances, has begun courting Estella.

Years go by and Pip is still living the same wasteful life of a wealthy young man in the city. A rough sea-worn man of sixty comes to Pip's home on a stormy night soon after Pip's twenty-fourth birthday. Pip invites him in, treats him with courteous disdain, but then begins to recognize him as the convict that he fed in the marshes when he was a child. The man, Magwitch, reveals that he is Pip's benefactor. Since the day that Pip helped him, he swore to himself that every cent he earned would go to Pip.

"I've made a gentleman out of you," the man exclaims. Pip is horrified. All of his expectations are demolished. There is no grand design by Miss Havisham to make Pip happy and rich, living in harmonious marriage to Estella.

The convict tells Pip that he has come back to see him under threat of his life, since the law will execute him if they find him in England. Pip is disgusted with him, but wants to protect him and make sure he isn't found and put to death. Herbert and Pip decide that Pip will try and convince Magwitch to leave England with him.

Magwitch tells them the story of his life. From a very young age, he was alone and got into trouble. In one of his brief stints actually out of jail, Magwitch met a young well-to-do gentleman named Compeyson who had his hand in everything illegal: swindling, forgery, and other white collar crime. Compeyson recruited Magwitch to do his dirty work and landed Magwitch into trouble with the law. Magwitch hates the man. Herbert passes a note to Pip telling him that Compeyson was the name of the man who left Miss Havisham on her wedding day.

Pip goes back to Satis House and finds Miss Havisham and Estella in the same banquet room. Pip breaks down and confesses his love for Estella. Estella tells him straight that she is incapable of love — she has warned him of as much before — and she will soon be married to Drummle.

Back in London, Wemmick tells Pip things he has learned from the prisoners at Newgate. Pip is being watched, he says, and may be in some danger. As well, Compeyson has made his presence known in London. Wemmick has already warned Herbert as well. Heeding the warning, Herbert has hidden Magwitch in his fiancé Clara's house.

Pip has dinner with Jaggers and Wemmick at Jaggers' home. During the dinner, Pip finally realises the similarities between Estella and Jaggers' servant woman. Jaggers' servant woman is Estella's mother!

On their way home together, Wemmick tells the story of Jaggers' servant woman. It was Jaggers' first big break-through case, the case that made him. He was defending this woman in a case where she was accused of killing another woman by strangulation. The woman was also said to have killed her own child, a girl, at about the same time as the murder.

Miss Havisham asks Pip to come visit her. He finds her again sitting by the fire, but this time she looks very lonely. Pip tells her how he was giving some of his money to help Herbert with his future, but now must stop since he himself is no longer taking money from his benefactor. Miss Havisham wants to help, and she gives Pip nine hundred pounds to help Herbert out. She then asks Pip for forgiveness. Pip tells her she is already forgiven and that he needs too much forgiving himself not to be able to forgive others.

Pip goes for a walk around the garden then comes back to find Miss Havisham on fire! Pip puts the fire out, burning himself badly in the process. The doctors come and announce that she will live.

Pip goes home and Herbert takes care of his burns. Herbert has been spending some time with Magwitch at Clara's and has been told the whole Magwitch story. Magwitch was the husband of Jaggers' servant woman, the Tigress. The woman had come to Magwitch on the day she murdered the other woman and told him she was going to kill their child and that Magwitch would never see her. And Magwitch never did. Pip puts is all together and tells Herbert that Magwitch is Estella's father.

It is time to escape with Magwitchapter Herbert and Pip get up the next morning and start rowing down the river, picking up Magwitch at the preappointed time. They are within a few feet of a steamer that they hope to board when another boat pulls alongside to stop them. In the confusion, Pip sees Compeyson leading the other boat, but the steamer is on top of them. The steamer crushes Pip's boat, Compeyson and Magwitch disappear under water, and Pip and Herbert find themselves in a police boat of sorts. Magwitch finally comes up from the water. He and Compeyson wrestled for a while, but Magwitch had let him go and he is presumably drowned. Once again, Magwitch is shackled and arrested.

Magwitch is in jail and quite ill. Pip attends to the ailing Magwitch daily in prison. Pip whispers to him one day that the daughter he thought was dead is quite alive. "She is a lady and very beautiful," Pip says. "And I love her." Magwitch gives up the ghost.

Pip falls into a fever for nearly a month. Creditors and Joe fall in and out of his dreams and his reality. Finally, he regains his senses and sees that, indeed, Joe has been there the whole time, nursing him back to health. Joe tells him that Miss Havisham died during his illness, that she left Estella nearly all, and Matthew Pocket a great deal. Joe slips away one morning leaving only a note. Pip discovers that Joe has paid off all his debtors.

Pip is committed to returning to Joe, asking for forgiveness foreverything he has done, and to ask Biddy to marry him.

Pip goes to Joe and indeed finds happiness — but the happiness is Joe and Biddy's. It is their wedding day. Pip wishes them well, truly, and asks them for their forgiveness in all his actions. They happily give it.

Pip goes to work for Herbert's' firm and lives with the now married Clara and Herbert. Within a year, he becomes a partner. He pays off his debts and works hard.

Eleven years later, Pip returns from his work overseas. He visits Joe and Biddy and meets their son, a little Pip, sitting by the fire with Joe just like Pip himself did years ago. Pip tells Biddy that he is quite the settled old bachelor, living with Clara and Herbert and he thinks he will never marry. Nevertheless, he goes to the Satis House that night to think once again of the girl who got away. And there he meets Estella. Drummle treated her roughly and recently died. She tells Pip that she has learned the feeling of heartbreak the hard way and now seeks his forgiveness for what she did to him. The two walk out of the garden hand in hand, and Pip "saw the shadow of no parting from her."

Chapter 13

Summary and Analysis

PART I

Chapter 1

The story opens with the narrator, Pip, who introduces himself and describes an image of himself as a boy, standing alone and crying in a churchyard near some marshes. Young Pip is staring at the gravestones of his parents, who died soon after his birth. This tiny, shivering bundle of a boy is suddenly terrified by the voice of large, bedraggled man who threatens to cut Pip's throat if he does not stop crying.

The man, dressed in a prison uniform with a great iron shackle around his leg, grabs the boy and shakes him upside down, emptying his pockets. The man devours a piece of bread which falls from the boy, then barks questions at him. Pip tells him that yes, he is an orphan and that he lives with his sister, Mrs. Joe Gargery, the wife of a blacksmith, about a mile from the churchapter. The man tells Pip that if he wants to live, he will go down to his house, bring him back some food and a file for the shackle on his leg. Pip agrees to meet him early the next morning and the man walks back into the marshes.

Analysis

Dickens introduces us immediately to Pip, who serves as both the young protagonist of Great Expectations and the story's narrator looking back on his own story as an adult. With this two-level approach, Dickens leads the reader through young Pip's life with the immediacy and surprise of a first person narration while at the same time guiding with an omnipotent narrator who knows how it will all turn out. The adult narrator Pip will foreshadow future events throughout the story by using signs and symbols.

Dickens uses this duality to great effect in the first chapter, where we are personally introduced to Pip as if we were in a pleasant conversation with him: "I give Pirrip as my father's family name..." Immediately after this, however, we are thrown into the point of view of a terrified young child being mauled by an escaped convict.

The narrator Pip then presents an interesting, and prophetic, relationship between the boy and the bullying man. At first, the relationship appears to be based solely on power and fear. The man yells at the boy only to get what he wants, a file and some food, and the boy only responds for fear of his life. And yet, after they part, the young Pip keeps looking back at the man as he walks alone into the marshes.

The image of the man holding his arms around him, alone on the horizon save a pole associated with the death of criminals, is strikingly familiar to the initial image of young Pip, holding himself in the cold, alone in the churchyard with the stones of his dead parents. For a moment, then, the relationship seems to warm. They share a common loneliness and a common marginalization from society, the orphan and the escaped convict. Even while he is afraid, Pip instinctively displays a sympathetic reaction.

This initial meeting, between a small boy and a convict, will develop into the central relationship in the book. It is the relationship which will cause Pip's great expectations for himself to rise and fall.

Chapter 2

Pip runs home to his sister, Mrs. Joe Gargery, and his adoptive father, Joe Gargery. Mrs. Joe is a loud, angry, nagging woman who constantly reminds Pip and her husband Joe of the difficulties she has gone through to raise Pip and take care of the house. Pip finds solace from these rages in Joe, who is more his equal than a paternal figure, and they are united under a common oppression.

During the dinner, Pip nervously steals a piece of bread. Early the next morning, Pip steals food and a pork pie from the pantry shelf and a file from Joe's forge and runs back to the marshes.

Analysis

The reader's sympathy once again is directed at Pip who not only lost his parents but is being raised by a raging, bitter woman. A common criticism inherent in many of Dickens' novels is the abuse of children in society at large. Although he paints Mrs. Joe in a rather humorous light at times, the reader is still keenly aware of the fear in which this poor child grew up.

Character names in Dickens' works are often codes which reflect a characteristic of the person or their station. Mrs. Joe's name can be decoded to reflect humorous irony on Dicken's part. Although the wife of Joe has taken both his names in the classic patriarchal manner (usually connoting that the wife is the property of the man) the Gragery household is anything but patriarchal. In fact, her husband is treated as little more than a child and Pip and he are the submissive ones.

Chapter 3

The next morning, Pip sneaks out of the house and back to the marshes. He finds a man, wet and cold and dressed like a convict, but he turns out to be a different convict from the man who had threatened him the night before. This man has a badly bruised face and wears a broad-brimmed hat. He runs away from Pip without speaking to him. Pip finally finds his man and gives him the food. The man reacts with anger when Pip tells him about the other convict. Pip leaves him filing at his shackle and returns home.

Analysis

The second meeting of Pip and the convict is much more civil and sympathetic than the first. Pip even puts away his fear to say, "I am glad you enjoy it," as the convict eats. Since he stole the food and file, Pip is now the convict's partner in crime and feels closer to the man.

Great Expectations is sometimes called, among other things, a mystery or suspense novel, and in this chapter we see elements of that genre. Dickens uses secrets as a way of heightening suspense throughout the novel. Someone is always hiding something from someone else. Sometimes these secrets are clear to the reader and makes the reader a partner in crime with the characters, as we are with Pip last as he sneaks around his house, terrified of getting caught, stealing food. Other times the reader is left out of the secret but we are given the impression that it is an important thing that we need to find out, as in the case of the two convicts. We know that there is some connection between the two that is important to the story but we are given very few clues to help us.

Chapter 4

Pip returns home to find Mrs. Joe preparing the house for Christmas dinner. She has invited Mr. Wopsle, the church clerk, Mr. Hubble the wheelwright and Mrs. Hubble and Uncle Pumblechook who was a "well to do corn-chandler" who "drove his own chaise-cart." The discussion over dinner was how fortunate Pip should feel about being raised "by hand" by Mrs. Joe and how much trouble she has gone through in that endeavor, though Pip's opinion was never requested. Mr. Pumblechook nearly chokes on some brandy after the meal and Pip realises that he poured tar water in the brandy bottle when he stole some for the convict. Mrs. Joe becomes too busy in the kitchen to afford a full investigation, but then announces that she is going to present the pork pie. Sure that he is going to get caught, Pip jumps up from the table and runs to the door, only to meet face to face with a group of soldiers who appear to be there to arrest him.

Analysis

The suspense grows in this chapter as the reader and Pip fearfully await the discovery by Mrs. Joe of the things which are missing from the kitchen. The apprehension is kept light, however, with a foolish dialogue between the adults over how much trouble Pip is to raise for Mrs. Joe. Mr. Pumblechook is presented as a loud mouth idiot, full of himself. The only sympathetic character is Joe, who continues to make gestures of support toward Pip. Dicken's little social commentary here is clear: It is often the dim witted and poor (Joe) who act with more grace and charity than wealthy loud mouths (Mr. Pumblechook and Mr. Wopsle) who claim that they do.

Chapter 5

The soldiers do not want to arrest Pip but they do need a pair of handcuffs fixed by Joe. They are invited in, Mr. Pumblechook offers up Mrs. Joe's sherry and port, and Joe gets to work on the handcuffs in the forge. They are, in fact, hunting two convicts who were seen recently in the marshes. After Joe fixes the handcuffs, he, Pip, and Mr. Wopsle are allowed to follow the soldiers into the marshes. They soon find the two convicts wrestling each other in the mud. The one with the hat accuses the other, Pip's convict, of trying to kill him, but the other replies that he would have done it if he really wanted to. Instead, he had been the one who had called for the soldiers and was willing to sacrifice himself just so the one with the hat would get caught again.

The bring the two back to a boathouse where Pip's convict, eyeing Pip, admits to stealing Mrs. Joe's pork pie by himself, thus getting Pip off the hook.

Joe and Pip watch as the two convicts are brought back to the prison ship.

Analysis

The reader is presented with the question of why the two convcts are fightng each other. Pip's convict goes so far as to say that he deliberately got himself caught, just so he could make sure the man with the hat would go back to prison. What hatred did this man have that would make him go back to prison just to see another suffer as well?

The relationship between the convict and Pip continues to grow as well, even though they do not speak and the convict hardly looks at him. The convict obviously wants to protect the boy and, suspecting Pip may be threatened, takes the blame for stealing the pork pie. The two are, once again, united in secrecy.

Chapter 6

Joe, Pip, and Mr. Wopsle walk back home. Pop decides not to tell Joe the truth about his file and the pork pie — he is afraid of losing his respect. When they return, the topic of discussion is the question of how the convict managed to get into the locked house. Through his bombastic overbearance, Mr. Pumblechook's argument wins: the convict crawled down the chimney. Mrs. Joe sends Pip to bed.

Analysis

Pip's fear that Joe would "think worse of me than I was" if Pip told him about the file and pork pie is a fear that Pip will revisit throughout his young life. Joe is the only friend in the world for Pip, he is his entire society. Pip fears to lose this companionship by telling the truth. In the future, Pip will struggle with telling the truth because of the fear that society will think less of him.

Chapter 7

Pip describes a little of his education with Mr. Wopsle's great aunt, a "ridiculous old lady" who had started a small school in her cottage. The education, as Pip describes it, is less than satisfactory, but Pip does learn some basics from Biddy, an orphan girl who works for Mrs. Wopsle.

While doing his homework one night, Pip discovers that Joe is illiterate. Joe explains that he never stayed in school long because his father, a drunk and physically abusive to him and his mother, kept him out. Joe goes on to explain to Pip that, because of his father, Joe stays humble to Mrs. Joe. "I'm dead afeerd of going wrong in the way of not doing what's right by a woman," he says. He let's Mrs. Joe "Ram-page" over him because he sees how difficult it is to be a woman, remembering his mother, and he wants to do the right thing as a man. Pip has new understanding and respect for Joe.

Mrs. Joe comes home, quite excited, and proclaims that Pip is going to "play" for Miss Havisham, "a rich and grim lady who lived in a large and dismal house." Uncle Pumblechook suggested Pip to Miss Havisham when she asked if he knew any small boys. Pip was to go tomorrow and spend the evening at Uncle Pumblechook's in town.

Analysis

Chapter Seven and Chapter Eight mark a key turning point in the novel, separating Pip's young childhood in the humble company of Joe from the beginnings of greater expectations in the company of higher society.

The chapter presents a relationship between Joe and Pip which is growing in love and respect. Joe is at the bottom of the social hierarchy, and, particularly, at the bottom of his household's hierarchy but Pip finds new respect for his position. "I had a new sensation of feeling conscious that I was looking up to Joe in my heart." The image is almost ideal: the young Pip and Joe sitting next to the fire, Pip admiring him and teaching him the alphabet.

Dickens contrasts this humble setting with the opportunity presented at the end of the chapter by the noisy entrance and rather insolent announcement by Mrs. Joe. She introduces the first of Pip's "great expectations" in the form of the job given to Pip "to play" for Miss Havisham: "...this boy's fortune may be made by his going to Miss Havisham's." Although little is known about the wealthy woman, and less is known exactly how Pip is supposed to "play," the opportunity is one where Pip will be in the company of a higher social and economic class of people.

Chapter 8

Pip spends the evening at Mr. Pumblechook's and is brought to Miss Havisham's after a meager breakfast. They are met at the gate by a young woman, Estella, "who was very pretty and seemed very proud." Estella lets Pip in, but sends Mr. Pumblechook on his way. She leads him through a dark house by candle and leaves him outside a door. He knocks and is let in. There he meets Miss Havisham, a willowy, yellowed woman dressed in an old wedding gown. She calls for Estella and the two play cards, despite Estella's objection that Fip was just a "common labouring-boy." "Well," says Miss

Havisham, "you can break his heart." Estella insults Pip's coarse hands and his thick boots as they play.

Smarting from the insults, Pip later cries as he eats lunch in the great house's yard. He explores the yard and the garden, always seeing Estella in the distance walking ahead of him. Finally, she lets him out of the yard and he walks the four miles home, feeling low.

Analysis

Dickens uses strong imagery to describe Miss Havisham's house ("The Manor House" or the "Satis House") as barren of feelings or even life, even before we meet the bitter Miss Havisham and the rude Estella: "The cold wind seemed to blow colder there, than outside the gate..." Again we have a strange mystery: Why is this woman always in the dark, and dressed in a wedding gown? Who is the young and pretty Estella and what is she doing in such a morbid place?

Pip's first taste of "higher society" is a bitter one, and it leaves him ashamed and embarrassed rather than justifiably angry. Pip is, in fact, just a toy for both Miss Havisham, who wants him to "play," and Estella, who treats him roughly while at the same time flirts. Pip, torn between being insulted and his attraction to Estella, opts to feel ashamed of his upbringing — so much so that he "wished Joe had been rather more genteelly brought up." His new found respect and love for Joe was being spoiled by his embarrassment of being brought up in a lower class family.

Chapter 9

Pip is forced to talk about his day to Mrs. Joe and Mr. Pumblechook. Pip lies in a fantastical matter, making up stories about dogs being fed veal and Miss Havisham lounging on a velvet couchapter He lies, partly in spite, but also because he is sure that the two would not understand the situation at the Satis House even if he described it in detail..

Later, Pip tells Joe the truth, and also confesses that he is embarrassed about being a "commoner" because of his attraction to Estella.

Joe reassures him that he is not common, he is uncommon small and an uncommon scholar. Referring to Pip's lies, he adds, "If you can not get to be oncommon through going straight, you'll never get to do it through going crooked."

Analysis

Joe's analysis, though phrased in what Pip would call "common" language, is accurate: Pip is trying to become "uncommon" by lying about his experiences. Pip made up lies about the Satis House with the intention of glorifying it in front of the eager Mr. Pumblechook and Mrs. Joe, both of whom eat it up. While Pip is naively honest in admitting to Joe that he wants to become uncommon, he is intelligent enough to know that he can become uncommon by being dishonest, or, as Joe would have it, "crooked."

One of the main themes of the book is spelled out in this chapter, specifically, the desire to rise above one's social station. Dickens, writing this book toward the end of his life, is speaking directly of his own youthful desires and those of his father as well. As the story of Pip unfolds and we witness the different ways in which Pip tries to climb the social ladder — by making up fantastical stories in this case. It will be interesting to listen to the running commentary made by the narrator, the older Pip, who, like Dickens himself, is looking back on this theme and reflecting on how it affected his happiness later on in life.

Chapter 10

Pip states plainly that he wants to be uncommon and so, taking to heart Joe's advice that "you must be a common scholar afore you can be a oncommon one," he asks Biddy at the small school to help him get educated. Mr. Wopsle's great-aunt's school is little more than a play school and Pip understands it will be hard to concentrate on some actual learning, but Biddy agrees and gives Pip some books to start with.

On the way home, Pip goes into a pub to pick up Joe. He finds Joe sitting with a stranger, a man with one eye pulled closed and a worn hat on his head. The man asks Joe all kinds of personal questions, some about Pip's relation to him, the whole time staring at Pip. At one point, the man stirs his drink with Joe's file — the file Pip stole to give to the convict! As Joe and Pip depart, the stranger hands Pip a coin wrapped in paper.

When they get home, Pip realises that the paper is actually a two pound note. Thinking it was a mistake (though Pip knows somehow that it wasn't) Joe runs back to the pub to give it back but the man is gone.

Analysis

Pip, excited at the beginning of the chapter by the prospect of educating himself to become uncommon, is reminded of his common, and somewhat illegitimate, past by the stranger in the pub. As he goes to sleep, he is bothered by the fact that it is uncommon to be "on secret terms of conspiracy with convicts."

The man clearly knew something about Pip assisting the convict and wanted Pip to know that he did. How he knows remains a mystery, but Pip's immediate fear is how his past will "haunt" him as he tries to climb out of his common background.

Chapter 11

A few days later, Pip returns to Miss Havisham's as directed. This time, the house seems full of people waiting to see her but she sees him first. She brings him into a great banquet hall where a table is set with food and large wedding cake. But the food and the cake are years old, untouched except by a vast array of rats, beetles and spiders which crawl freely through the room. Miss Havisham has Pip walk her around the room as four guests are brought in: Sarah Pocket, a "vicious," "dry, brown, corrugated woman;" Georgiana, "the grave lady;" Camilla, an old melodramatic woman; and her husband, Cousin Raymond. All are, apparently, the same age or a little younger than the withered Miss Havisham and all come to see her on the same day of the year: her birthday, which also happens to be the day when the cake was set out and the clocks were stopped so many years ago; i.e. the day Miss Havisham stopped living.

Miss Havisham continues walking around the room, saying little to her guests, until the mention of a certain Matthew, whereupon she stops short.

The guests leave, and Miss Havisham once again asks that Estella and Pip play cards as she watches.

As Pip is once again allowed to explore the yard, he runs into a pale, young gentleman who challenges him to fight. Despite the young man's jumping about and expert preparation (bringing some water and explaining the rules), Pip gives him a bloody nose, a black eye, and a general whopping. They end the fight and the boy, cheerful as ever, wishes Pip a good afternoon.

At the gate, Estella tells Pip that he may kiss her if he likes. Pip kisses her on the cheek.

Analysis

Pip is introduced to a number of strange characters in this chapter but, more importantly, he is given some more hints about Miss Havisham's strange lifestyle. It is clear that the decay of her and the house stem from her wedding day that none of her relatives dare to mention. Miss Havisham's relationship with her relatives — Georgiana, Sarah Pocket, Cousin Raymond, and Camilla — is even more loveless than her relationship with Pip. For her relatives, their visit to Miss Havisham is based on greed, hoping to please her enough to be given some of her money at her death. Miss Havisham is well aware of this, and a number of times refers to her dead body laid out as a meal for her relatives on the same table where her decaying cake now sits.

It is ironic that the loveless environment of the Satis House is representative of the higher society that Pip would like to rise to. The relationships of the house are based on money and power, while the relationship at the forge with Joe is based on mutual respect. Pip feels unnatural with how he acts with this kind of society, as is the case when he feels guilty for hitting the pale young gentleman. But he is rewarded for his violence by Estella's kiss, symbolic of society's rewarding of violent behaviour. Though unclear to young Pip, the narrator is making clear that Pip's desire to enter into higher society is a decision to choose empty relationships where people are tools (or, as in Pip's case, simple walking sticks). It is also a decision to choose death and decay, as reflected in the Satis House setting. Lastly, it is an environment where Pip instinctively feels he is going against his nature.

Chapter 12

Pip returns once again to Miss Havisham's, but he does not run into the boy again. He begins pushing Miss Havisham in a wheelchair from her room to the large banquet hall, and continues to do so over the course of eight months. Sometimes they are joined by Estella and the three sing little ditties together.

During this same time, Mr. Pumblechook makes a habit of visiting Mrs. Joe and discussing Pip's promising prospects, now that he is routinely seeing Miss Havisham.

But the prospects seem to fall away when one night Miss Havisham asks Pip to bring Joe to visit her in order that Pip may start his indenture as a blacksmith.

Analysis

By this time it is clear that Miss Havisham is bringing up Estella to "...break their hearts and have no mercy." That is, to break the hearts of men, like Pip, in revenge for what they have done to Miss Havisham. Although what they have done to Miss Havisham is not completely clear, we can assume that the reason for her unchanged state and the decaying state of the house is that she was jilted on her wedding day by a man. Estella, then, is to revenge this sin for Miss Havisham by causing men to fall in love with her and then breaking their hearts. With Pip, she is obviously succeeding, who is continuing to be abused and insulted by her while admitting that she grows prettier and more a part of his thoughts everyday.

Chapter 13

Joe accompanies Pip to the Satis House the next day. Miss Havisham gives Joe twenty five guineas for Pip's service to her and thus buys Pip's indenture as a blacksmith.

Returning to Mr. Pumblechook's house, where Mrs. Joe is also anxiously waiting, Joe produces the twenty five pounds much to everyone's — except Pip's — joy. Caught up in the excitement, Mr. Pumblechook insists that Pip be legally bound by law and drags Pip and the entourage down to the Town Hall to be bound. Mrs. Joe then brings everyone out for dinner.

At the meal, all but Pip seem to be enjoying themselves: "...I was truly wretched, and had a strong conviction on me that I should never like Joe's trade. I had liked it once, but once was not now."

Analysis

Throughout Great Expectations, Dickens uses meals as a reflection of the relationships at hand. The meal celebrating Pip's indenture is reminiscent of the Christmas meal in Chapter 4, where Pip feels none of the enjoyment, human companionship, and hospitality that is supposed to accompany meals. What is significant about these meals among friends is what they are not. The uneaten meal and cake in Miss Havisham's banquet hall stands as a starkly direct symbol of the lack of love and human companionship that meals commonly signify.

If we look, however, at the first "meal" of the story: the pork pie and "wittels" that Pip gives to the convict, we see something different. Though the setting of the meal is unglamorous, the cold, damp marshes, and the manners of the guest (the convict) are likened to a dog, there appears to be some genuine hospitality in Pip's words, "I am glad you enjoy it." And the convict answers sincerely, "Thankee, my boy, I do." The meal, in fact, joins the two inexorably.

Dickens will turn to the use of food and meals throughout the story to reflect on relationships on various levels of society.

Chapter 14

Pip explains his misery to his readers: He is ashamed of his home, ashamed of his trade. He wants to be uncommon, he wants to be a gentleman. He wants to be a part of the environment that he had a small taste of at the Satis House.

His greatest fear allies his greatest shame. He fears, beyond everything else, that Estella will see him in his current, dirty, blacksmith state.

Analysis

Throughout all of Dicken's books, criticism aimed specifically at the Victorian Society can be seen. In this case, Dickens is contrasting Pip's shame at having to do honest, hard work with his desire to be a gentleman which, up until this point, has meant acting as Miss Havisham's walking stick. In essence, Dickens is criticizing a Victorian tendency, seen even today, of looking down on the common labourer as dirty and of less value than the more urbane man leading a wealthy, leisurely lifestyle. Instead, the gentleman, and his sense of "work," is held up as ideal.

Dicken's criticism is on two levels: one, against the society, which enforces these values and two, against the individuals, like Pip, who adopt society's values despite their better judgment.

Chapter 15

Biddy continues to teach Pip all she knows including an ironic little ditty about a man who goes to London and lives a fancy life. Pip continues to teach Joe everything he has learned, though he doubts Joe is taking much of the information in.

Orlick, a gruff man that Joe employs around the forge, begins one day to insult Mrs. Joe within her hearing. There is a fight between Joe and Orlick, which Joe wins, but the two continue to work together as if it is all behind them.

About a year into his indenture, Pip revisits Miss Havisham at the Satis House ostensibly to thank her for paying for his indenture. He is disappointed at the meeting: Miss Havisham does see him for a few moments, but only to laugh at him when he looks around for Estella. Estella has, in fact, been sent abroad to be educated as a lady.

Pip returns home to find nearly the whole of the village gathered around his house. Mrs. Joe has been hit over the head, knocked senseless by some unknown assailant.

Analysis

Even while Pip dreams of an upper-class life, violence and crime continue to be events in his life. In this chapter, Pip is witness to a fight between Orlick and Joe, apparently egged on by Mrs. Joe, reminiscent of Estella complimenting with a kiss Pip's fight with the pale young gentleman. Violence comes quickly and rather unexpectedly throughout the novel and, as in this case, does little to solve anything.

Chapter 16

Pip immediately suspects Orlick, though, strangely, his sister was hit with the shackles that the convict filed off in the first chapter! Because of this connection, Pip also suspects the one-eyed man that Joe and he had met in the pub, and who had demonstrated his own knowledge of Pip's past by stirring his drink with the file used to free those same shackles.

His sister has suffered some serious brain damage, having lost much of voice, her hearing, and her memory. She communicates by writing letters and symbols on a slate. Furthermore, her "temper was greatly improved, and she was patient."

To help with the housework and to take care of Mrs. Joe, Biddy is employed and moves into the house and becomes "a blessing to the household."

Strangely, Pip's sister starts to treat Orlick extraordinarily well, inviting him to have something to drink, and watching him with an "air of humble propitiation."

Analysis

The seemingly distant episode of Pip helping the convict on the marshes continues to haunt him, even as he tries to distance himself by becoming educated and he dreams of being Estella's gentleman. The shackles in this chapter remind Pip of the episode and bring back his shame and guilt to the point where Pip feels like he is partly responsible for his sister's injury.

Dickens subtly changes how we view Mrs. Joe by referring to her now as "my sister." Before the accident, the readers almost forget the blood relationship between Pip and Mrs. Joe, but with the changing of Mrs. Joe's attitude and temper, her position reverts to Pip's sister.

Chapter 17

Pip notices that Biddy is turning into a woman, not very pretty, but very bright and wise. They go for a walk and Pip confesses his desire to be a gentleman. He also admits that he wants to be a gentleman so that he will be acceptable, and perhaps loved, by Estella. Biddy wisely suggests that becoming a gentleman to "gain over" a woman who thinks him course and common does not sound very logical.

Pip knows this instinctively, can not help himself and says as much, amidst tears in front of Biddy. He tells Biddy that he wishes he were more easily satisfied, he wishes he could fall in love with her, Biddy. "But you never will, you see," Biddy replies.

Analysis

This chapter lays out what has remained unspoken for some time to a somewhat relieving affect: Pip comes right out and says he loves Estella and that, foolish even to himself, he wants to become a gentleman to win her over. The discussion, symbolically, takes place among the marshes, which have, throughout the novel, represented Pip's past as well as his social position as a blacksmith's apprentice. The pastoral peacefulness that accompanies Pip's walk with Biddy is contrasted with the ships in the river, that Pip has always associated with some far away, expected future. Pip himself states his frustrated state when he says he wishes he were happy in his current position, including having Biddy close, but he is forever looking toward some impossible future.

Chapter 18

It is the fourth year of Pip's apprenticeship and he is sitting with Joe and Mr. Wopsle at the pub when they are approached by a stranger who wants to talk to Joe and Pip alone. Pip recognizes him, and his "smell of soap," as a man he had once run into at Miss Havisham's house years before.

Back at the forge, the man, Jaggers, explains that Pip now has "great expectations." He has been given a large amount of money, to be administered by Jaggers, by an anonymous sponsor whom Pip is never to try to discover. Fulfilling Pip's dreams, Jaggers explains that Pip is to be "brought up a gentleman" and will be tutored by Matthew Pocket — the same "Matthew" that had been mentioned at Miss Havisham's. Jaggers gives him money enough for new clothes and leaves, expecting to meet him in London within a week.

Pip spends an uncomfortable evening with Biddy and Joe, then retires to bed. There, despite having all his dreams come true, he finds himself feeling very lonely.

Analysis

The implication to Pip, and to the readers, is that Miss Havisham is the sponsor who is going to make all of Pip's dreams come true including, Pip imagines, training him as a gentleman so that he may be an appropriate mate for Estella.

Immediately after this dramatic change in fortune, however, Pip finds himself feeling lonely and isolated. The reason is clear: From the moments of Jagger's announcement, the relationship between he and Joe and Biddy has changed. In essence, Jagger's news fulfills the vanity that had been creeping up in Pip since he first worked at Miss Havisham's. That is, he thinks himself better, more intelligent, more qualified than the life which he was leading with Biddy and Joe. As the end of the chapter makes clear, however, Pip has marginalized himself with this vanity and made himself lonely.

Chapter 19

The word has spread through town that Pip has come into fortune and people are treating him distinctively different. Pip goes into town to buy clothes for his London trip and stores them at Pumblechook's house because he thinks it would be common of him to wear them in his own neighborhood. Even Pumblechook is treating him as if he is a king, and Pip, joining into the arena that he viewed as hypocrisy only a few chapters before, starts to enjoy it and even starts to like Pumblechook.

Relations between he and Biddy and Joe do not improve, however, especially when he asks Biddy if she would try and educate Joe so that he could bring him up to another social level once the full extent of Pip's sponsor's fortune is given to him. Biddy brusquely tells Pip that Joe has no need, and does not want, to be brought up to another social level.

Pip visits Miss Havisham. She hints subtly that she is his unknown sponsor, and does it in such a way that Sarah Pocket, standing near, is given to believe it.

The week finally over, Pip leaves for London. Even while he is in the carriage, however, he considers turning around and spending another day saying good-bye to Joe and Biddy.

Analysis

Pip is in the height of his own vanity here, and it is reflected in a new pomposity to his language. He even goes as far as to correct the grammar of Biddy, who was his first teacher. He feels himself being remeasured by society, just as the tailor in town remeasured him for clothing even though he already had Pip's sizes. At the same time, Pip is treating the people he meets differently as well, especially Joe and Biddy. He actually finds himself enjoying the bombastic idiot Pumblechook whom he had hated for most of his life.

Symbolically, Pip goes to say good-bye to the marshes, which have always represented his lowly past. This time, however, he finds them beautiful in a way he hadn't recognized before. Nevertheless, he wants to "get them done with." We are, of course, left with the feeling that Pip will never be done with the marshes, or his past.

PART II

Chapter 1

Pip goes to London and, compared with his last images of the marshes, finds it "ugly, crooked, narrow and dirty." He meets with Jaggers, who tells him that he will be boarding with Matthew Pocket. He meets Wemmick, Jagger's square-mouth clerk.

Analysis

Once again, Dickens is using place, and Pip's attitude toward it, as symbolism. In this case, London is the setting for Pip's great expectations, but immediately we find it rather ugly, unnatural, and suffocating, giving us an indication of how those great expectations may be played out. Ironically, Jagger's office is located in a place called "Little Britain" and it has all the trappings of death: a chair that looks like it was made of the same material as a coffin and death masks on the hearth. This, then, is Pip's grand future.

Chapter 2

Wemmick brings Pip to Bernard's Inn, where he will be staying when he is in town. The Inn appears to Pip to be a fairly run-down, decrepit place. There he meets his guide and roommate for the next few days, Matthew Pocket's son Herbert. Herbert Pocket and Pip recognize each other when they meet: Herbert is the pale young gentleman that Pip fought in the garden of Miss Havisham's so long ago.

Analysis

Though Pip grew up in what might be considered rural poverty, his new digs in the city seem much more poor in nature than the warmth of the forge. The only warm spot appears to be Herbert, whom Pip had first met under strange, and violent, circumstances.

Chapter 3

Herbert Pocket prepares a simple dinner and explains his relationship to Miss Havisham. His father, Matthew Pocket, is Miss Havisham's cousin. Miss Havisham was doted on by her father her whole life and shared her only with a half brother, the son of her father and the cook. Miss Havisham fell in love with a swindler and Matthew Pocket tried to warn her about him. Angrily, she demanded that Matthew leave the house and not return.

Miss Havisham is then jilted on the day of her wedding, her fiancé leaving her only a letter. The rumor was that the fiancé had worked in conspiracy with her younger brother, who may have wanted to exact revenge on the more favored.

Miss Havisham adopts Estella and raises her to wreak revenge on the male gender by making them fall in love with her, and then jilting them.

The next day, Herbert brings Pip to meet his father, and his seven siblings, in the outlying area of Hammersmith.

Analysis

The theme of the meal as a reflection of human companionship again returns in this chapter. The meal prepared by Herbert is simple and the table setting is balanced on a number of pieces of furniture, clearly showing it as a non-traditional set-up. And yet, Pip enjoys himself immensely, and feels that Herbert, despite the fact that he may have lost favour in Miss Havisham's eyes (and thus Pip has taken his inheritance), is honest and has no capability for bitterness at all.

Pip and the reader are again reminded none to subtly that the "lap of luxury" is, in fact, not material or social gain, but the simple joy of eating with sincere friends. In fact, we are given Matthew Pocket's definition of a gentleman, repeated by his son:"... no man who was not a true gentleman at heart, ever was... a true gentleman in manner." Young Pip, however, is not ready to learn this lesson.

Chapter 4

The Pocket household turns out to be a comical jumble of children, nurses, and boarders, all held together loosely under Matthew Pocket's weary gaze. Mrs. Pocket had been raised with high expectations herself and brought up to be "highly ornamental, but perfectly helpless and useless." She seems to have little idea of child rearing, leaving the young ones in the hands of two nurses. Pip observes the chaos over a meal.

Analysis

Dickens, pointedly, is making two criticisms here aimed at English society. The first is a humorous critique of England's obsession with titles in their class system. Mrs. Pocket is, in fact, so caught up in titles that she spends her whole day reading a book about them. She is disappointed by her own lot in life, though she seems not to have to do any household duties and has a good man for a husband. She is caught up in the class system in complete oblvion to what is going on around her. She is actually raised, Pip finds out, to be utterly useless and to be taken care of.

The second criticism is Dicken's continuing them of child abuse, and the many ways in which children are oppressed and marginalized. In the Pocket family the children are not necessarily physically abused (though their lives appear in danger sometimes from lack of supervision) or under fed or made to work, but there seems to be psychological abuse by there mere numbers. The parents, Matthew and Mrs. Pocket, have little to no time for a decent rearing of the children.

Chapter 5

Pip finds Matthew Pocket to be, like his son, serious, honest, and good. Because Matthew Pocket was earnest in teaching Pip, Pip feels earnest in learning and progresses well. At the same time, he is drawn by the city life within London and asks Jaggers if he can live permanently at the Bernard Inn with Herbert, instead of boarding in Hammersmith. Jaggers agrees.

Wemmick brings Pip to watch Jaggers in court, where Pip observes him "grinding the whole place in a mill."

Analysis

The honesty and earnestness of Matthew Pocket is contrasted in this chapter with the logical, though not necessarily honest, character of Jaggers. In fact, Jagger's morality is not based on what is actually just, it is only based on a game of words. Guilt or innocence is not decided in Jaggers' mind by who is actually guilty or innocent, or even who has the most evidence or not, it is based on the talent of the lawyer to massage out of the participants the desired verdict.

Again, Dicken's is taking a rather direct critical shot at the judicial system and lawyers in general.

Chapter 6

While at the Pockets, Pip comes to know the family surrounding Miss Havisham. Camilla is Matthew Pocket's sister, Georgiana is a cousin. Pip also grows close to Herbert.

Pip is invited to dinner at Wemmick's whose slogan seems to be "Office is one thing, private life is another." Indeed, Wemmick has a fantastical private life. Although he lives in a small cottage, the cottage has been modified to look a bit like a castle, complete with moat, drawbridge, and a firing cannon. Pip finds Wemmick an entertaining host, far different from the Wemmick at the office.

Analysis

Dicken's humorously uses Wemmick to show how conforming to society, in this case Wemmick's job at Jaggers, can twist a person so much as to make them unidentifiable. It is almost as if Wemmick's private and life and public life have made him a split personality. The one, a grim clerk with a dry callousness, the other, an imaginative, caring, generous esoteric.

Literally, Wemmick's home is his castle, and Wemmick talks in terms of def4ending this private home against the encroachment of the hard city life. Pip's meal there, complete with the customary cannon firing, continues the thematic use of meals with a series that introduces Part II of the novel. In this meal, Pip is brought to understand the entertaining imagination, as well as the caring humanity, of an acquaintance whom he presumed was a dull clog in the city machine.

Chapter 7

The next day, Jaggers himself invites Pip and friends to dinner. Pip brings Herbert as well as the other Pocket boarders, including Startop and Drummle, a mopey depressed aristocrat. Pip and his friends find themselves revealing their relationships quite clearly, specifically all of their irritation at the insulting Drummle.

Pip, on Wemmick's suggestion, looks carefully at Jagger's servant woman — a "tigress" according to Wemmick. She is about forty, and seems to regard Jaggers with a mix of fear and duty.

Analysis

Dickens uses this chapter to once again present mysteries that the narrator Pip hints will be solved in upcoming issues. Of all the young men invited to Jagger's house, Jaggers is especially pleased and interested in the unfriendly Drummle. It is a strange choice for Jaggers and we are led to believe that Drummle will become a more important character later in the novel. As well, Wemmick's singling the servant woman out as one to be watched and Jagger's own proud demonstration of her scarred wrists, indicate that she too will reoccur.

This chapter presents yet another meal, this one serving as an airing of dirty laundry, much to the enjoyment of the host Jaggers. The evening ends in an argument between the boarders and we learn nothing personal about Jaggers himself. Used as a comparison to Pip's meal with Wemmick, it appears that Jaggers is what he seems to be: a nearly mechanical rationalist, with a cold scientific fascination for the psychology of people, but with a complete lack of emotional involvement with them. In fact, we are given the feeling that a good insulting argument is more entertaining to Jaggers than a peaceful communion of friends.

Chapter 8

Biddy write to Pip to tell him Joe is coming into London and would like to visit him. Pip does not look "with pleasure" on this.

Joe shows up for breakfast and tells Pip that Miss Havisham wants him to know Estella is back at the Satis House. The conversation is apologetic and stilted, Joe addresses Pip as "sir," and Joe stays only for a few minutes. He tells Pip that he is out of his element, and that if Pip would like to see the real Joe and sit down and talk like old times, he should visit the forge.

Analysis

Once again, we are presented with the meal theme, this meal an uncomfortable clash between Pip's new "gentlemanly" life and his "common" life at the forge. Joe even uses the word "wittles," which was last used by the convict that Pip met in the marshes, symbolizing all of Pip's past that he is trying to separate from.

Joe, like Dickens, knows the importance of place and invites Pip back to the forge where the two of them could be natural around one another.

Chapter 9

Pip journeys back to this hometown to see Estella. He shares the carriage with two convicts who sit behind him. Pip recognizes one of them as the one-eyed man Pip met in the tavern years before who stirred his drink with the file and gave Pip a one pound note. The convict does not recognize him, but Pip overhears him tell the other convict about the note that a stranger had given him to bring to Pip.

Analysis

We are given a number of answers to earlier mysteries in this chapter. The convict riding with Pip in this chapter was given the pound note, and, presumably, the file by the convict who Pip had helped in the opening few chapters. Other than being a fellow convict, it appears that the one-eyed man has no real relationship with that first convict.

Still, Pip feels uneasy. By the mere proximity of the convicts and their story, Pip is reminded how his past will always cling to him.

Chapter 10

Pip imagines that Miss Havisham has adopted both he and Estella to raise them to be with each other. Pip imagines he and Estella inhabiting the old Satis House and flinging open the windows to let the sun and the breeze in.

He meets Orlick at the gate of The Satis House and learns that he is now working for Miss Havisham. He goes in to meet her and Estella, who is now older and so much more beautiful that he does not recognize her at first. Facing her now, he slips back "into the coarse and common voice" of his youth and she, in return, treated him like the boy he used to be. She is coming from France and on her way to live in London. They talk of his new friends and his old friends: "Who is fit for you then is not fit for you now," Estella said, asking about Joe. Pip agrees and, at that moment, decides not to go see Joe and Biddy.

It is here that Pip sees something strikingly familiar in Estella's face. He can not quite place the look, but an expression on her face reminds him of someone.

Later, they all have dinner with Jaggers, who, curiously, does not look at Estella the whole meal.

Analysis

We are given a much greater look into the character of Estella in this chapter. It is evident, or at least Estella wants to be convinced of the fact, that Miss Havisham has been successful in raising her as a beautiful but emotionless woman. "I have no heart," she tells Pip.

Miss Havisham will have her revenge on the male gender: "I developed her into what she is, that she might be loved," she tells Pip. "Love her!"

The master-apprentice archetype is seen in a number of different relationships through Great Expectations, sometimes demonstrating the positive nature of the relationships, sometimes demonstrating the negative. The Miss Havisham/ Estella master-apprentice relationship is decidedly negative. Miss Havisham raised Estella not as an individual, but as an extension of herself to fulfill that which she had not in her own life (not to find love, however, but to revenge love).

In contrast, Pip was an apprentice to Joe, but Joe raised him out of generosity and love as opposed to any selfish reasons. Other master/apprentice relationships — Mr. Trabb and his boy, Pip's own "Avenger" servant boy — are more of a comment on the abusive treatment of children in Victorian times.

Chapter 11

Pip and Jaggers return to the inn in town. Pip mentions to Jaggers that Orlick may not be a trustworthy assistant to Miss Havisham and Jaggers tells Pip that he will see him fired.

Pip stays away from Joe and Biddy's house and the forge, but walks around town, enjoying the admiring looks he gets from his past neighbours. This pleasant walk is disturbed by the Trabb boy who makes fun of Pip, imitating the snobbish way he walks and barking out, "Don't know yah!" to onlookers.

Pip returns to London and talks to Herbert about Estella. Herbert himself reveals that he is in love with a woman named Clara, though it must be kept secret because his mother would think he was marrying "below station."

Analysis

Although Pip continues to make decisions based on how he thinks society wants him to act — not going to see Joe and Biddy while he is home — we recognize the fact that he feels guilt and shame about these same decisions. Unlike Estella, Pip seems to wear his guilt on his sleeve, but his guilt shows him to have a conscience at least. Dickens uses guilt in Pip — who seems to be the only one in the novel who experiences it — to signal moments when Pip feels himself acting against his nature.

The Trabb boy's pranks nail Pip's shame right on the head, and his antics reflect what is going on in Pip's conscious. Pip feels he has become a parody, a proud peacock who "does not know yah."

At the same time, Pip confesses to Herbert that he cannot let it go. He desires Estella deeply and can not seem to shake her. As long as he tries to be the person that Estella — and society — want, he will be acting against his nature.

Chapter 12

Herbert and Pip go to see Wopsle in Hamlet, which turns out to be a horrible piece of theater, but a very humorous evening nonetheless because of the crowd's wisecracks.

They invite Wopsle home for dinner and listen to him rant about his performance.

Analysis

Dickens presents a light hearted critique of overacted theater in this chapter. Wopsle's Hamlet is laugh-out-loud comedy. Dickens was an actor and a producer of theatrical productions himself, and there is no doubt he was probably targeting certain actors that he knew personally in this parody.

Part II Chapter 13

Pip receives a note from Estella that she is coming to London. She asks if he will meet her at the carriage stop.

While waiting for the carriage, Pip meets Wemmick who is on his way to Newgate prison to conduct some business. The prisoners are friendly with Wemmick, even offering to send him presents before their executions.

As Pip returns to wait for Estella, he wonders at the fact that things associated with the criminal element have strangely intercepted his life at various times, starting with the convict at the beginning of the story. He feels as if the stain of criminality is still on him from his visit to Newgate prison and how that contrasts with the beautiful Estella.

As the carriage pulls up, Pip once again sees a familiar expression in Estella's face, but cannot place it.

Analysis

Pip reflects on how criminals have intercepted his life at various points, starting with the convict that he fed at the beginning and the one-eyed convict that gave him the pound note from the first convict. Now he is involved in men, Wemmick and Jaggers, who make convicts their livelihood. These thoughts are interrupted by the strangely abrupt entrance of Estella's carriage. It is strangely abrupt since Pip spent the whole chapter in anticipation, waiting for nearly six hours for it, but when it finally comes, Pip is involved in other thoughts.

Narrator Pip is hinting with these thoughts that Young Pip's interaction with criminals is not over. Their surprising involvement in his life will continue. Dicken's placing the abrupt intervention of Estella's entrance in these thoughts foreshadows a little more specifically: Estella, too, will have something to do with criminality.

Chapter 14

Estella is to go on to Richmond, accompanied by Pip, and the two sit in a nearby cafe as they wait for the outgoing coachapter Estella is to educated by a wealthy woman in Richmond with a single daughter.

Estella tells Pip that all of Miss Havisham's relatives hate him because they Miss Havisham to be his benefactor. They are always gossiping jealously, but Estella believes that Pip is still alright in Miss Havisham's eyes.

The carriage comes and they ride to Richmond talking of trivial things. Pip believes that if he were to be with her forever that he would be blissfully happy — but this contradicts his knowledge that whenever he is with her he is "always miserable."

Analysis

"We are not free to follow our own devices, you and I," says Estella, meaning that she has been given instructions for the day and they must not deviate from them. The statement, however, is a projection of how both their lives are controlled in general.

Estella is not free "to follow her own devices" not only because Miss Havisham is her adoptive mother and she should do as she says, but because Estella has been raised to actually think, feel, and act exactly as Miss Havisham wishes. In raising Estella, Miss Havisham created a puppet, an individual who indeed cannot choose her own destiny because she will act that way she has been conditioned to act.

Pip, on the other hand, is also trapped and cannot freely choose, but his lack of independence is wholly his own fault. Pip is not free to follow "his own devices" because he has trapped himself in how he thinks he needs to act, think, and feel. He believes himself to have great expectations, among these, someday, the hand of Estella, and this belief has forced him into acting a certain way (snobbishly, especially toward his past), feeling a certain way (that he is happy with Estella even if he is not), and thinking a certain way (proud and wasteful).

As hinted in the previous chapter, both Pip and Estella will find their destinies intricately tied up in their pasts. This, too, will bind them to certain actions.

The irony is that, though they think themselves trapped, both can escape their current lifestyles if they truly wanted too, just as easily as they could ignore Miss Havisham's instructions and change the plans for the day. Estella can shake off her upbringing and try to find her emotions, Pip can stop acting like an ass and lead a life which feels more natural to him.

Chapter 15

Pip's conscience bothers him with regard to Joe and Biddy who he continues to ignore. As well, he feels guilty for leading Herbert into a life of debt by carrying him along on a very expensive lifestyle of dinners, drinks and shows.

Pip describes his life at Bernard's Inn with Herbert: "We spent as much money as we could, and got as little for it as people could make up their minds to give us. We were always more or less miserable and most of our acquaintances were in the same condition... our case was in the last aspect a common one."

They "check their affairs" by shuffling papers and bills and realise that, though they are in far in debt both, are quite unsure just how far in debt they have gone.

After one evening of "checking their affairs," a letter comes for Pip announcing the death of Mrs. Joe Gargery.

Analysis

Pip makes clear in this chapter that, in general, he is not happy with his lifestyle. He is not happy with his state of mind, feeling guilty about Joe and Biddy, nor with his day-to-day life as a young gentleman about town. A symbol of the emptiness he feels with being a gentleman around town is indicated by his joining a men's club called "Finches of the Grove." The group meets over dinner, argues, and gets drunk and Narrator Pip does not respect the group of young gentleman enough to even introduce their names.

The only true friend Pip has met is Herbert, and Pip feels that he is betraying even that relationship by living the high life with a man who cannot afford it.

The chapter reinforces what the reader already knows about Pip: He has chosen a lifestyle which alienates himself from the people he loves, and even alienates him from his true self.

Chapter 16

Pip returns home to attend the funeral — which turns out to be a ridiculous affair put on by Trabb the tailor and made worse by the pompous Pumblechook and the foolish Hubbles.

Later, however, Joe and Pip sit comfortably by the fire like times of old. Pip finds out that before she died, his sister put her head on Joe and said, "Joe... Pardon... Pip."

Later, Biddy and Pip go for a walk and Pip asks what she will do now. She tells him she is going to open her own school. Biddy insinuates that Pip will not be returning soon as he promises. Pip leaves insulted.

Analysis

As Joe predicted, the environment of the forge was a better environment for an honest relationship between he and Pip. Joe is much more comfortable with Pip in the comfort of his own home, smoking his pipe by the fire.

Discomfort continues, however, between Pip and Biddy. Biddy's honest evaluations of Pip are the cause of this discomfort. It is like talking to his own conscience. Biddy seems to be able to see right through Pip, as when she predicts that he will not be back too often, while at the same time she seems to sympathize with his position. Biddy's relationship with Pip appears as a contrast to Estella's relationship with him. In the former, Pip is loved by a woman who knows him better than anyone, both his strength and his failings. In the latter, Pip is a mere play thing to a woman who apparently, and admittedly, has been conditioned not to love.

Chapter 17

Pip "comes of age," that is, turns twenty one, and hopes that his benefactor will present her/himself. His hopes seem to be on the mark when Jaggers makes an appointment with him for early that evening.

In fact, Jaggers reveals nothing about Pip's benefactor and tells him that he does not know when the benefactor will chose to reveal themselves. The only thing that has changed is that Pip is now in charge of his own stipend which is now set at five hundred pounds a year.

Jaggers then dines with Herbert and Pip at the Bernard Inn. After he leaves, Herbert echoes both he and Pip's thoughts: When they are in Jagger's presence, you always feel as though you've committed some outrageous crime that not even you yourself are aware of.

Analysis

Once again, the irony of the title of the book is echoed in the events in Pip's life. Expectations, great or small, will be crushed. Pip expects his benefactor — whom he continues to believe is Miss Havisham — will reveal themselves on his birthday. Though Herbert's twenty-first birthday was only a few months ago, it was not anticipated or celebrated with as much anxiousness as Pip's — because of the great expectations which preceded it.

The motif of expectations crushed is paralleled with the continuing theme of guilt and shame in Pip's life. Herbert and Pip both share in a rather humorous feeling that any conversation with Jaggers makes you feel like your hiding something, but in Pip's case, he has felt like he is hiding something for most of his life.

Chapter 18

Pip goes to Wemmick's castle for dinner and is introduced to Miss Skiffins (whose face, like Wemmick's, also looks like a post office box). Pip asks Wemmick for advice on how to give anonymously give Herbert some of his yearly stipend (one hundred pounds a year).

With help from Miss Skiffins' brother, who is in finance, Wemmick and Pip put together a plan whereby Herbert will be given a job with a young merchant.

Analysis

The distinction between how we treat people in the public arena versus how we treat them in private is made stark clear by Wemmick's initial reaction in the previous chapter when Pip first approaches him about helping Herbert. Pip spoke with him in Jaggers' office, where Wemmick told him that giving money to help a friend is like throwing money into the Thames. When Pip approaches him about the same subject in his own home, Wemmick tells him that the gesture is "devilish good" of him. Wemmick demonstrates that not only does society force us to act a certain way, in a great part against our nature, it also forces us to denigrate our fellow humans to the level of positive or negative investments. The narrator certainly does not fault Wemmick for this, but Young Pip is being given clear lessons about life in the city.

Chapter 19

Pip dedicates a chapter, thin as it is, to his relationship with Estella while he lives in the city and she lives in Hammersmith. "I suffered every kind and degree of torture that Estella could cause me," he says.

On a number of occasions, he accompanies Estella on her frequent visits to Miss Havisham. In his presence, Miss Havisham demands to hear of all the hearts that Estella has broken, complete with names and details.

Pip blindly interprets this as meaning that after Estella has wreaked appropriate revenge on the male gender, the two of them will be given to each other by Miss Havisham as a reward.

Miss Havisham's concentrated effort to raise a child who can feel no love comes back to work against her, however, as Pip witnesses an argument between them. Miss Havisham, an older woman from when Pip first met her, has moments when she needs to be loved and appreciated. Unfortunately, Estella is incapable of love and cannot, therefore, give affection to even her adoptive mother. Miss Havisham did her job too well.

While fraternizing with his men's club, "the Finches of the Grove," Pip finds out that Drummle has begun courting Estella. Despite knowing how Estella treats men, Pip is miserably upset that Estella has begun seeing the most repulsive of Pip's acquaintances.

Analysis

Though Pip continues to dream of Miss Havisham revealing herself as his benefactor and, as well, revealing her plan of bringing he and Estella to live together in perfect domestic bliss, he admits that he "...never had one hour of happiness in her (Estella's) society..."

The torture that Pip feels, however, may in a great part be the torture that he brings on himself. Estella tells him that of all the men that she toys with, and of all the hearts that she breaks, she has never deceived or entrapped Pip.

Chapter 20

Pip has his twenty-third birthday and seems to be doing very little with his life. He no longer is tutored by Mr. Pocket, though they remain on good terms. He tries a few occupations, but does not stick to any of them. Instead, he finds that he is spending a lot of time reading.

A rough sea-worn man of sixty comes to Pip's home on a stormy night. Pip invites him in, treats him with courteous disdain, but then begins to recognize him as the convict that he fed in the marshes when he was a child.

The man reveals that he is Pip's benefactor. He has been living in Australia all these years and making money as a sheep herder. But since the day that Pip helped him, he swore to himself that every cent he earned would go to Pip.

"I've made a gentleman out of you," the man exclaims. Pip is horrified. All of his expectations are demolished. He has been living his life off the hard workings of a convict. There is no grand design by Miss Havisham to make Pip happy and rich, living in harmonious marriage to Estella.

The convict tells Pip that he has come back to see him under threat of his life, since the law will execute him if they find him in England. Pip gives the convict Herbert's empty bed, then sits by the fire by himself, pondering his miserable position.

Analysis

The chapter closing the second part of the novel closes as well Pip's great expectations. The irony is that the convict lived his life for Pip, worked his fingers to the bone to make Pip a gentleman. He did this based on the true act of kindness that Pip demonstrated when he gave the convict wittles to eat in the marshes. ("You acted noble, my boy. Noble Pip!") With all of his money and education, however, Pip has become much less of a noble "gentleman" than when he was a child. Pip has become less prone to kind acts than when he was a poor shivering orphan in a lonely courtyard. As seen by Pip's decaying relationship with his adoptive father Joe and his true friend Biddy, but most strongly by his horrified reaction to his benefactor in this chapter, Pip has become an unkind, ungenerous, pompous ass.

Considering his situation, Pip first becomes angry at Miss Havisham, who used him and deliberately led her relatives and himself into believing that he was destined for her fortune. But his anger soon turns to himself, when he realises how badly he treated Biddy and Joe, his true friends. He saw Joe as common and low class when all the time he was being supported by the lowest of the classes, a convict.

Although Pip learns that his expectations were all a sham and he realises that he has mistreated Biddy and Joe, he is still basing his thoughts on the class system, society's ideas of "gentleman " and "common." Although Pip's future seems to have changed, internally he still has not learned that the hierarchy of the class system says nothing about the nobleness of a person or how to lead a happy life. Indeed, he thinks he is ruined because he now associates himself with a convict, even though the convict has shown him nothing but kindness. He does not know what crime the convict committed, he only classifies him as less than common because of his label of "convict." Even his guilt about how he treated Joe is based on the fact that the money which brought him great expectaiions is somehow less pure than money from Miss Havisham. Yet the convict has shown Pip more generosity and care than Miss Havisham ever did: "Look'ee here, Pip. I'm your second father." Dicken's finishes this part with the line, "This is the end of the second stage of Pip's expectations."

PART III

Chapter 1

Pip gets up and eats breakfast with the convict, who tells him his name is Magwitch though he is going by Provis while in England. Pip is disgusted with him, though, at the same time, he wants to protect him and make sure he isn't found and put to death. Pip buys some clothes for him that will make him look like a "prosperous farmer."

Pip goes to Jaggers to verify that this man is his benefactor. Indeed, Jaggers assures him that Miss Havisham had nothing to do with his great expectations.

Analysis

Pip is closer to Magwitch than he knows since they both base the value of people on societally structured hierarchies. Pip still believes that one's value is decided by the class one is born, or adopted, into. Because he thinks of Magwitch as the lowest of the low, he thinks himself the lowest of the low because of his association with him. Magwitch does not see it this way. Instead, he believes that the amount of money you have, and how ostentatiously you spend it, is what gives one value. Thus, he has spent his life working for money to make a poor blacksmith boy a "gentleman."

Chapter 2

Herbert meets Magwitchapter Pip brings Magwitch to a nearby inn, then returns to discuss with Herbert "what is to be done."

Pip feels he cannot take any more of Magwitch's money, mostly because Pip is still proud and it is the money of a criminal. At the same time, Pip does not want Magwitch's execution on his hands which will surely occur if it is discovered he is back in England. Pip wants to protect Magwitch since he has risked his life to come back to see him.

The two decide that Pip will try and convince Magwitch to leave England with him. After that, they'll see what happens. Magwitch returns for breakfast the next morning, and Pip asks him about the other convict that Pip had seen him fighting with in the marshes on the Christmas day long in the past.

Analysis

The reader has been shown very few moments when Young Pip has been happy. Pip was unhappy even when he should have been happy — during his apprenticeship with Joe — and continued to be unhappy even when great expectations were announced for him. Now a great mystery has been solved in the way of the appearance of Pip's benefactor, and Pip is, once again, unhappy. We notice, however, that Pip is unhappy not so much because of his circumstances but because of how he views those circumstances. And although many in the novel are living a much worse life than he — Joe and Biddy, Magwitch himself, Wemmick and Jaggers, Herbert and the rest of the Pockets — they do not seem to demonstrate the same unhappiness with their lot in life. Magwitch, his life in danger, seems strangely happy to be in the company of Pip, a person he had met under dire circumstances for just a few moments many years before.

Only Pip has yet to reach within himself to find a happiness that neither society, nor romantic concepts of home, can offer him.

Chapter 3

Magwitch tells them the story of his life. From a very young age, he was alone and got into trouble. Mostly, he stole out of hunger and cold. At that same young age, he was impressed with the fact that others referred to him as hard, as a criminal, and predicted that he would spend his life in and out of jail. Indeed, his life ran along this very path.

In one of his brief stints actually out of jail, Magwitch met a young well-to-do gentleman named Compeyson who "had the head of the devil." Compeyson had his hand in everything illegal: swindling, forgery, and other white collar crime. When Magwitch met him, Compeyson was working with a half-crazed man called Arthur, who saw visions of a woman dressed all in white, with a broken heart, who came to haunt him. On one of these haunts, Arthur gave up his own ghost and died.

Compeyson then recruits Magwitch to do his dirty work and soon gets Magwitch into trouble with the law. Both standing before the judge, Compeyson, being a gentleman, is given a lesser sentence than Magwitch, a career criminal. Magwitch hates the man.

Herbert passes a note to Pip: "Young Havisham's name was Arthur. Compeyson is the man who professed to be Miss Havisham's lover."

Analysis

Previously non related story lines now come together and into focus. Magwitch worked with the man who had jilted Miss Havisham on her wedding day. And Compeyson's work horse Arthur turns out to be Miss Havisham's half brother who worked against her, haunted by her until the end.

Magwitch hates Compeyson with a self-sacrificing vengeance, and yet the reason for his hatred — that Compeyson was the mastermind behind the crimes yet received less of a sentence — is tied to his sacrifice for Pip. Compeyson got a lighter sentence because he was considered by society to be a gentleman. So Magwitch sets out on a life of sacrifice to provide the same advantages for Pip. Magwitch both hates this societal label and accepts it, as is demonstrated by his constant reference to himself as "low." Indeed, Dickens seems to hint that Magwitch may have been a much different man if people had not told him since a young age that he would come to no good. Yet he wants to exploit the societal labeling by promoting Young Pip into gentleman hood.

Magwitch, a sympathetic character, is a reflection of what Pip, or any of us, could become if we take societal labels to heart.

Chapter 4

Pip finds out that Estella is at the Satis House and feels he needs to go back to visit both she and Miss Havisham.

He returns to his home town and, at the town inn, meets Drummle, who is obviously courting Estella. The two pass rude words to each other, then they depart on their own ways.

Analysis

Magwitch has turned Pip's world upside down, just as he had turned the Young Pip upside down to get some bread when they first ran into each other in the churchyard. But even if Magwitch had not presented himself as benefactor, it is clear that Pip would not have lived a satisfying life. With or without Magwitch, Estella was not being grommed for Pip. She was being groomed as a lady for a man of greater fotune, in this case, the insolent Drummle. The high-class life that Pip thought he wanted is not a very pleasant place to be with people like Drummle taken as models. But Pip's world had to be turned upside down for him to start seeing that.

Chapter 5

Pip finds Miss Havisham and Estella in the same banquet room in the Satis. Pip tells Miss Havisham that he is unhappy with the way she led him on to thinking that she was his benefactor and the manner in which she hinted that he and Estella were destined to be together. It was his own fault, says Miss Havisham, just like it was the fault of her relatives to believe this was the case as well.

Pip tells her that Herbert and Matthew Pocket are different from her other relatives. They are the same blood but they are kind and upright. Pip breaks down and confesses his love for Estella. Estella tells him straight that she is incapable of love

— she had warned him of as much before — and she will soon be married to Drummle.

Even Miss Havisham seems to be finally feeling sympathy toward Pip, holding her heart as if remember how her own was broken.

Pip walks back to London. At the gate to his house he is given a note by the Porter written by Wemmick: "Don't Go Home."

Analysis

Pip is justifyably angry at both Miss Havisham and Estella, though he forgives them both without them even asking because he realises it was his own folly that brought him to unreal expectations. Estella's and Miss Havisham have vastly different reactions to Pip's break down in front of them. Miss Havisham appears to be touched, finally, and Pip's broken heart strikes a chord in her own heart. Estella, on the other hand, appears amazed at the show of emotion and does not seem to understand it. She is not angry, she is curious, as she really does not know what it means to love as Pip is now loving her.

Their reactions may also be an indication of culpability, in the sense that some characters are more guilty of their sins than others because of the level consciousness in their actions. Miss Havisham deliberately set out to break Pip's heart through Estella. Estella, on the other hand, is unconscious of what she did. She only acted as she was brought up to act.

Chapter 6

Pip gets a room at a nearby inn and in the morning visits Wemmick at his castle. Wemmick tells Pip things he has learned from the prisoners at Newgate. Pip is being watched, he says, and may be in some danger. As well, Compeyson has made his presence known in London.

Wemmick has already warned Herbert as well who, heeding the warning, brought Magwitch to his fiancé Clara's house in a neighborhood that Pip does not frequent. As well, the house is right next to a dock on the Thames, making an escape by river more easily accomplished.

Pip spends the day with Wemmick's deaf old relative, the "Aged," and leaves as it starts to grow dark.

Analysis

As the threat on Magwitch's life grows, so does Pip's affection and worry for him. Pip is no longer worried about himself, or even about having the blood of Magwitch on his hands, he is worried about the man at hand.

In this crisis, Pip is reminded who his true friends are: Wemmick, who is willing to be unprofessional and ask questions around the criminal areas of town and Herbert, who is risking his own life by helping Pip harbor a wanted man.

Chapter 7

Pip goes down to Clara's to find Magwitch and Herbert. Herbert introduces him to Clara. Clara has no relatives except her father, a drunk, bed-ridden old sailor who lives on the second floor (Herbert has never met him) and constantly claims Clara's attention.

Pip tells Magwitch that he is being watched and this is the best place for him now. In order to stay safe, Pip and Magwitch must only have contact through Herbert. Pip is a little sad to leave him. The rough old convict appears to have "softened" a bit.

Analysis

In this chapter, Pip actually misses Magwitch and wants to be closer to him. We are reminded of a parrallel moment in the first chapter when young Pip looked back on the marshes he was running from and saw Magwitch walking away into the cold night. That singular figure on the horizon struck a sympathetic chord in young Pip and made the two of them unified in their abandonment by the world. Here, too, Pip has changed from fear (and disgust) of the convict, to sympathy and genuine companionship.

Chapter 8

Pip goes to dinner alone one night, then to the theater where he sees Mr. Wopsle in one of his productions. Mr.

Wopsle stares strangely at Pip throughout the play, getting quite out of character.

Afterwards, Mr. Wopsle asks Pip who it was that he came with. Pip says he came alone. Mr. Wopsle tells him that there was man sitting behind Pip for much of the production and that he recognized him as the second convict that he, Pip, and Joe had hunted with the soldiers when Pip was just a child. Compeyson!

Analysis

Things are coming together quickly in the next few chapters. Pip is learning mysteries that have been unknown since the beginning of the novel. At the same time, the suspense is growing because there is a sense that all of these subplots are going to collide soon. Compeyson and Magwitch's ongoing hatred, Miss Havisham's "creation" of Estella, Pip's snubbing of Joe and Biddy.

The rhythm of the novel and its subplots — the introduction of mysterious events, their explanations, and the reaction of these explanations by the various characters — lends itself well to the series genre in which this story, and all of Dickens' novels, were first published. Only one or two chapters, in the form of a magazine, were presented to the public at a time. One week a mystery would be introduced, the next week suspense would build, the week after that solutions and new problems, plus new characters, would come to light.

It is easy to see how all of England waited eagerly for the next issue of Dickens' story, much like some today discuss the ongoing plots and subplots of soap operas.

One can imagine that when the different issues of Great Expectations were first published, the readers felt, and probably talked, about Pip and all the characters as if they knew them personally. Pip was made all the more real by the fact that, in many cases, Dickens was creating the story as he went along. Therefore anything really could happen to Pip from one issue to the next when not even the author knew all the details.

Chapter 9

Pip has dinner with Jaggers and Wemmick at Jaggers' home and learns from the host that Drummle has indeed married Estella. Jaggers' verdict on the subject is that Drummle, because of his "spidery" character, will either beat her or "cringe," that is, become a brow-beaten husband himself. The whole conversation pains Pip, who has been trying to avoid the subject even with Herbert.

During the dinner, Pip finally realises what had been so familiar about a certain look he had seen in Estella. It was a look that he had seen in Jaggers' servant woman as well. Pip knows instinctively now that Jaggers' servant woman is Estella's mother!

On their way home together, Wemmick tells the story of Jaggers' woman servant, the "tigress" as Wemmick refers to her. It was Jaggers' first big break-through case, the case that made him. He was defending this woman in a case where she was accused of killing another woman by strangulation. This is why Jaggers' likes to show off the poor woman's hands to company. The woman was also said to have killed her own child, a girl, at about the same time as the murder.

Analysis:

Once again, Pip sees his life colliding with criminality and violence as he realises that his love is the daughter of a murderess. The solutions to all the mysteries of the novel are starting to pour out now. For each one, Pip's life is being disassembled. Things are not how he first saw them. People are not how he first defined them.

Convicts are kind and ladies are the daughters of criminals. Gentleman are scoundrels and blacksmiths are loyal. He has started letting go of the societal definitions for these people and started seeing them for who they are: individuals beyond labeling.

Chapter 10

Miss Havisham asks that Pip come visit her. He finds her again sitting by the fire, but this time she looks very lonely. In fact, as she begins to speak, Pip sees that a big change has come over the cold woman. She seems almost afraid of Pip. Pip tells her how he was giving some of his money to help Herbert with his future, but now must stop since he himself is no longer taking money from his benefactor. Miss Havisham wants to help, and she gives Pip nine hundred pounds to continue to assist Herbert.

She then asks Pip for forgiveness. Pip tells her she is already forgiven and that he needs too much forgiving himself to be able not to forgive others.

"What have I done?" Miss Havisham repeats again and again. "What have I done?"

Pip asks her about the history of Estella. Miss Havisham says that she was brought as a mere infant by Jaggers during the night.

Pip goes for a walk around the garden then comes back to find Miss Havisham on fire! Pip takes his jacket, and the tablecloth from the old banquet table, and puts the fire out, burning himself badly in the process. The doctors come, announce that she will live. they put her on the banquet table to care for her (where she said she would always lie when she died.)

Analysis

Repentance and forgiveness is a common theme among the relationships in the novel and it is interesting to see the instances where forgiveness is given and where it is refused. We are reminded of Mrs. Joe's last words to Joe, seeming to imply a request for forgiveness for her actions toward he and Pip.

In this chapter, Miss Havisham is asking for forgiveness from Pip for having been a part of breaking his heart. She commiserates with him because her own heart had been so broken once. Pip immediately forgives, but believes her to have been much more of a disservice to herself and to Estella in her actions. She took away the light (both daylight and a spiritual sense of joy) from both their lives. In so doing, she destroyed a young girl's capacity to love, and she herself is growing old with none to love her.

Miss Havisham's request for forgiveness, of course, reminds Pip of his own need to reconcile and ask for forgiveness from Joe and Biddy and his treatment of them.

Reflecting the Christian influence in Victorian morality, those that do not seek reconciliation will sooner or later destroy themselves. We will see this in the upcoming chapters with Magwitch's hatred for Compeyson and Orlick's hatred for Pip.

Chapter 11

Pip goes home and Herbert takes care of his burns. Herbert has been spending some time with Magwitch at Clara's and has been told the whole Magwitch story.

Magwitch was the husband of Jaggers' servant woman, the Tigress. The woman had come to Magwitch on the day she murdered the other woman and told him she was going to kill their child and that Magwitch would never see the baby again. And Magwitch never did. Pip puts it all together and tells Herbert that Magwitch is Estella's father.

Analysis

Though this chapter is short, it drops such a bomb that it takes longer to realise all the ironies and implications of that bomb than it does to actually read the chapter. Estella is the daughter of a convict and a murderous tigress! Pip's idea of all that is desirable in this life — Estella, wealthy, beautiful, uncommon Estella — is more closely related to the world of criminals and convicts than even he. Pip has been blindly headed towards what he thought he was running away from in the first place.

Of course, he does not feel any less respect or love for Estella. He cannot, because he knows her to be a lady. And so he must start to reevaluate how he judges people. He has judged himself harshly, at times, because he feels he has always been surrounded by criminals and violence and this is a reflection of his value as a person. But he can no longer do that, now that he sees that his benefactor is the father of the woman he loves.

Strangely, Pip feels he has not become what Magwitch had hoped for: a gentlemanly son. Unconsciously, however, Magwitch has given the world a ladylike daughter, in all ways very upper-class and uncommon.

Chapter 12

Pip wants to make sure he has the whole thing straight and goes to see Jaggers the next morning.

Pip tells Jaggers that he knows his servant woman is the mother of Estella and that Jaggers brought her to Miss Havisham. He also tells him Magwitch is the father. Jaggers was not aware of this and is as visibly amazed as Jaggers can get. Then Pip asks him to give him more details on the story and appeals to Wemmick, standing by, to help him. While doing so, he tells Jaggers of Wemmick's warm castle and of his "Aged" relative. Jaggers is amazed at this as well, and tells Pip more of the story.

Jaggers had, in fact, talked (or rather threatened) his servant woman out of keeping the child and knew that Miss Havisham was looking to adopt. His reasoning amazes Pip, and Wemmick moreso, with its humanity. Jaggers says he wanted to save the child, to give it a chance in life, because he had seen too many children in her situation grow up in and out of jails and surrounded by the dangerous world of crime.

Analysis

The solving of the mysteries is coupled with the unveiling of the true personalities of the characters involved. In this chapter, we are pleased to learn that Jaggers does indeed have a heart, and his heart went out to little Estella. Before this scene, Young Pip had often imagined that the face casts of the two dead criminals in Jaggers' office had a different expression everytime he walked in, implying that the masks of two dead men had more feelings and emotions than the living occupant of the room, Jaggers. Now, Jaggers is revealed, though only for a moment.

Wemmick's private self, too, is revealed in the presence of his employer. In a humorous commentary, Pip describes how uncomfortable they are with their new relationship. By berating a harried convict for his show of emotion, the two revert immediately to their old selves and find themselves on a much more comfortable plane.

Chapter 13

Wemmick sends Pip a note indicating that now may be a good time to escape with Magwitch and get him out of the country.

Herbert and Pip plan to take the boat out with Magwitch in a few days, take him down the Thames until they run into a steamer headed for a foreign port.

In the meantime, Pip gets another letter, this one by an anonymous author, telling him to come down to the limekiln in the marshes that night. Once again, Pip goes to his hometown and walks out to the marshes.

Analysis

On returning his village yet again, Pip hears his own story from an innkeeper who didn't know his identity. The story was about a young man from the village who had come into some property. This young man would often come back, but would give a cold-shoulder to the man who had been his initial benefactor and protector. The innkeeper is talking about Pumblechook as Pip's initial benefactor as Pumblechook in his loud mouth likes to identify himself. But for Pip it is yet another reminder of the "cold shoulder" that he has given Joe all these years. Joe truly was his benefactor and never asked for anything in return (unlike Pumblechook). With his reflections on Joe and on Magwitch, Pip is now examining the great relationships in his life as opposed to his great expectations.

Chapter 14

Pip goes to the marshes to a shack near the limekiln where he is to meet the anonymous writer. There Pip is jumped by Orlick who ties him up and tells him that he is going to promptly kill him. Pip does not want to die, not because he values his own life, but because he still has moral obligations to fulfill with Magwitch (getting him out of the country) and Joe (asking for forgiveness).

Orlick admits to hitting Mrs. Joe over the head, but says it was Pip's fault because Pip was the favoured one and Orlick was jealous. Orlick says he is working for Compeyson and assures Pip that Compeyson will make sure that Magwitch does not leave the country.

Just as it appears Orlick is going to kill him, Herbert, Startop and Trabb's boy burst through the door. Orlick escapes.

Pip had dropped the anonymous letter at home and Herbert found it. He and Startop came to the town and got Trabb's boy to show them where the shack was. Pip rests a day at home; the following day they plan to escape with Magwitchapter

Analysis

Orlick represents random violence and is probably the only truly evil character in the novel. He acts simply on his anger — first with Mrs. Joe, now with Pip. At the same time, if there is a character that Pip would truly like to kill, it would be Orlick. Orlick, after all, was responsible for the death of his sister and was considered a threat to Biddy. Now Orlick threatened to take away the time Pip wants to set his life straight with the important people in his life.

Hatred begets hatred. The only way Pip sees as dealing with Orlick is violently. Fortunately, the only expression of violence that Pip is capable of in his current predicament is a ferocious scream.

Chapter 15

They get up the next morning and start rowing down the river, picking up Magwitch at the preappointed time. They row downstream all day and put in on shore at an inn for the night.

They start off the next day and are within a few feet of a steamer that they hope to board when another boat pulls alongside to stop them. In the confusion, Pip sees Compeyson leading the other boat, but the steamer is on top of them. The steamer crushes Pip's boat, Compeyson and Magwitch disappear under the water, and Pip, Startop and Herbert find themselves in a police boat of sorts.

Magwitch finally comes up from the water. He and Compeyson and wrestled for a while, but Magwitch let him go and now Compeyson is presumably drowned. Once again, Magwitch is shackled and arrested.

Pip sits down next to the injured and exhausted Magwitch, and feels that he will stay by Magwitch's side until the end. Pip also realises that the English government will take all of Magwitch's fortune.

Analysis

The chapter begins with Magwitch and Pip sitting together in the boat, Magwitch seemingly unworried about the future: "...we can no more see to the bottom of the next few hours, than we can see to the bottom of this river what I catches hold of." But Magwitch is content to be free for the moment and sitting next to the boy he considers a son.

By the end of the chapter, with Magwitch in chains, Pip too feels that he is where he should be, sitting next to his adopted father. Pip, too, does not know what is in store for him in the future, with all his expectations dashed, but he is content to stand by the man who risked his life to be near him.

The single fact that the loss of Magwitch's fortune does not bother Pip demonstrates the power of his transformation. Even the generous Wemmick laments its loss to the crown, but Pip seems to take it as a mixed blessing. He will not live off the money of others again.

Chapter 16

Magwitch is in jail and quite ill. Herbert is leaving for Egypt with the firm in the position that Pip, and now Miss Havisham, had secretly set up for him. Herbert plans to marry Clara as soon as her drunk old father dies. He offers Pip a job as his clerk in the company as well as a place to stay — with he and Clara, once they get settled. Pip cannot give his answer for the job until he sees the Magwitch situation through, but asks Herbert to keep the position open for a few months for him.

Wemmick invites Pip to his castle on a Monday, the first holiday Wemmick has taken in over twelve years. He and Pip go for a walk.

They walk to a church where Miss Skiffins and Wemmick's "Aged" relative are waiting. With Pip as witness, Miss Skiffins and Wemmick proceed to get married.

Analysis

Two of Pip's best friends have found happiness: Herbert in his job and in his pending matrimony to the fairy-like Clara and Wemmick in the completion of his castle fantasy with a queen in Miss Skiffins. In contrast, Pip is in the worst of straits. He has no employment, he no longer has a pending fortune, Estella has married someone else, and his adoptive father is dying in prison.

A Victorian moral lesson is being taught here. Herbert is a cheerful, hard working, honest man with limited resources but large dreams. His kindness to Pip and his sincere love of a woman below his status demonstrates that he is a moral, upright man. Good things, then, have come to the man who has lived an honest life. Likewise Wemmick has also showed kindness and incredible generosity to Pip and his "Aged" relative with nearly superhuman cheerfulness. He, too, has earned a good life with a good woman.

Pip, with his great expectations, has failed to achieve any of them, and now does not have even the smallest expectation of a good honest living with a good loving wife.

Through his difficulties, however, Pip is being transformed from a proud boy to an actual gentleman, with respect for good relationships and rejection of societal value judgments. Being witness to two beautifully caring love matches — the romantic Herbert and Clara and the rather comical Wemmick and Miss Skiffins — Pip is starting to learn what is important.

Chapter 17

Pip attends to the ailing Magwitch daily in prison. "The kind of... resignation that he (Magwitch) showed, was that of a man who was tired out."

Magwitch is condemned to die and the sentencing is carried out with thirty two other convicts also condemned to die. Within ten days of the sentencing, Magwitch dies in prison. Before he does, Pip whispers to him that the daughter he thought was dead is quite alive. "She is a lady and very beautiful," Pip says. "And I love her." Magwitch kisses Pip's hand in response and passes away.

Analysis

Pip's transformation is made graphically clear during the trial and sentencing of Magwitchapter Throughout the trial, Pip holds Magwitch's hand. At the sentencing, Pip assists Magwitch out of the chambers while onlookers point their fingers at them. Pip is no longer the proud boy afraid of what people will think of his associates and his past. He is, literally, embracing his past. He honestly loves Magwitch and therefore does not fear showing this love in public. This Pip is a much different Pip from the one who would not visit Joe and Biddy in the privacy of the forge for fear that people would talk.

Chapter 18

Pip, weakened by his burns, the fight with Orlick, and the general psychological stress, falls into a fever for nearly a month. Creditors and Joe fall in and out of his dreams and his reality. Finally, he regains his senses and sees that, indeed, Joe has been there the whole time, nursing him back to health.

Joe tells him that Miss Havisham died during his illness, that she left Estella nearly all, and Matthew Pocket a great deal. The rest of the relatives were given very little. Orlick has been put in jail because he broke into Pumblechook's house.

Pip slowly regains his strength. Seeing this, Joe slips away one morning leaving only a note. Pip discovers that Joe has paid off all his debtors.

Pip is committed to returning to the forge and to ask for forgiveness foreverything he has done. He also wants to ask Biddy to marry him.

Analysis

As in his childhood, Pip is assisted by the irreplaceable help of Joe. Through this action, Joe has already forgiven Pip.

Joe is most comfortable when Pip is at his weakest. As Pip grows stronger, Joe begins to distance himself. Finally, he leaves. Joe has proved his friendship, it is now Pip's turn to show his true colours.

Other endings are wrapped up. Miss Havisham makes good in the end by giving money to the one relative that she didn't allow to visit her. All the other relatives are given rather humorous inheritances to help with their faulty characters.

Chapter 19

Pip returns to his home town and is treated with a certain coldness by the town that was so kind to him when he was on his way to great expectations. He meets Pumblechook, who tells Pip his misfortune is due to him because he was ungracious and ungrateful to his earliest benefactor and friend — meaning, of course, not Joe but himself, Pumplechook.

Pip walks toward the forge, creating a picture in his mind of the simply happy life he will have with Biddy.

Pip comes to the forge and indeed finds happiness — but the happiness is Joe and Biddy's. It is their wedding day.

Pip wishes them well, truly, and asks them for their forgiveness in all his actions. They happily give it.

Pip goes to work for Herbert's' firm and lives with the now married Clara and Herbert. Within a year, he becomes a partner. He pays off his debts and works hard.

Analysis

Poor Pip has one last lesson to learn and he learns it in Biddy's marriage to Joe. The lesson appears to be that one should not have expectations at all, simple or grand.

Pip, walking in his old neighborhood, is struck by the simple beauty of the place. He develops expectations of the place as much as he creates an expectation of an idyllic marriage to Biddy.

The expectation fails because, once again, Pip is adhering to societal concepts of what is happiness (this one taking place in a simple village with a simple wife) instead of seeing people for who they really are and appreciating the relationship beyond its societal label.

Pip sees the simple village, he remembers his simple and happy life in the forge with Joe. The idyllic vision in his head has nothing to do with the actual people involved, including himself. Pip, in fact, is not thinking of Biddy when he imagines their life together. He does not examine or appreciate that relationship for what it is. If he had been more attentive to the actual relationships involved instead of his idyllic view of them, he would have seen Biddy's love for Joe and Joe's love for her. He would have seen that Pip's place at the forge was as a friend, not as a husband or a brother.

In the end, there is a feeling that Pip's life is actually just beginning. The journey through his great expectations was in preparation for what would become a fuller life. Pip will now adhere to the Victorian standards of working honestly for his money, of being loyal to his friends, of being generous and kind even to those whom societal may view as low or common. In essence, Pip has made the past a part of his life and has more realistic expectations of the future. He can now live more fully in the present, developing and appreciating relationships.

Pip seems to have finally learned all he needs to learn. But we have one more chapter...

Chapter 20

Being out of the country working for Herbert's firm, Pip has not seen Biddy or Joe in eleven years. He visits them finally and meets their son, a little Pip, sitting by the fire with Joe just like Pip himself did years ago.

Pip tells Biddy that he is quite the settled old bachelor, living with Clara and Herbert and he thinks he will never marry.

Nevertheless, he goes to the Satis House that night to think once again of the girl who got away.

And there he meets Estella. Drummle treated her roughly and recently died. She tells Pip that she has learned the feeling of heartbreak the hard way and now seeks his forgiveness for what she did to him.

The two walk out of the garden hand in hand, and Pip "saw no shadow of another parting from her."

Analysis

The final chapter of Great Expectations remains a controversy with critics even today. Dickens had initially written a different ending in which Pip runs into Estella on a London street but she has not changed at all and he, in turn, feels none of the old feelings for her. Though much more depressing, many critics consider the first ending more true to the story's themes. Their argument, in some cases, is that the entire point of the book was that Pip must come to realise happiness through his own internal process and not through some external situation (such as position or wealth) or person (like Estella).

Nevertheless, there is some justice in Estella and Pip finally finding love in each other. Because of their difficulties, they seem both to have come to a realization of what it means to be happy and therefore are ready for a healthy relationship with each other. Chapter Nineteen demonstrated that Pip had been living an upright life for 11 years when he finally runs into Estella again. Estella might be seen as the final reward for a true Victorian gentleman.

And, although we are not witness to Estella's transformation from ice queen to sensitive lady, we, as readers, must in the end forgive her for her treatment of Pip. Estella, more so than Pip, represents the abused child, the true victim of circumstance that Dickens presents in many other characters throughout his novels. Estella had no choice in her lot in life — she was born to criminals and brought up to be emotionless by a cold, vengeful woman. Even Estella's marriage to Drummle, and her abuse in that relationship, is pre-designed by powers beyond her control. While Pip had good friends in Joe and Herbert and Wemmick, Estella had only jealously bitter relatives.

Estella's life, in fact, is nearly identical to the lives of both her criminal parents. She has been trapped, nearly imprisoned, throughout her life, but literally and figuratively. Estella is trapped in a house without daylight for her entire childhood and then moved, like a prisoner herself, to houses in Paris and then London. Finally, she ends up trapped in an abusive marriage. Estella's past, her roots, her beginnings, are symbolized not by the warm fire of the forge, as is Pip's case, but in the barren empty lot where the Satis House once stood.

Estella is the true victim of society's values. It is a miracle that she emerged sane or with any feelings at all. And so, like Pip, we must forgive her and wish the two of them well.

Chapter 14

Study Questions

Q. Discuss Pip's unrealistic expectations in Dickens' Great Expectations

One of the most important and common tools that authors use to illustrate the themes of their works is a character that undergoes several major changes throughout the story. In Great Expectations, Charles Dickens introduces the reader to many intriguing and memorable characters. Including the eccentric recluse, Miss Havisham, the shrewd and careful lawyer, Mr. Jaggers, and the benevolent convict, Abel Magwitchapter However, without a doubt, Great Expectations is the story of Pip and his initial dreams and resulting disappointments that eventually lead to him becoming a genuinely good man.

The significant changes that Pip's character goes through are very important to one of the novel's many themes. Dickens uses Pip's deterioration from an innocent boy into an arrogant gentleman and his redemption as a good-natured person to illustrate the idea that unrealistic hopes and expectations can lead to undesirable traits.

In the beginning of the novel, Pip is characterized as a harmless, caring boy, who draws much sympathy from the reader even though he is at that point content with his common life. The reader most likely develops warm and sympathetic feelings toward Pip after only the first two pages of the novel, which introduce the fact that Pip's parents are "dead and buried" and that the orphan has never seen "any likeness of either of them". Pip's confrontation with the convict presents his harmless, innocent nature. As Magwitch first seizes the young boy, Pip simply responds, "Oh! Don't cut my throat, sir, Ö Pray don't do it sir" (p. 2). Then, Pip is forced into submitting to the convict's demands, mainly due to his naive fear of Magwitch's fictitious companion who "has a secret way peculiar to himself of getting at a boy, and at his heart, and at his liver" (p. 4). Even though he aids the convict, the reader's sympathy for Pip soon increases, as his robbery of his own home weighs greatly on his conscience.

For example, when Mrs. Joe leaves the Sunday dinner to retrieve the "savoury pork pie," which Magwitch had enjoyed heartily, Pip is tortured by the thought of his actions, while his mind screams, "Must they! Let them not hope to taste it!" (p. 27). He seems to sincerely regret his actions and the fact that he "had been too cowardly to avoid doing what I knew to be wrong" (p. 40). Approximately one year after his encounter with the convict, Pip is still shown to be an innocent, caring boy. One night, when Pip and Joe are alone at the forge, Joe explains his various reasons for enduring Mrs. Joe's constant abuse. .

After their conversation, Pip realises that he cares deeply for Joe and appreciates everything that the blacksmith does for him. Also, he develops "a new admiration of Joe from that night" and "a new sensation of feeling conscious that I was looking up to Joe in my heart" (p. 48). Unfortunately, as Pip develops unrealistic hopes and expectations for his life, these positive characteristics are replaced by undesirable ones.

The expectations that cause Pip's character to become less likable are those that he develops after being introduced to Miss Havisham and Estella. During his first visit to the Satis House, Estella, who considers herself much too refined and well-bred to associate with a common boy, scorns Pip. On the other hand, Pip seems to fall in love with Estella during that first meeting. He even admits to Miss Havisham that he thinks her adopted daughter is not only "very proud" and "very insulting," but also "very pretty" and that he should "like to see her again" (p. 59). After just one afternoon at the Satis House, Pip develops a desire to become more acceptable to Estella, in hopes that her callous attitude toward him would change. As a result, while walking back to the forge, Pip begins to feel ashamed of his life. His mind is filled with regretful thoughts such as "that I was a common labouring-boy; that my hands were coarse; that my boots were thick; and generally that I was in a low-lived bad way" (p. 63). Pip realises that his personality and outlook on his life is changing as he states, "That was a memorable day to me, for it made great changes in me" (p.70).

When his visits to the Satis House cease and he is apprenticed to Joe, Pip becomes even more deeply ashamed of his position in society because he believes that it will ruin his hopes of Estella loving him. He constantly worries that Estella will see him at the "unlucky hour" when he is at his "grimiest and commonest" (p.107), but he endures his shame with an irrational hope, "that perhaps Miss Havisham was going to make my fortune when my time was out" (p. 133). Then, when Mr. Jaggers informs Pip of the "great expectations" that have been placed on him, Pip thinks, without a doubt, "Miss Havisham was going to make my fortune on a grand scale" (p.139). Also, he begins to believe that Miss Havisham has destined him to be married to Estella. Almost immediately, Pip's ego grows tremendously, and he becomes arrogant as he looks down on his "common," yet caring and loyal friends. For example, in a private conversation with Biddy, Pip tells his good friend that Joe "is rather backward in some things. For instance in his learning and his manners" (p. 149). In addition, when Pip is finally ready to depart for London, he tells Joe that he "wished to walk away all alone" because he privately fears the "contrast there would be between me and Joe" (p. 159).

As the arrogant and ungrateful Pip continues to believe that Miss Havisham has chosen him to be the recipient of her money and, hopefully, of Estella's hand in marriage, he also continues to be ashamed of and look down on his past life. On one occasion, Pip receives word that Joe will be visiting London and would like to see him. However, Pip is not at all overjoyed to receive this news. In fact, he looks forward to Joe's visit "with considerable disturbance, some mortification, and a keen sense of incongruity," and he states that he "certainly would have paid money" in order to keep Joe away (p.217). Pip is distraught over the prospect of others, especially Bentley Drummle, seeing him with the common blacksmith. After Joe's departure, Pip decides that he should return to the forge, but the next day, he resolves to stay at the Blue Boar Inn, rather than at his old home. His snobbish reasoning is simply, "I should be an inconvenience at Joe's; I was not expected, and my bed would not be ready" (p. 225). Then, Pip is so concerned with gaining Estella's favour that he visits Miss Havisham's home and returns to London while never stopping at the forge.

The negative attitudes and traits that Pip develops as a result of his unrealistic expectations are portrayed in ways other than his view of his past life. In London, while living as a "gentleman," Pip has trouble managing his new way of life. Both he and Herbert "went on from bad to worse, in the way of increasing our debts, looking into our affairs, leaving margins, and the like exemplary transactions" (p. 287). Also, during a dinner with other gentlemen, Pip has an irrational confrontation with his nemesis, Drummle. After Drummle proposes a toast to Estella, who has allowed "the Spider" to attach himself to her, Pip loses control of his emotions and accuses him of lying. Drummle is then able to provide proof that he has danced with Estella on several occasions, and Pip is forced to apologize for his outrageous actions. However, he and Drummle sit "snorting at one another for an hour" because Pip can "not endure the thought of her stooping to that hound" (p. 310). For many years, Pip had believed that he and Estella were destined to be married, but now his hopes and expectations are just beginning to fade.

When Pip finally learns that Abel Magwitch, not Miss Havisham, is his benefactor, his unrealistic expectations cease and his genuinely good nature begins to overcome the negative traits that he had developed. Also, he realises that he was at fault for his non-realistic hopes. During a visit to the Satis House, Pip is able to hold no harsh feelings toward Miss Havisham for the misfortunes of his life. He refuses her offer to financially compensate him for his unhappy life, and instead, he requests that she provide aid to Herbert's business situation. Then, he confesses that he can forgive her, stating, "There have been many sore mistakes; and my life has been a blind and thankless one; and I want forgiveness and direction far too much to be bitter with you" (p. 400). Later, Pip revisits Miss Havisham's room to check on her and finds that she had been too close to the fire, as her aged garments are ignited in flames. Pip immediately risks his own life to save the old woman. She receives serious burns and nerve damage, but she remains alive. Pip is also seriously burned and states, "I was astonished to see that both my hands were burnt, for I had no knowledge of it through the sense of feeling" (p. 404).

Pip's positive characteristics are also evident in his treatment of his benefactor, the convict Magwitchapter Initially after the revelation, Pip's reaction had been one of shock, disbelief, and even repugnance. However, he realises and somewhat appreciates that Magwitch had tried to greatly repay him for the practically insignificant favour that Pip had provided for the convict as a child. Over time, Pip's hard feelings toward his benefactor fade, and at one point he confesses that Magwitch "was softened indefinably, for I could not have said how, and could never afterwards recall how when I tried, but certainly" (p. 379). As he had done while saving Miss Havisham, Pip puts himself through great personal risks and inconveniences to save Magwitchapter He is unsuccessful in fleeing the country with Magwitch, but his caring and devotion for the kind convict are unwavering, even though he will not receive any money after Harwich's death. Every day, Pip visits him in the infirmary in efforts to comfort Magwitch and to make the prisoner's last days as peaceful as possible. During one visit, Pip notices, "a smile crossed his face then, and he turned his eyes on me with a trustful look, as if he were confident that I had seen some small redeeming touch in him, even so long ago as when I was a little child" (p. 461). Pip believes that his visits are somewhat cheering to Magwitch, and he goes to the infirmary every day until the convict's tranquil death which is almost a blessing.

Just as Pip's feelings toward Magwitch soften, so does his attitude toward his old life after the burden of his expectations is lifted. Soon after Magwitch dies, Pip becomes seriously ill. When he recovers, he learns that Joe had traveled to London to care for him. As he continues to nurse Pip back to good health, Joe remains formal and awkward around Pip, as he had acted while visiting Pip in London several years earlier. On the other hand, Pip begins to feel as if he had never left the forge. He realises and appreciates that "there was no change whatever in Joe. Exactly what he had been in my eyes then, he was in my eyes still; just as simply faithful, just as simply right" (p. 472). When Joe unexpectedly leaves London to return to the forge, Pip follows him as soon as he is physically able. At the forge, Pip no longer shows any feelings of shame or arrogance because he is now content and cheerful in his old surroundings. In fact, he even requests, "Now let me go up and look at my old room Ö And then when I have eaten and drunk with you, go with me as far as the finger post, dear Joe and Biddy, before we say good-bye" (p. 484).

At the conclusion of Great Expectations, the reader most likely finds Pip's fate acceptable and enjoyable. Earlier in his life, he had changed from an innocent, caring boy into an arrogant young man as a result of his nonrealistic hopes and expectations. However, when those expectations come to an end, so do his undesirable traits, as he is shown to be a truly good-natured person. Therefore, it is fitting that, in both of Dickens' final episodes, Pip is happy and content with his life.

Q. What is the situation that makes Pip feel his guilt?
Or
Q. Is this sense of guilt justified or not in the life of Pip?
Or
Q. Do you think that Pip is over exploited in the whim of life?

The frightened Pip is tormented by a sense of guilt, which some readers have found excessive, for it is not justified by the events in his life. Julian Moynahan asserts, "Pip has certainly one of the guiltiest consciences in literature." They explain this guilt in terms of Dickens's biography and attribute it to Dickens's own guilt over his affair with Ellen Ternan and the breakup of his marriage of over twenty years. But is Pip's guilt excessive, and is it unjustified by the events in his life? First of all, this question assumes that our sense of guilt is always proportionate to our actions, but is this true. Do we sometimes feel guilty over behaviour, feelings, or thoughts which are natural, which are minor transgressions, or which we have no control over? Do children, for instance, take responsibility for their parents' divorce or a parent's alcoholism and feel guilty?

Second, is there indeed no justification in his life for his sense of guilt? Consider the way that he is physically, verbally, and emotionally abused by his sister. Could such treatment give a child a sense of being somehow wrong and deserving to be punished? A close reading of the opening chapters suggests other possible causes for Pip's guilt:

- His behaviour at times causes his sister to assault Joe; when Joe's oblique references to Pip's supposed bolting of his bread drive her to knock Joe's head against the wall, Pip looks on helplessly and "guiltily" (page 10).
- In taking food to the convict, Pip is stealing, and he certainly knows that stealing is a crime.
- When Pip asks what a convict is, the only word Pip understands of Joe's explanation is "Pip." Reinforcing Pip's identification of himself as a criminal, his sister says criminals who murder and rob (which Pip intends to do) always start by asking questions (which Pip has been doing). A little later, he thinks he has somehow murdered Pumblechook with the doctored brandy. When he runs into the sergeant, he thinks the handcuffs are for him.
- Pip is made to feel that his very existence is a crime: "I was always treated as if I had insisted on being born in opposition to the dictates of reason, religion, and morality, and against the dissuading arguments of my best friends" (page 21). His sister tells the Christmas dinner guests about the acts of sleeplessness. I had committed and all the high places I had tumbled from,

and all the low places I had tumbled into, and all the injuries I had done myself, and all the times she had wished me in my gave, and I had contumaciously refused to go there (page 26).

She constructs a scenario of the ordinary actions of childhood as crimes; the final crime is his continuing to live. The guests all acquiesce. Only Joe, who is powerless to protect Pip, offers solace; he ineffectually spoons more gravy onto his plate.

- Pip several times refers to the corruptness of his own nature.
- The adult Pip wonders what terrible acts he might have committed as a child, under the pressure of fear and the consciousness of having no adult to turn to for help: "I was in mortal terror of myself... I am afraid to think of what I might have done on requirement, in the secrecy of my terror" (page 13).
- He does not confess the theft to Joe because he is afraid of losing Joe's love and trust. He sees this failure and the theft as examples of deliberate moral transgressions: "In a word, I was too cowardly to do what I knew what was right, as I had been too cowardly to avoid doing what I knew to be wrong" (page 40).
- In the fight with the pale young gentleman in Miss Havisham's garden, Pip confesses, "I am sorry to record that the more I hit him, the harder I hit him." Looking back, the adult Pip hopes that he regarded himself "as a species of savage young wolf, or other wild beast" (page 90). The young Pip suffers agonies afterwards, expecting to be arrested or otherwise punished for the young gentleman's injuries.
- The culmination of Pip's being treated as a criminal occurs with his apprenticeship. Pumblechook takes Pip "into custody" and physically handles Pip as if he committed a crime; bystanders in court think he has been caught "redhanded"; one comments he "looks bad, don't he?" and another gives him a tract written for young criminals (page 103).

- After his visit to Satis House, Pip becomes ashamed of himself, his home, and Joe and dreams of becoming a gentleman. Would the rejection of the loving Joe, his true friend and constant companion, contribute to a child's feeling guilty?

Q. How the plans of Pip counter attack on him itself?
Or
Q. How does the play portrayed become a blessing in disguise for Pip?

Pip's internalization of guilt is expressed in his reaction to the assault on his sister. He agrees to participate in Wopsle's reading of *The Tragedy of George Barnwell*, in which an apprentice murders his uncle; Pip is, of course, an apprentice. Though he is annoyed at Wopsel's identifying him with the murder, at the same time he accepts the identification because of the way Wopsle and Pumblechook treat him: "When Barnwell began to go wrong, I declare I felt positively apologetic." He describes the murderous apprentice's actions as his own, "Even after I was happily hanged" (page 117).

When Pip first hears of the assault on his sister, his immediate thought is that he must have attacked her or that he will be suspected as the assailant. He explains that he was still thinking of the play. But is it possible, at a psychological level, that Pip is expressing guilt at his own hostility toward and resentment against his sister? Wouldn't anger and perhaps a desire for revenge be natural responses to his sister's abuses? Another connection between Pip and the assault is his belief that the weapon is the leg iron his convict filed off using the file Pip stole for him

Q Compare and contrast the various settings, situations and characters of Chapter 1 and 39 of the novel.

Introduction

In both of these chapters (Chapter 1 and Chapter 39), the main theme is the arrival of the convict, and in both chapters Dickens goes in to a lot of detail, not only in describing the convict, but in other areas, such as setting the scene. In this essay I will be looking at both chapters in detail, and be comparing them to see whether there are any similarities or differences in the way that Dickens had written them.

Comparison

Within this section, I will be comparing aspects from both the chapters looking for similarities or differences. The aspects that I will be comparing are; circumstances, setting, how the characters are presented, what this tells us about 19th century life and Dickens's message to his readers.

Circumstances

The circumstances in which the two characters met were very different within each chapter. For example; The first time that the two characters met was purely coincidental, Pip just happened to be in the graveyard at the same time that the convict (Magwitch) was there. However, in chapter 39, Magwitch actively sought out Pip, which provided Dickens with the opportunity to give the characters more depth, regarding the time that had passed between them "I've been a sheep farmer, stock-breeder, other trades besides, away in the new world".

In chapter 1, Magwitch was on the run from the law, and subsequently everything he said had a direct meaning to the cause at hand and he had no time for subtleties, " 'Blacksmith eh' said he. And he looked down at his leg." He had no time to explain that he needed to get the chains off his leg, so made do with this very short and abrupt sentence. However, in chapter 39, Magwitch had plenty of time to do as he pleased, as he was merely avoiding being seen, not actively on the run. This meant that he had a lot of time to speak with Pip, and his style of conversation differed immensely because of this "Some lawyer, maybe. As to the first letter of that lawyer's name now. Would it be J?" This quote also shows that Magwitch was intelligent, he was toying with Pip, not telling him directly but letting him have little pieces of information at a time. If this were in the same circumstances as the first chapter this sentence would

would never have occurred, Magwitch would have just told Pip that he was his benefactor.

Setting

The settings in these particular two chapters are worlds apart and make each chapter very different.

When Pip first met Magwitch in chapter 1, he was on a lonely marsh in the middle of a graveyard! Yet, when he met Magwitch for the second time, he was inside a warm room with a warm fire, but the weather outside was dark and dreary "I might have fancied myself in a storm-beaten lighthouse". This suggests that Dickens was implying that Pip was a recluse; he was hiding away from his past within the small, warm shelter of his good fortune, but that his past (the weather) was catching up with him. This would also explain why Pip did not recognise Magwitch, as you would expect the fear instilled in him from the first meeting to remain with him indefinitely.

The first meeting was also 'set' in Pips childhood, which meant that Magwitch had to check whether Pip understood him "You know what a file is?" However, in the second meeting Pip was a much older and well educated character, so Magwitch could talk to Pip in full confidence that he understood what he was saying. In fact, Magwitch even presumes that Pips intelligence outstrips his own "And if they're in foreign languages wot I don't understand"

This book was set in the 19th century, and there are many indicators to show this. However, there are few of these indicators in the first chapter, with the only main clues being the language and the treatment of Pip, not by Magwitch, but by his sister. However, the clues are mostly in the language "and my sister - Mrs Joe Gargery" this is an unlikely phrase for a child to use nowadays, as women generally use their own first name (instead of taking their husbands). There are many other examples of phrases or words that would not be used nowadays, for example "Ours was the marsh country" and "wittles".

The clue in the treatment of Pip is that he had been told very little about his parents by his sister, and has had to make his own assumptions on what little knowledge he had "my first fancies regarding what they were like, were unreasonably derived from their tombstones". Nowadays it would be presumed that Pip's sister would have told him all about his parents, even if there were photographs of them.

There are also few indicators in chapter 39 that this book was set in the 19th century, as Dickens probably presumed that the reader knew this by now. However, there are some indicators, yet they are all in the style of language. For example "the forge" "gentlemen" and "neckerchief" are all words that would not be used nowadays

Q. How the characters are presented?

Or

Q. Describe Dickens's art of characterization in the novel.

In the first chapter, Pip was presented as a naive little boy who, caught up in the moment, would believe anything that Magwitch told him "I looked all round for the horrible young man", Pip was clearly frightened by the prospect of the horrible young man, when it is clear to the reader that the individual does not exist. No reference is made to him in chapter 39 because Pip had matured and probably realised that the "young man" did not exist. In chapter 1 Pip was also presented as very gullible, as he made no attempt to escape from Magwitch, even though he could probably have escaped, as Magwitch was shackled by a chain between his legs "a great iron on his leg". Also, at one point Magwitch began to run off "He started, made a short run", and Pip did not try to escape, but informed Magwitch that his mother was dead "Also Georgiana". This shows that Pip was very honest, as he could have just let Magwitch presume that his mother was nearby and made his escape.

Magwitch was presented as a very callous individual in the chapter 1, with only the slightest hint of compassion when he learns that Pips mother was dead, "Oh!" He was also presented as an impatient character "'tell us your name!' said the man. 'Quick!' ", and he scared Pip in to giving him what he wanted, not caring what psychological harm he inflicted upon a small vulnerable child. "Or I'll have your heart and liver out"

By chapter 39 Pip had matured and become a much more distrustful character, and asked Magwitch what he wanted before asking him to come in "Pray, what is your business? Do you wish to come in?", whilst the young Pip would have probably done things the other way round.

This is due to the fact that Joe was his role model when he was young, but as an adult, and as he grew up, he encountered a much more distrusting world - London, and in turn, he became more shrewd. Pip was also portrayed as an ungrateful person, and when Magwitch revealed to Pip that he was his benefactor, Pip does not feel any gratitude, only "repugnance" and "abhorring him". Although this reaction was understandable to some extents, when Pip was younger he would probably have shown at least some gratitude, unlike his adult self.

Image

In chapter 39 Magwitch was portrayed very differently, in fact, he was almost like a new character, he was kind "dear boy",

caring ""He caught me, drew me to the sofa" and he respected Pip with an almost godlike reverence ""he took both my hands and put them to his lips" "bent on one knee before me". He was also willing to risk his life to see Pip, as returning to England was punishable by death "By G, it's Death!" This was probably more true to Magwitch's real personality than when Pip met him on the marshes, as at this point he was no longer starving or on the run.

However his love for Pip was so great that it had exaggerated his good qualities by an incredible amount, making the reader forget that he was a convict, and had done wrong. Subsequently, the reader gets the image of an old, lonely man who was blinded by love for the young boy who helped him survive on the marshes. However, by making Pip a gentleman, Magwitch had done the one thing that he wished not to do - change Pip in to a completely different person, who had lost some of the qualities that had made him so endearing.

19th century life

These two chapters tell us many things about 19th century life. One of the main things that Chapter 1 told us about this period was the treatment of children, as mentioned previously under settings. Another thing this chapter tells us about is that mortality rates were high, especially for the lower class people such as Pip's family, and subsequently living conditions were probably poor, as Pips mother, Father and five brothers had all died. No mention of the circumstances of their deaths leads to the assumption that they were, in all probability, due poor sanitation.

Chapter 39 reveals more about the upper class and convict's way of life - two huge extremes. Being a gentleman, Pip lived a life of luxury, in an apartment in the middle of London, with a roaring fire and many books "mounting up, on their shelves, by hundreds!" Pip also wore high quality clothes and linen (unlike when he was a child) and had expensive jewellery "a gold 'un". This shows that in a gentleman's lifestyle it was important to keep up appearances, with fine clothes, expensive jewellery and well preened homes.

Magwitch's lifestyle as a convict was completely different. He was shipped off to Australia "away in the new world" and used almost as a slave "my master" until his "master" died. He lived in a hut "a solitary hut" and was treated terribly by the colonists "them colonists might fling up the dust over me". This tells us that the convicts were treated appallingly, and were shipped over to Australia to dispose of them.

Dickens's message to his readers

Dickens conveyed many of his own ideas to his readers, via his books.

The message to Dickens's readers in this particular novel is plain - not all convicts are malevolent. This idea comes across very strongly in chapter 39, when Pip realises that it was Magwitch that had been his benefactor all along. The fact that Magwitch "lived rough, that you should live smooth" also shows that not all convicts are selfish; in fact, Magwitch is one of the most generous people that Pip had met!

Chapter 1 portrays the idea that not all convicts are inherently wrong, they are just driven to do wrong by the circumstances that they are in, just like Magwitchapter

The reason that Dickens wanted to portray this particular message may be due to the fact that he, and all his family, were imprisoned for his father's debt. He may even have met someone who helped him whilst he was in prison, and subsequently he based the character of Magwitch on them, realising that not all convicts are the evil people we think of, and some are kind generous people.

Conclusion

I conclude that although these two chapters are about as different as you can get (whilst still using the same characters), they both contribute to the same moral, just in entirely different ways.

Q. Comment on Dickens' use of setting focusing on the opening graveyard scene and the scenes with Miss Havisham set in the Satis house.

As a skilled writer, Dickens has chosen a perfect setting, which corresponds to the involvement of his characters. The dark isolated graveyard associates with death, and provides a backdrop that is very similar to the appearance of a criminal, in the society in Dickens' time. Dickens describes the marshes as being a dark, flat wilderness. This creates the opportunity to become lost and isolated, it emphasises the danger for someone who is alone, such as Pip. Pip is far from the safety of the town and from the higher class in society, therefore he is very vulnerable to criminality.

The society in Dickens' time was very different to the society now, it was portrayed in the places he used, such as the town. This was to show the higher classed side of society, where all people who were nice, honest and normal lived. The marshes were used because of its vast emptiness and the danger involved in being out there. This was completely cut off from the town. The people who lived there were outcasts and were once criminals. The Victorians wanted this complete separation physicaliy and metaphorically. Once you were a criminal, you can never change and you are lost forever.

In the opening scene, Dickens purposely creates a dark, desolate atmosphere that surrounds young Pip. He also uses the idea of a black horizontal landscape. This emphasises doom and danger, as Pip is alone. Dickens uses red, black, angry colours to describe the marshes and skyline. This links the atmosphere with death and blood, and brings Pip into the life of a criminal in the society of Dickens' time.

The beacon and the gibbet are the only things that are verticals and standing, as they are very important and have to stand out. This is because the beacons light guides in good people who will be saved from the distant savage lair, criminals being the savage beasts. The gibbet is the place where criminals will go, and they will not be saved. This, in Dickens' view, is what will happen between the two groups of people. If Pip does steel he will go to the gibbet.

Dickens cleverly associates the graveyard with the dark, mist and the rushing winds. These provide the right atmosphere that corresponds to the gloomy, course, grey appearance of Magwitch, a criminal. Magwitch is described as being a fearful man, with a terrible voice and shuddering body. This is Dickens' view on what a criminal was like in the society in the Victorian times.

Dickens puts across the idea of going across the marshes is a path you would not want to take as it hurts, it's unpleasant, it's wild and cold, it's not attractive and it's lonely. This also means that being a criminal is a path you would not want to take for the same reasons.

When Magwitch turns Pip upside down, it is like Pips life being turned around. From being, a well brought up boy to a criminal. Dickens wrote this to show the idea of the change in Pip's behaviour and manner towards criminality. The appearance of Magwitch, cut and stung by nettles, scares Pip, because he does not want to become like him and look like that.

Pip is about to undergo a disturbing experience as he enters Miss Havisham's garden, as it is overgrown and tangled with weeds. Dickens describes it like this to show that it has not been cared for and there is no love, like the appearance of Miss Havisham. The courtyard is described as being lifeless and desolate; there are no pigeons, no horses and no pigs. This gives the idea that the place is abandoned and empty. The noise of the wind is compared to the noise of the wind in the rigging of a ship. This shows how quiet and scary the atmosphere was and how lonely Pip must have felt.

All the surrounding walls are very high, this gives Pip the feeling that he is trapped and there is no way out. The windows on the Satis house are all walled up and covered in rusty iron bars. Dickens has written this to portray his views on society at his time. It gives across the idea that the higher class (in the house) cannot see out at people in the lower class, and the lower class cannot see in. It is also like a divide between the two groups. The main gate was also locked. Dickens' view on society is that the only way to enter the house is by money, because if you had money you would be in the higher class and therefore can enter.

Next to the house is a deserted brewery; that had not worked for a long time. Dickens uses this idea to show that the brewery had once worked and was once nice, now all celebration and better days have gone from the higher class. All that is left are memories.

The passages leading to Miss Havisham's room were very dark, this is a very unpleasant atmosphere for Pip to enter. The only little bit of hope in the house, in Dickens' view, is Estella, as she had left a candle burning.

As Pip entered Miss Havisham's room there was no glimpse of daylight, Dickens has written this to show his views on how the higher class has been cut off from the outside world. The objects in Miss Havisham's room were decayed, yellow and had lost their luster. They had faded over time like Miss Havisham. She was dressed in a bridal dress, vale and shoes that had once been white and fitted her properly, but were now yellow and she had shriveled and shrunk inside her dress. Dickens has described her like this to show that she does not want to change she wants to stay in the upper class. That is why she carries on wearing her best dress, because she does not want to fall down. Even though the bridal flowers in her hair had withered with the dress and the bride. Nothings changed in Miss Havisham's room, like the positioning of her half-packed trunks, her prayer book and the time on her clocks, this also shows that she does not want to change, and she wants things to stay the same.

When Pip is in the Satis house, Estella says to him, 'that whoever has this house could want nothing else'. This means that if you do own the house it is enough, which is what Satis means. You would also have wealth, education, refinement and position. In Dickens' view on society in the Victorian times, this is enough for someone in the upper class; they do not need love, care and compassion.

My observations, from how society was for Dickens in the Victorian times to how society is now, are very different. In Dickens' time, there were classes and different groups and divides. He shows this by having criminals living on the marshes in the harsh, wild, unpleasant conditions. He has the upper class people living in the town in well-established houses such as the Satis house. Dickens has created a perfect metaphoric society that corresponds to the physical society he lives in and the atmosphere and living conditions are right for that period of time.

Q. Do you agree that the delianation of the characters is according to the themes?

Or

Q. What themes do the characters of the novel portray?

In this book, Great Expectations by Charles Dickens, we are exposed to various types of affections. We encounter obsession, love and friendship. These three emotions are explored through the relations that develop between the main characters. The relationship between Pip, Estella, Joe and Mrs. Joe, changes as additional characters are introduced into the story.

One love relationship that Dickens tells us about is between Pip and Estella. Pip is obsessed by her and would do anything to please her. For instance Pip strives to become a gentleman when Estella tells him that she finds him to be common and dumb. Also Pip becomes very jealous when another man, especially Drummble, pursues her. Pips obsession is shown again when Estella wants to see him and he drops everything that he is doing to get to her as quickly as possible. He would do anything or go anywhere that Estella told him too. In Great Expectations Pip has another relationship with another character named Joe.

Joe Gargery and Pip have a kinship of love and friendship. Joe is Pips brother-in-law, and is much older than Pip. When Pip was a young boy, he and Joe were the best of friends, and would always back each other up. Latter in the story Pip becomes embarrassed of Joe when he becomes a gentleman and he considers Joe to be a lowly blacksmith. As the story unfolds, Pip feels ashamed of the way he has treated Joe and tries to make up for his bad treatment of him. Joe also has an another relationship with a harsh character named Mrs. Joe, his wife.

Joe and Mrs. Joe, Pips sister, are married with no children of their own who took care of Pip when he was young. Mrs. Joe treats Joe badly, but no matter how much abuse he receives from her, he stills thinks of her as a fine figure of a woman. He shows his love for her by fighting any man who offends her. He fights one of his employees, Orlick, when he talks badly of Mrs. Joe. When Mrs. Joe is seriously injured by Oarlock, Joe takes care of her until her death. This demonstrates Joe's love and dedication for his wife. In these three examples, Dickens shows obsession between Pip and Estella, friendship between Joe and Pip, and devotion between Joe and Mrs. Joe. Although these types of affection are different they all fall under the same category, Love.

Q. Comment upon the social criticism portrayed in Dickens's Hard Times

Or

Q. Describe the exploitation of poor by rich in the 19th century society.

Or

Q. Discuss the affect of Utilitarianism in Victorian age on the education and on society as a whole.

In the midst of the industrialization era in Victorian Times, an educational system known as the Utilitarian Model was introduced in order to produce "the greatest good for the greatest number." Founded by Jeremy Benthan, it consisted of strict discipline, rote education and "facts alone". Creativity was not encouraged. Social criticism in Dickens's Hard Times exposes how people were turning into machines. Dickens effectively uses caricature in writing to mock the educational system at that time. There are also elements of exaggeration, repetition and allusions to emphasize the mockery against utilitarianism. Factory imageries and measuring imagery is used to objectify and depersonalizes characters and thus, to create a false logic in the text. "Teach these boys and girls nothing but facts." From the very beginning,

Dickens establishes himself within a contemporary debate on the nature of learning, knowledge and education. Utilitarianism was based mainly upon the learning of facts and only facts. This is acknowledged by the constant repetition of the word fact in the first chapter, especially in the first paragraph. The repetition is used to emphasize the importance of facts and that nothing else will ever be of any service to the students. This emphasis is further on stressed by the description of the body language of the speaker. "The emphasis was helped by the speaker's square wall of forehead..." At the same time, an anaphora is used at the beginning of each sentence to put an extra emphasis to the emphasis. Clearly, Dickens does this on purpose to exaggerate this ridiculous emphasis on facts, the one thing needful, according to utilitarianism.

The actual scene is depicted as plain, bare, monotonous vault of a schoolroom. This contrasts with the idea of sowing and to the biblical allusion of the parable of the Sower. The schoolroom description matches with the wayside, stony places and thorns as metaphorically explained in the parable. Dickens means to say that there is no true sowing taking place in the vault of a schoolroom. The adjectives plain and bare also explain that there is no place for creativity, art or leisure. This is an another characteristic of utilitarianism. "The speaker's obstinate carriage, square coat, square legs, square shoulders..." is described against the archetype of youth (spring, sowing, leisure). The older men are "square;" yet are ironically depicted that their head[s] had scarcely warehouse-room for the hard facts stored inside. Dickens' hyperbole makes architecture out of the physical description of The Speaker. Dickens wants to demonstrate that the idea of the child's mind as a "vessel" that is "ready to have imperial gallons of facts poured" will eventually destroy the child's mind once they are "full to the brim". This directly alludes to the story of Ali Baba, where Morgiana, his girl servant pours hot oil to kill the forty thieves hiding in the vessels. Likewise, the pouring of facts on the children's minds will also make this eventually happen.

Murdering of the innocents is another allusion to the biblical story of King Herod's genocide in fear for his throne. Although students are literally in danger, the educational system has their childish imagination targeted for annihilation. The children are always expected to do what they are told and to be "regulated and governed by fact". This slowly destroys their independent character of free will. This new chapter is introduced to us with the characters names and social identities. The characters' names are usually an immediate indication of where the character fits on Dickens' moral spectrum. Thomas Gradgrind, "a man of realities" is a hard educator who grinds his students through a factory-like process, hoping to produce graduates. He is also constantly objectified as a "kind of cannon loaded to the muzzle with facts" or as a "galvanizing apparatus."

This exemplifies the perfect result of someone being mechanized and filled of facts. Additionally, Gradgrind is a "doubting Thomas" much like the Biblical apostle who resisted belief in the resurrection. This Thomas urges that students depend exclusively upon the evidence in sight. He dismisses faith, fancy, belief, emotion and trust at once. Mr. M'Choakumchild is plainly villainous and his own name resembles the choking of a child. The hard consonants used have an effective onomatopoeic effect representing the sound of the choking of a child. This government officer, "a mighty man at cutting and drying", "ready to fight all England" and a master in 13 subjects at the ends of his ten chilled fingers represents the finished result of someone "filled" with facts. The exaggeration and hyperbole used to describe him and his intelligence mocks the unimportance of such perfection of knowledge and criticizes the mode of factory-style, mind-numbing, grad-grinding production that takes the fun out of life. Students are unable exploit fully their intelligence, since they are filled by too many facts and many bits of everything. They are unable to think for themselves and process these facts into their brains. One clear example is Bitzer, who when he is asked to define a horse he responds monotonously with bits of information: "Quadruped, Graminivorous, forty teeth...age known by marks in mouth".

Bitzer's short sentences and nervous response shows that he is not confident in his answer and that he has extracted his information from something he has read or facts alone. Additionally, he uses another person's words to work out his definition to please Mr. Gradgrind's expectation. "Girl number twenty possessed of no facts". Further, Gradgrind does not only distort the intelligence and the thinking of a child but objectifies and takes away their self-confidence. Cecilia (Sissy) Jupe is unlike the other character in almost every possible way.

While there are other female students, she is the only female identified thus far in the novel. Her character is a romanticized figure. Her last name, "Jupe," comes from the French word for "skirts" and her first name, Cecilia, represents the sainted patroness of music and clearly, Cecilia represents Art in opposition to mechanization. "Thou wilt always kill outright the robber Fancy lurking within." Ultimately, a last critique is made to the utilitarian model of education. The last sentences stresses that Fancy, a word connoting feelings, art and personal opinion would be "maim" and distorted.. Dickens brilliantly plays out the two opposites of 'hard fact' and 'feeling' to lead the reader to the inevitable conclusion that sentiment is more important than factual knowledge. Aiding him in this idea/are the language features used and the characters of this moral fable, each personified in such a way that they represent, or symbolize, a particular positive or negative notion that Dickens encourages or criticizes.

Q. How industrialization gave birth to colonization in the 19th century?

Or

Q. Describe the detailed condition of the poor in the Victorian era.

Or

Q. "The settings play a very important role in movement of story" Explain

The empire was a favoured topic of many Victorian novelists, and Dickens was no exception. Like many other authors, Dickens found it a useful narrative device - as Leon Litvack observes in 'Dickens, Australia and Magwitch' (*Dickensian* 93, 1998), the colonies could function as a kind of theatrical 'green room' from which characters could appear, or to which they could vanish having fulfilled their dramatic function. Either way, Britain's imperial hold of so many far-off places meant that characters could appear and disappear with impunity - if an English gentleman decided he would go to Africa, it was perfectly acceptable that he should do so. Hence we get Walter Gay's departure and return in *Dombey and Son*, the Micawbers' and Peggottys' emigration in *David Copperfield* and of course, Pip's 'getting away from it all' in Clarriker's in Egypt with Herbert Pocket in *Great Expectations*.

All these examples play very minor roles in Dickens' fiction - they serve as narrative devices and little else. However, one other consequence of Britain's colonial process - the policy of transportation - plays a far more fundamental part in *Great Expectations*. It is true, however, that, as Donald Simpson asserts in 'Charles Dickens and the Empire', the concept of transportation offered Dickens a perfect plot device - 'a transported convict exactly meets the need for a benefactor who can make a substantial fortune yet who has to remain anonymous, and of whom Pip will eventually be ashamed.

The capital law against returning from transportation sharpens the impact of the later chapters, when Pip sheds his pretensions as well as his wealth.' Thus Dickens, like so many Victorian authors who used the colonies as 'places to transfer burned-out characters or from which to retrieve characters', uses this aspect of colonialism as the dramatic cornerstone for his novel.

The fact that Dickens sees the peripheral edge as merely a place for European characters to sojourn, ignoring any indigenous peoples which might occupy it, is not unusual - Raskin believes that 'for the Victorians, existence meant existence in England... going to India was like falling off a cliff.' This attitude - that nothing which happened away from the metropolitan centre could really be said to have happened at all - directly affects Magwitch and Pip in the novel. Magwitch may have earned his fortune by honest labour, but because he has done it in 'the vulgar colonial fashion' (Sadrin in *Great Expectations*), he can never be accepted into English society where standards are more demanding. The lax morality and classless system of the colony can not be transferred to the centre, at least not yet - therefore Magwitch, though he may achieve success on the periphery, cannot hope to be welcome in England - and Pip, by his association with 'colony money' will never be a true gentleman.

Dickens' Australia is a place of opportunity for the hardworking penitent - although it is worth noting that, like his contemporaries, very little attention is paid to the ethics of the colonial project - the landscape is seen as a place which exists only to be exploited by the coloniser. It is also interesting that the colony is a completely different world, with different social and moral structures, and therefore those who dwell there cannot easily be reintegrated into 'real' English society. Although the periphery is a potential paradise, this is seemingly only so for those who are misfits at home, and the metropolitan centre maintains complete dominance both socially and culturally.

Themes

Love

Pip is tormented by Estella. She has been taught not to love, but to break hearts. Miss Havisham was devastated when her fiance (Compeyson, see above) left her on her wedding day. Only Biddy and Joe are happy.

Gentlemen

Pip wants to be a gentleman. Herbert Pocket is a real gentleman and is an honest hard worker. Drummle is false, as is Uncle Pumblechook.

Money

Pip needs it to impress Estella. Some have it and use it to get their way- such as Drummle. Some use it but need power more, such as Jaggers. Some have it and use it to take power over others- such as Miss Havisham. Some have it and give it away- Magwitchapter

The Corrupting Power Of Wealth

Pip is corrupted by wealth. He forgets his family and the people that are important to him. He worries more about trying to impress people than being moral.

Double Lives (Appearances Can Be Decieving)

Wemmick leads a double life. He is a hard accounting clerk at Jaggers' office, yet at home he lives in a castle with an aging parent that he takes care of and love. He is an excellent friend to Pip. Jaggers also leads a double life, as he is secure on the outside but really longs for respect and needs to impress. Pip pretends to be someone he's not while in London. Magwitch seems to be a cruel, violent convict but is really a kind and generous, simple honest person. Uncle Pumblechook is a hypocrite. Compeyson seems to be a gentleman, well learned and intelligent when he is a hardened criminal. Estella seems to be cold and heartless, but somewhere she finds it in her to become a real person.

Death

Miss Havisham and the crumbling Stasis Manor are symbols of death throughout the book. Pip's parents are dead, so he must fight with the world. Jaggers and Wemmick work around death constantly and expose Pip to it. Estella is dead inside. Magwitch's death is a wake-up call to Pip that he must move into the world on his own.

Expectations

Pip expects things to be one way and then finds out they are quite another. This is also true for Mrs. Joe- who did not know what she was getting into when she married him. Miss Havisham certainly thought her life was going to be one way and found it completely different- as did Estella. Magwitch had expectations for Pip that were too high to be met, and he also had expected a different life. Miss Havisham has expectations for Estella that could not possibly work.

Pip's Growth and Maturation

Pip learns a lot throughout the novel as he grows up and matures. So do Estella and Herbert, and Orlick as well. Pip and Estella learn from their mistakes, Orlick does not and thus their respective fates. Both Pip and Estella grow morally while they are growing up. Pip learns the true meaning of life, and Estella learns to have a heart. Orlick keeps making the same mistakes, and after he kills Mrs. Joe he tries to kill Pip and is arrested.

The Three Stages of Pip's Great Expectations

In the first stage, Pip meets Magwitch and is scared, and meets and visits with Miss Havisham. In this stage he is still a child, and is still bound to his present life (he is apprenticed to Joe). This stage ends when Jaggers shows up to take him out of his life and into a new life, as a young fellow of great expectations. Here Pip is still immature and inexperienced- he is always afraid that he will be punished and that if he does anything wrong he would be caught anyway.

The second stage involves Pip's adventures in London. There he meets new people, finds out what its like to have money, gets educated and learns to be a gentleman, and pawns after Estella. He still has ties to his other world, but not his family only Miss Havisham and Estella. He wastes his fortune and becomes a self-centreed idle rich jerk. He experiences Jaggers utilitarianism and Wemmick's strange world, and he sees Estella fall to Drummle. He also begins to realise how poorly he has treated those that love him, especially Joe who takes care of him when he is sick. At the end of this stage, he finds out about Magwitch, that Estella was not designed for him and Miss Havisham never intended to make him a gentleman.

In the third stage Pip has to deal with hiding Magwitch to protect him from the law. He also has to forgive Miss Havisham and keep her from trying to kill herself as a result of the grief she has had from what she has done. He ends up back in the place where he has started his journey, sees Magwitch kill Compeyson and escapes being killed by Orlick. He also watches how unfairly Magwitch is treated at his trial, holds his hand when he dies, and tells him about Estella. Then he loses all of his money and returns to an honest, earned lifestyle in a counting house- all great expectations lost. He finds out how unhappy Estella was with Drummle and. depending on the ending you read he either marries her or sees her married to a doctor.

Pip's Moral Development

Throughout Great Expectations, we are shown Pip's progress toward developing his own morality. hen the story opens, Pip is a skittish and uncertain little kid. He is frightened by Magwitch, so he steals him food and tools. Then he regrets it, but his morality at this point is more connected to getting caught- rather than seeing that he has done anything wrong, he fears he will be punished. He reacts the same way to his fight with Herbert. Pip becomes selfish and priggish once he becomes a young man of great expectations. He does things only for himself, and he does not think of others that he should care about. He treats Joe terribly and is ashamed of him, and he only feels a little bad. At this point, Pip's morality is connected to how others feel about him. If others, such as Biddy, feel that he has done a bad thing, then he feels bad. Otherwise, he does not notice that he has hurt Joe.

Then Magwitch reveals himself, Pip feels wronged. He accuses Miss Havisham of leading him on with Estella. He realises, however, that they used him as he used them- and he was only misleading himself. In the beginning Pip is resentful of Magwitch and sullen about where his prospects come from. He does not heed Jaggers' or Wemmick's advice. He begins to realise that Magwitch is an honest and generous man that just wants the best for him. He first attempts to sneak him out of the country out of duty. Pip's morality is now tied to what he believes is right- his sense of right and wrong, though there, is based only on superficial impressions. He begins to do good things for people- get Matthew Pocket into Miss Havisham's will, set Herbert up in a business, etc. hen Pip is nearly killed several times- when saving Miss Havisham, when kidnapped by Orlick and in the river- and becomes very ill, his perception of life changes.

He is by Magwitch's side as he dies not because he should be but because he wants to be. He feels as if Magwitch were his second father. When he loses his fortune, he repents. When Joe takes care of him, he is grateful. He accepts that Joe has married Biddy and Estella has married Drummle. He is prepared to live his life on his own terms, on his own sense of what is right and wrong. Pip has finally developed his own personality.

Pip's Moral Development, Continued

The message Dickens is sending is that the people in our lives are important to us, and we do not always know how much or why. We should not do things just for personal gain, or at the harm of others. We should also be happy with what we have. Dickens asks the question- what if you had everything you ever wanted? How would you treat the people you love? Would your priorities change? Is it really what you wanted after all. We can see this through Pip's moral development throughout the novel.

When Pip is frightened by the convict and steals food, he feels guilty. When Estella calls him coarse and common, he feels ashamed. In both ways, Pip is willing to take action to reverse the situation. While he lies about the food, he goes to Biddy to learn to be more uncommon. Pip also feels guilty when he lies about Estella and Miss Havisham and when he fights with Estella.

When Pip is granted his expectations, he is still not granted Estella. He is involved in a stage of self-gratification-acting selfish, priggish and getting into horrible debt. Here he learns that his worst act can be to impress the person he most despises- Drummle. He hurts Joe's feelings. When Joe comes to take care of him, Magwitch returns and Estella marries Drummle, he changes.

Pip turns altruistic around the time Magwitch shows up. He suddenly is responsible for someone else. He takes care of Magwitch and tries to sneak him out of the country. He stays with him on his deathbed. Pip's altruistic actions intensify throughout the novel- he works to get Herbert into a partnership, he saves Miss Havisham from the fire, he tries to save Magwitch and he accepts the fact that his money is gone. Pip goes to work with Herbert, and marries Estella despite the way she treated him.

Redemption

Great Expectations is not just about criminality and guilt but also about redemption [*redemption*: atonement for guilt, deliverance from sin or crime]. Redemption in this novel comes from love; it may be selfless love for a particular individual, like Joe's love for Pip, or compassion for other human beings, like Joe's kind feelings for the convict Magwitchapter Redemption should not be confused with happiness; redemption may be the result of disillusionment or may even result in death. The greatest symbol of redemption in Western culture is Christ, who offered human beings the possibility of redemption from original sin by suffering the agonies of crucifixion and sacrificing his life.

Miss Havisham

Confronted by Estella's inability to love her and seeing Pip's torment because of his hopeless love for Estella, Miss Havisham comes to understand the enormity of her actions. More, she wants to make amends. She asks Pip if there is anything she can do for him, not just for his friend. (Why does does Pip refuse her money? Does it indicate growth in Pip, subconscious anger against her, or some other motives?) She generously gives Pip the money he needs for Herbert. In the agony of remorse, she kneels to Pip, cries, falls to the ground, while repeating, "What have I done!" (page 401). Until released by death, the delirious Miss Havisham repeats, like a mantra, three sentences: "What have I done!," "When she first came, I meant to save her from misery like mine," and "Take the pencil and write under my name, 'I forgive her!'" (page 405). Is Miss Havisham finally redeemed?

A related question is whether Pip fully forgives her. At a conscious level, he certainly is moved by her remorse and seems to forgive her. Is this true at a subconscious level? Is his vision of her hanging caused by resentment and hostility toward her? Are the same feelings suggested in his description of extinguishing the flames engulfing her, in their "struggling like desperate enemies" (page 404)? Or does this reading push psychological interpretation too far and should Pip's description of his last visits to Miss Havisham be taken at face value?

Magwitch

As a result of the concern of Herbert and Pip for Magwitch's safety and Pip's growing affection, Magwitch becomes, in Pip's terms, softer or humanized. In court when he is referred to as a desperate criminal, he looks at Pip

> with a trustful look, as if he were confident that I had seen some small redeeming touch in him, even so long ago as when I was a little child. As to the rest, he was humble and contrite, and I never knew him to complain (page 461).

As he lies dying in the prison infirmary, Magwitch appreciates the fact that Pip has been closer to him and more accepting of him in his fall than in his prosperity. Despite the fact that Magwitch was involved in, perhaps caused, the death of Compeyson, is he redeemed by Pip's love for him and/or his love for Pip?

Pip

The process of Pip's redemption brings up the question, how complete is his transformation? Does he truly give up his snobbery and society's false values, and if he does, at what point(s) does he give them up?

Pip's redemption begins with his relationship with Magwitch; he moves from revulsion at Magwitch's appearance, manners, and social status to perceiving his humanity and to finally loving him selflessly.

> For now my repugnance to him had all melted away, and in the hunted wounded shackled creature who held my hand in his, I only saw a man who had meant to be my benefactor, and who had felt affectionately, gratefully, and generously towards me with great constancy through a series of years. I only saw in him a much better man than I had been to Joe (page 450).

He no longer cares about his status as a gentleman and accepts a condemned criminal as his second father. Compare this attitude with his unease at having visited Newgate with Wemmick as he waits to meet Estella. Not until the end of the novel does the irony of his response on that occasion become clear; the larger irony is that Magwitch is the source of all Pip's dreams, as the father of Estella and the provider of his great expectations.

When Magwitch dies, Pip prays, "O Lord, be merciful to him a sinner!" (page 465). This prayer is a misquotation of the New Testament verse, "O Lord, be merciful to me, a sinner!". Does Pip's substitution of *me* for *him* indicate some remaining condescension and snobbery toward Magwitch? Or has Dickens merely remembered the text incorrectly, so that the misquotation has no significance in our understanding of Pip's growth? Paul Pickering believes "The last stage of Pip's progression is reached when he learns to love the criminal and to accept his own implication in the common guilt." Is Pickering's view of Pip's regeneration accurate, or does Pip still have to come to terms with his rejection of Joe? Is it enough for Pip to wholeheartedly and unreservedly love Magwitch? Must he also be able to love Joe in the same way? He has come to accept Magwitch's love; does he still have to accept Joe's unconditional love?

Pip falls ill with brain fever. His hallucinations express his passivity and his loss of identity or self in becoming a gentleman; his distress at his social elevation and his inability to control or even direct his life comes out in his cries to be released from his place as a brick in the wall or a steel beam whirling over a gulf. Joe nurses him back to health and protects him. Temporarily as helpless as a child, Pip accepts Joe's love and attentions again.

Does Pip's convalesence give Pip the opportunity to give up any remaining false pride and social values in his relationship with Joe, his first father? When he chooses not to tell Joe about his debts, does he want to keep Joe from paying his debts, which the narrator Pip looking back hopes was his motive, and/or is he motivated by pride, a desire not to let Joe see how he has fallen? Realizing that Joe is pulling away as he recovers, he decides to trust Joe completely and share the full truth of his situation–on the next day. Is postponing his confession a valid decision or does it show reluctance to admit his fall? Does the postponement, with the opportunity it gives Joe to leave, foreshadow the fact that it is too late for Pip to return to his old life or any part of his life with Joe? Is this why the adult Pip finds another Pip sitting on his stool before the fire, when he returns to England after eleven years in the East? The fires of his childhood home and the forge have symbolized love, in contrast to the cold light of the stars and Stella.

In Edgar Johnson's view of Pip's redemption, the virtues that ultimately save him are mainly those he unconsciously absorbed from Joe in his childhood, and his return to a life of modest usefulness is a repudiation of the ideal of living off of other people's work. Pip comes to realise that his society and its grandiose material dreams cheapen, distort, and deny human values. Humphrey House raises an interesting point in connection with Pip's snobbery, which is one of Pip's moral and emotional crimes. He denies that Pip is a snob:

The real snobs are the characters blinded to human considerations by the worship of wealth and social position, [they] are Pumblechook and Mrs. Pocket, and Pip sees through them from the start....to call him a snob is to suggest that he was wrong to feel discontented with life on the marshes and could have chosen to act otherwise than he did. Whereas much of the energy of Dickens's imagination in the early part of the novel goes in showing how mean and limiting that life is, and how helpless Pip himself is in face of the contradictory forces at work on him.

Is it true that Pip does not become "blinded to human considerations by the worship of wealth and social position"? And is the moral crime of snobbery one of degree, that is, does the fact that Pumblechook and Mrs. Pocket may be greater snobs than Pip mean that he is not a snob? Alternately, if Pip is a snob, is at least some of his alienation from his childhood home and Joe justified by the "mean and limiting" life he led as a child? Does House's analysis free Pip of some of his guilt or even most of it?

Estella

After Estella's announcement of her marriage, Estella disappears till the end, several hundred pages later. The history of her suffering in an abusive marriage is briefly summarized; we do not see any of it. In other words, we are presented only with the end result and none of the process whereby she changed. The issue of her change is complicated by there being two endings. In both endings, she is chastened and shows feeling for Pip. Clearly she has changed, but is her change convincing? Does Dickens intend the reader to see her as redeemed? If so, is her redemption believable?

Jaggers And Wemmick

Are Jaggers and Wemmick in need of redemption, and if so, are they redeemed?

Jaggers sees but cannot accept the cruelty of his society and "the atmosphere of evil" in which he lives (page 416). He makes one compassionate effort to change the fates of a mother and child. In comparison with Joe, does he accept full or limited responsibility? He makes the mother his servant and gives the child up for adoption, whereas Joe marries the sister or mother-figure and accepts full responsibility and suffers all the consequences of trying to save the child, whom he loves. Certainly, there is a difference in their situations, for one mother is a murderess who threatened to destroy her own child and Mrs. Joe's criminality consists of emotional and physical abuse of the child and her husband as well as her self-serving pretense of martyrdom.

Except for his involvement with Estella and her mother, Jaggers refuses to accept responsibility by looking only at the facts, which he can control. This system does not seem to be completely effective; he still needs to dissociate himself from the immorality and viciousness of his surroundings, as is expressed by his washing his hands, using scented soap, and even, upon occasion, gargling and cleaning his fingernails.

His clerk Wemmick leads a divided life; at the office, he is unfeeling efficiency personified, as his mechanical post-office mouth symbolizes. As Jaggers's representative, he walks through Newgate, shaking hands only with the condemned prisoners and accepting gifts of "portable property" from them. At home, however, he is a different man; he loves his father and imaginatively transforms his home into a castle. In his Walworth life, he becomes Pip's friend and confidant. Does his love for his father and Miss Skiffins redeem him? Or does it at least preserve him from the dehumanization and isolation that afflict Jaggers?

The harmony in which Jaggers and Wemmick work is temporarily disrupted when each learns of the softer or feeling side of the other. Their normal impersonal relationship is reestablished when Wemmick ejects a sniveling client from the office, "I'll have no feelings here" (page 418). Dickens uses this incident to do more than characterize Jaggers and Wemmick and their working relationship; he is also attacking the lack of feeling in business and business relationships. T.A. Jackson believes that Jaggers reflected "Dickens's deepening sense that success in business in the bourgeois world can be won only at the expense of everything nobly generous, elevating, sympathetic, and humane."

Mrs. Joe

Disabled after her attack, Mrs. Joe intensely wants to see Orlick. When he appears, she kneels before him. Is she expressing remorse for past unjust actions? As a consequence of her suffering, is she redeemed? or, in her disabled state, is she beyond redemption?

Society

Society, in the form of the legal system, continues to be cruel, unjust–in a word, criminal. Jaggers tells of children being raised by society to grow up to be criminals and finally transported or executed. The casts of the hanged men in Jaggers's office, which for Pip are inseparable from official proceedings, form a continuum with the mass condemnation of thirty-two men and women to death. The bond that connects all human beings is repudiated by the legal system; the institutionalization of such a procedure condemns the legal system and the society,which created and perpetuates it. Dickens writes an impassioned denunciation of the legal system and affirmation of the bond connecting the condemned and the judge:

The sun was striking in at the great windows of the court, through the glittering drops of rain upon the glass, and it made a broad shaft of light between the two-and-thirty and the judge, linking both together, and perhaps reminding some among the audience how both were passing on, with absolute equality, to the greater Judgment that knoweth all things and cannot err (page 462).

Society is unredeemed. Do you find any hints that society is redeemable or even reformable? Does the commonplace of Dickens criticism that he was not a systematic thinker and lacked a social programme apply to *Great Expectations*? Does the fact that individuals are redeemable imply that society as a whole is?

Q. Discuss the social entrapment in the novel Great Expectations.

Throughout *Great Expectations*, Dickens utilizes the description of nature and weather in order to set a tone of oppression that often characterizes Pip's experiences. This first passage occurs in the beginning of the book when Pip is on the way, under severe threat, to provide food for the convict:

It was a rimy morning, and very damp. I had seen the damp lying on the outside of my little window, as if some goblin had been crying there all night, and using the window for a pocket-handkerchief. Now, I saw the damp lying on the bare hedges and spare grass, like a coarser sort of spiders' webs; hanging itself from twig to twig and blade to blade. On every rail and gate, wet lay clammy; and the marsh-mist was so thick, that the wooden finger on the post directing people to our village, for they never came here—a direction which they never accepted—was invisible to me until I was quite close under it. Then as I looked up at it, while it dripped, it seemed to my oppressed conscience like a phantom devoting me to the hulks.

The exchange between Pip and the convict is the underlying force of the novel. Magwitch becomes forever indebted to the young Pip and pays him back by providing him with "great expectations." While Magwitch's resources enable Pip to rise to the social station that he had dreamed of since encountering Estella, his newfound status is accompanied by a sense of entrapment. Pip not only falls quickly into debt once he as a gentleman, and thus becomes entangled financially, but he also struggles with his own sense of guilt for deserting Joe and Biddy. Even before Pip can possibly conceive that he will one day have "great expectations," Dickens uses ominous description of weather to foreshadow Pip's future.

A similar use of weather description as foreshadowing occurs just prior to when Magwitch appears and reveals that he is Pip's benefactor:

It was wretched weather; stormy and wet, stormy and wet; mud, mud, mud, deep in all the streets. Day after day, a vast heavy veil had been driving over London from the east, and it drove still, as if in the east there were an eternity of cloud and wind. [Charles Dickens, *Great Expectations*, 292]

Once aware that his patron is an escaped criminal, Pip becomes conscious of the hard realities of his "expectations." He believes himself now forever bound to what he thinks the lowest of society.

Both passages utilize repetition of certain words, such as "mud," "stormy" and "wet," to create a mood of gloominess. London, soaked and enshrouded by the weather, heavy and distorting, recalls Pip's village on the fateful day when he binds himself to his convict. In addition, each passage precedes an encounter with Magwitchapter Another part of the novel that pertains to this particular theme in *Great expectations* appears in Pip's final association with Orlick, when Orlick takes Pip hostage with the intent to kill him.

Pip's natural surroundings at that moment are such that "a stranger would have found them insupportable, and even to me they were so oppressive that I hesitated, half-inclined to go back" (*Great Expectations,* 392). Pip does not go back, and as a result Orlick captures him.

This motif in *Great Expectations* hints at the rigid class structure of Victorian England. The sense of entrapment that precedes Pip's encounters with Magwitch stems from the fact that Magwitch produces Pip's source of increased social status. As a result of Magwitch's generosity, Pip becomes a so-called gentleman. He does not work and can not perform any specific job or have a certain career due to his gentleman's education.

As Victorian England was increasingly capitalistic, placing greater value on the ability to gain more capital, it seems as though the gentleman would become increasingly obsolete. To succeed in a capitalistic society, it is necessary to have a means through which to make money, in other words, a job.

The oppressive quality of Pip's situation derives from the fact that he is thrown into London, a centre of capitalism, with apparently no ability to do anything valued by that society. At the end of the novel, Pip becomes a clerk for Herbert Pocket's company. This new station in his life coincides with a time of true happiness, having been reconciled with Joe and Biddy and more or less freed from the binding life he tried to lead in London.

Q. Who were the challenging figures of Dickens's?
Or
Q. Can they be called as marginal women?

Introduction

Among the multitude of characters that people Dickens' novels, it has often been remarked; few mature adult women are portrayed in any convincing way as sexual beings, although critics such as Michael Slater, and, more recently, David Holbrook, Rita Lubitz, and Patricia Ingham have all explored Dickens' presentation of women in his novels. Yet little attention has been given to such marginal but significant characters as Rosa Dartle in *David Copperfield,* Miss Wade in *Little Dorrit,* and Lady Dedlock's French maid, Hortense, in *Bleak House.* I shall argue that such women all challenge the moral schemes and values, the resolutions, and sometimes, the linguistic norms and conventions of the novels.

They are rarely, if ever, seen sympathetically by the novels' narrators, or by their other characters, or, presumably, by Dickens himself. But they force their way into the novels nonetheless, and, like other marginal characters in Dickens' fiction, they articulate criticisms of the some of the most basic tenets of his philosophy, like the value and validity of Christian charity, the necessity of knowing and keeping to one's place in the social hierarchy, and the ultimate defensibility of the sexual double standard. These criticisms may be seen to be undermined to a certain extent by the nature of the women and men who utter them, but they are made nonetheless, and to examine the characters who make them is, in a certain sense, to read Dickens against himself.

Rosa, Miss Wade, and Hortense are all described, like many of Dickens' characters, through their outward appearance,which acts as a transparent sign or set of signs of their internal nature. As Ingham notes, in the pseudo-sciences of physiognomy (and, it might be added, phrenology), Dickens, like other nineteenth-century novelists, found a ready-made code of signification. As befits women who all in some way or other challenge social norms and conventions in Dickens' novels, and indeed, in nineteenth-century novels generally, all are dark, proud, passionate, unhappy, and repressed, although all of them overcome the usual repression of their feelings at certain points in the novels, in various ways and in varying degrees. Hortense, Lady Dedlock's French maid, rebels by murdering Tulkinghorn, Sir Leicester Dedlock's lawyer, and a bastion of the British legal system at the end of *Bleak House.* Rosa and Miss Wade express their repressed anger and desire only through verbal violence, although in certain scenes, for example when Rosa tells David the story of what has happened to Emily and when she confronts Emily towards the end of the novel, that verbal violence is extreme. In all three cases, the women's anger is provoked at least partly by feelings of a perceived inferiority of class and gender (and race, in Hortense's case), and in two cases out of three, with Rosa and Miss Wade, it is also partly a product of jealousy.

In their cases, their anger against the men who play with their feelings and then abandon them is displaced and transformed into jealousy of the women who have supplanted them (who are then either abandoned or mistreated in their turn), and into anger against the other women who embody the social hierarchy which condemns them as inferior. In the case of Hortense, jealousy of a younger woman is part of the pattern, but her animosity is more explicitly and logically directed at the man who has exploited her and dominated her. Since I shall not have time here today to examine all three cases in detail, I will focus on Rosa and, to a lesser extent on Miss Wade, although I shall discuss the significance of Hortense's murder of Tulkinghorn briefly before concluding.

Rosa Dartle (David Copperfield)

Rosa Dartle is the female companion to Mrs. Steerforth, James Steerforth's mother in *David Copperfield*. We first meet Rosa when David visits the Steerforth home on his way to visit Mr. Peggotty and his family in Yarmouth. It is through David's innocent and idealistic yet also casually callous and sexist hermeneutic categories that she is first seen and 'placed' for us. Fascinated by her, but not sure why, David describes her in some detail, with a mixture of attraction and repulsion and with an insistence upon one particular physical feature, a scar.[6]

From the start, there is a contradiction both in how David sees Rosa and in his response to what he sees. She is 'of a slight short figure, dark, and not agreeable to look at, but with some appearance of good looks', the final phrase being repeated later in the same passage. Having mentioned her 'black hair and eager black eyes', he focuses on the one unusual aspect of her face, the scar, which he describes in detail: 'It was an old scar - I should rather call it seam, for it was not discoloured and had healed years ago - which had once cut through her mouth, downward towards the chin, but was now barely visible across the table, except above and on her upper lip, the shape of which it had altered'. He concludes that 'she was about thirty years of age, and that she wished to be married.

She was a little dilapidated — like a house - with having been so long to let' (350). David's conclusion about Rosa's desire to be married tells the reader more about his conventional view of women than it does about Rosa, and the comparison of her to a dilapidated house which has been too long to let is both immensely suggestive in its visual clarity and callous and sexist in the way it treats Rosa as a less-than-desirable object. David concludes his initial presentation of her by noting that 'Her thinness seemed to be the effect of some wasting fire within her, which found a vent in her gaunt eyes' (350). The 'wasting fire' is of course the fire of sexual passion, unnaturally consuming its own substance and forcing itself out through eyes which are all but destroyed by it.

But it is the scar which most fascinates David, and it is the scar which in fact is an indication of the cause of Rosa's 'wasting fire'. An exchange between David and Steerforth explains things. When David comments on the scar, Steerforth is forced to admit: 'I did that'. He explains: 'I was a young boy, and she exasperated me, and I threw a hammer at her. A promising young angel I must have been!' Steerforth then adds his own explanation of Rosa: 'She has borne the mark ever since, as you see... and she'll bear it to her grave, if she ever rests in one - though I can hardly believe she will ever rest anywhere. She was the motherless child of a sort of cousin of my father's. He died one day. My mother, who was then a widow, brought her here to be company to her. She has a couple of thousand pounds of her own, and saves the interest of it every year, to add to the principal. There's the history of Miss Rosa Duarte for you'. David responds to this with the extraordinarily stupid remark, 'And I have no doubt she loves you like a brother', which draws from Steerforth the sardonic reply 'Humph!...some brothers are not loved over much; and some love -' (353).

The exchange is remarkable for Steerforth's characterisation of Rosa as a kind of vampire, whom he doubts will ever rest in a grave, or, indeed, 'anywhere', and for his awareness that Rosa's love for him is certainly neither brotherly nor innocent. Seduced and subjected to the violence of Steerforth as a girl, Rosa bears and will bear forever the traces of the conflicting passions she felt for him as a girl and still feels for him as a woman, while Steerforth knows exactly what is at stake, even if David does not.

It is in Rosa's language that these conflicting feelings are most notably, if not most directly, expressed. David notes that 'It appeared to me that she never said anything she wanted to say, outright; but hinted it, and made a great deal more of it by this practice' (350). The most interesting example of this indirectness occurs during the conversation about Peggotty and his family, when David proposes that Steerforth should accompany him on his visit to them. Steerforth declares that such a journey would be worthwhile '"to see that sort of people together, and to make one of 'em"'. In connection with the phrase, 'that sort of people', David says:

Miss Dartle, whose sparkling eyes had been watchful of us, now broke in again.

'Oh, but, really? Do tell me. Are they, though?' she said.

'Are they what? And are who what?' said Steerforth.

'That sort of people. - Are they really animals and clods, and beings of another order? I want to know so muchapter'

'Why, there's a pretty wide separation between them and us,' said Steerforth, with indifference. 'They are not to be expected to be as sensitive as we are. Their delicacy is not to be shocked, or hurt easily. They are wonderfully virtuous, I dare say - some people contend for that at least; and I am sure I don't want to contradict them - but they have not very fine natures, and they may be thankful that, like their coarse rough skins, they are not easily wounded.'

'Really!' said Miss Dartle. 'Well, I don't know, now, when I have been better pleased than to hear that. It's so consoling! It's such a delight to know that, when they suffer, they don't feel! Sometimes I have been quite uneasy for that sort of people; but now I shall just dismiss the idea of them, altogether. Live and learn. I had my doubts, I confess, but now they are cleared up. I didn't know, and now I do know, and that shows the advantage of asking - don't it?'(352) Steerforth's words reveal his unreconstructed sense of class superiority, which is later to lead to his seduction of Emily, and all that ensues. Rosa's challenge to the hierarchy of class and feeling to which Steerforth appeals should not be interpreted primarily as an intervention on behalf of the people being discussed, but as an indirect reminder to Steerforth of her own dependent position as the (relatively) poor relation in the family and as a negative and equally indirect questioning of what he says.

By reducing Steerforth's arguments to complete absurdity when she says, "It's so consoling! It's such a delight to know that, when they suffer, they don't feel!"', Rosa both obliquely questions their validity and reminds him of the pain he has inflicted on her. The indirectness of her language in this scene shows that, while she is marked forever by the conflicting feelings of desire and anger which she feels for Steerforth, she is unable to express those feelings directly. Since they would be unacceptable not only to Steerforth himself but, more importantly, to his mother; that is, she cannot offer any overt challenge either to his authority as the man in the house or to the authority of his mother as the older, richer woman. Constrained by her privileged yet also restricted position as companion to Mrs. Steerforth, Rosa, as Steerforth says '"[wears] herself away by constant sharpening"' until she is '"all edge"' (352), since propriety demands that she repress both her desire for Steerforth and her discontent with her subordinate position.

Later in the novel, confronting Emily in London, Rosa is not restrained by any such considerations and, in David's hearing, is allowed to rebuke and revile Emily at length. This can be seen as the first part of the punishment which is later to see Emily exiled to Australia. Rosa's words represent a particularly uncharitable and cruel version of the traditional double standard of sexual behaviour, and while both David and his creator deplore the cruelty, they do not disclaim the double standard; indeed, they reinforce it. Steerforth is ennobled in death, Emily exiled to Australia.

Miss Wade (Little Dorrit)

Miss Wade in *Little Dorrit* is another case of suppressed female resentment and anger, although the emotions are caused more by the treatment which she receives because of her illegitimacy and the position of social insecurity and inferiority which derives from it than by any sexual entanglement or feelings. Whereas Rosa's anger has a primarily sexual cause, Miss Wade's comes from a sense of hurt pride. Like Rosa, Miss Wade is dark, proud, and angry (Dickens 1991: 19-20). Even more effectively than Rosa, however, she marginalises herself. Whereas Rosa is affiliated through a somewhat distant family link to Steerforth and his mother, Miss Wade has no known relations of any kind. She reveals in the document, which she gives to Arthur Clennam, she has purposely cut herself off from the company of those who have loved and tried to help her, since she believed that their kindness to her was motivated by a perverse pride and pleasure in their own sense of social superiority, rather than uncomplicated goodness.

Dickens entitles this document 'The History of a Self-Tormentor', in order to make the narrative perspective on Miss Wade clear, and the narrative descriptions of both her and Tattycoram, the orphan girl she shelters for a time, emphasise the self-destructive nature of both the woman and the younger girl. They are described as 'two natures... constantly tearing the other to pieces' (553), an image which has already occurred in relation to Tattycoram who threatens on several occasions to '"tear [herself] to pieces"' before consenting to stay with her employers and benefactors, the Meagles (277). Unlike Rosa, Miss Wade is allowed to express herself in her own (written) words, but the text she produces is both placed and undermined by the narrator and the title he gives it, which serves to undercut the criticisms it and its author make.

Yet there is a sense in which Tattycoram (and perhaps Miss Wade too) are right to protest against the way they are treated; the former is taken from the Foundling Hospital to be a maid to the Meagles' daughter, Pet, and despite all the Meagles' good intentions, she is both an object of charity and an employee. There is no question of equality; benevolence cannot (and the novel implies should not) include equality: the object of charity is still an object, and an object of an inferior class, at that. In Miss Wade's case, it is harder to judge the issue, since all we have is her, grossly biased, narrative of her experiences, rather than any dramatisation which might allow diverging views. It is clear, however, even from her account, that she is the governess who rebels against the only means by which she could find a way out of her situation of social inferiority, marriage to a socially acceptable man, and consequent emigration to India. Of course, her rebellion is self-destructive: she meets Henry Gowan, who understands her as Steerforth understands Rosa, and who seduces and abandons her.

Dickens shows himself ready to contemplate a woman who will not follow the accepted and expected channels of action, but, not surprisingly, can find no positive role for her. That this should be so should scarcely surprise us. George Eliot, writing ten years later, can find no other solution than to drown Maggie Tulliver at the end of *The Mill on the Floss* when Maggie refuses to accept the only way to make her behaviour conventionally acceptable. That is to marry Stephen Guest, while Charlotte Bronte's solution in *Jane Eyre* is to have the once-rebellious governess marry her social superior, Rochester, after he has been suitably chastised.

Hortense (Bleak House)

Finally, there is Hortense like Rosa and Miss Wade; she is dark, proud, and angry (Dickens 1985: 209, 372-3). She is initially described as having a 'feline mouth' and as being 'a very neat She-Wolf imperfectly tamed' (209), and subsequently she is often defined by other animal imagery. To Tulkinghorn she is 'a vixen' (643), while the narrator describes her as 'that feline personage' (642), with a 'tigerish expansion' about the mouth (646, 794) and, on one occasion, as 'panting, tigress-like', when she hears how Mrs. Bucket has deceived her. Her discontent is manifested in various scenes and in a variety of ways earlier in the novel (209, 311-2).

She is explicitly associated with a potential for violence at several points in the book (209, 312).but it is of course her murder of Tulkinghorn, Sir Leicester Dedlock's lawyer and the representative of the status quo which expresses her rebellion most concretely. Moreover, in addition to challenging the status quo through the murder, she also explicitly criticises the hypocrisies and suppressions on which the status quo relies. At the very moment when Bucket, the detective, is about to lead her away to prison, she challenges him to tell her that he can reassert the rightness and stability. The old order of things after the murder has forced out the truth that Lady Dedlock had a lover and an illegitimate child before she married Sir Leicester, and that her noble husband has been deceived and betrayed. '"Can you restore [Tulkinghorn] back to life?"' '"Can you make a honourable lady of Her?"', '"Or a haughty gentieman of *Him*?"' she asks (799, emphasis in the original). Neither Bucket, nor the narrator, nor presumably Dickens, has an answer to any of these questions. All Bucket can do is to say, rather helplessly, '"Come, come, why this is worse Parlaying than the other"' (799), before he leads her away.

Hortense may have been found out and arrested, but she has forced out into the open the dirty secrets which Bucket, Tulkinghorn and Sir Leicester would have much preferred to keep silent. Perhaps Dickens can imagine such a crime since Hortense is French, and therefore different or 'Other' not only in terms of gender but also in terms of race. As a French woman, she is, as it were, double beyond the pale.

Conclusion

What can one conclude from these three marginal women? That they are anomalies, not to be given too much attention in any final evaluation of Dickens' work? That they are manifestations of Dickens' own anxieties and fears about women's sexuality as Holbrook suggests (1993: 10, 20, 21, 23, 166, 170)? Neither, I think. I prefer to read them as signs of those immense female energies which cannot be accommodated in the conventional forms of the family and the community in Dickens' world, but which seem to force their way out of his head and into the novels nonetheless. As they do so, these characters criticise the model of bourgeois benevolence which Dickens cherished, and the class hierarchy which, ultimately, he endorsed; they also show the crudity and injustice of the sexual double standard of which he also approved in ways which his narrators deplore and yet which they seem powerless to oppose. Through them, Dickens is his own best critic.

Subversion of Gender Identity in *Great Expectations*

Q. How do the physical descriptions of the female characters depict such women in a masculine fashion? How do the male characters in Dicken's work provide a visible contrast to such masculine portraitures of the female characters? Ex. Joe, Herbert, Matthew Pocket, etc.

Or

Q. What is Dicken's purpose in subverting stereotypical notions of Victorian gender identity and relations in *Great Expectations*? Do you think that the author does actually mean to oppose such stereotypes in the novel, or do you believe that they are actually upheld in the course of the novel? Is gendered space stronger than gendered disposition?

Or

Q. Do you feel Estella and Ms. Havisham present an antithetical example of Victorian femininity? Or are these characters actually indicative of the feminine plight in the nineteenth-century English societal setting?

Or

Q. How is Pip's gender identity contradicted and affirmed throughout the novel? How is he conflicted about his

place in a gender-divided society, both growing up at the forge and during his life in London?

In *Great Expectations,* Charles Dickens subverts stereotypical Victorian ideals of motherhood, femininity, and masculinity while concurrently maintaining his characters within the overarching strict framework of a gendered society in nineteenth-century England. In one sense, the actors in Dicken's work do maintain their gendered identities and live within the prescribed social space appropriate to each sex. Females in the novel are indubitably confined to the domestic realm throughout the book. Ms. Havisham is an extreme example of this reality, as she has not left Satis House since the morning when she was abandoned by her callous, pilfering fiancé. Pip's sister, Mrs. Joe Gargery, repetitively emphasizes her confinement to the forge, evidenced by such complaints as, "Perhaps if I warn't a blacksmith's wife, and (what's the same thing) a slave with her apron never off, I should have been to hear the Carols" (23). Biddy's persona is defined by her role as a domestic servant — her life revolves around hearth and home. And Estella, though more widely traveled than other the other women in the book, is confined between locations of a foreign school, Satis House, and Mrs.

Brandley's home in Richmond. In contrast, the Dickensian men folk are more or less free to go at will. Though Joe Gargery's movements are strongly confined by his wife's dictates, Joe still has the liberty to escape to the Three Jolly Bargemen or attend errands uptown on occasion. Pip, though also suffering the demands of his sister's will, is also free to attend night school, play upon the marshes and attend Ms. Havisham's house at Satis "for the good of the family". The males residing in London have an innate freedom to come and go as they will, as Wemmick and Jaggers are both bachelors, unconstrained by domestic demands or female counterparts. Herbert, though poor, is also at liberty to do what he pleases during his residence in Barnard's Inn.

However, though this notion of gendered space does effectively concur with Victorian modes of masculine and feminine propriety, it also contrasts sharply with more essential gender relations in the novel. Many of Dicken's female characters exist as an antithesis to Victorian ideals of fair womanhood and angelic femininity, while many of the male personages take on definitively female roles in the course of the novel. Pip himself is explicitly affected by this confusion of gender identity, and seems caught between prescriptions of masculine strength and feminine vulnerability during the course of his interactions with the strong female characters of *Great Expectations*.

Mrs. Joe Gargery, though adept at housekeeping at the forge, is very much the "man of the house". Pip describes his sister as a woman with "black hair and eyes" and a face with "such a prevailing redness of skin that I sometimes used to wonder whether it was possible she washed herself with a nutmeg-grater instead of soap. She was tall and bony, and almost always wore a coarse apron, fastened over her figure behind with two loops, and having a square, impregnable bib in front that was stuck full of pins and needles." (13). Furthermore, Mrs. Gargery's appearance is supplemented by such unmotherly declarations as "I may truly say that I've never had this apron of mine off, since born you were. It's bad enough to be a blacksmith's wife (and him a Gargery), without being your mother".

In similar fashion, Ms. Havisham inhabits the adornments of Victorian femininity, but Pip portrays this garb once again in a singularly unwomanly fashion.

It was not in the first moments that I saw all these things, though I saw more of them in the first moments than might be supposed. But, I saw that everything within my view which ought to be white, had been white long a go, and had lost its luster, and was faded and yellow. I saw that the bride within the bridal dress had withered like the dress, and like the flowers, and had no brightness left but the brightness of her sunken eyes. I saw that the dress had been put upon the rounded figure of a young woman, and that the figure upon which it now hung loose, had shrunk to skin and bone.

Finally, Estella is neither docile nor a fragile flower of Victorian femininity. She is a "femme fatale", who is repeatedly cajoled by Ms. Havisham to wreak havoc on the hearts of the opposite sex.

And sometimes, when her moods were so many and so contradictory of one another than I was puzzled what to say or do, Miss Havisham would embrace her [Estella] with lavish fondness, murmuring something in her ear that sounded like, "Break their hearts, my pride and hope, break their hearts and have no mercy!"

Q. Briefly describe the separate spheres of Dickens.

Or

Q. What do they show about the Victorian society?

In *Great Expectations,* Charles Dickens depicts men and women as existing within different social spaces. With the exception of Estella, who travels from Satis House to London, all of Dickens's female characters are contained within the home. Men, on the other hand, have a social existence, which their female counterparts lack. Pip, for example, constantly moves between the private space of the home and the public space of London itself. Joe Gargery, though often confined to the forge, has a social existence at the Three Jolly Bargemen, the local tavern. Unlike Dickens, Elizabeth Barrett Browning does not confine her female characters to the home in her novel-poem *Aurora Leigh.* Aurora is a woman who lives independently in London and whose writing earns her a space in the public world. Marian Erle is likewise independent and not confined to the local space of the home. Despite these different depictions of men's and women's spaces in the social order, Barrett Browning's notion of womanhood and femininity resembles Dickens's more than it differs from it. We shall explore how, for both Dickens and Barrett Browning, the ideal woman is a moral repository, a being whose function is to infuse men with spirituality and to protect them from the evils of the social world.

Recent historiography of gender constructions of the nineteenth century focuses on the different spheres in which men and women lived. Mary Shanley points out that "Husband and wife occupied 'separate spheres,' and each had distinct, but complementary, functions to perform. In addition to bearing children, middle-class women directed, and working-class women performed, the work involved in maintaining the household—care of the children, sewing, cooking, and cleaning. Men earned the money to purchase goods needed by their households and debated matters of public concern". The historian Catherine Hall has observed that women in the domestic sphere did more than just sew, cook, and clean. They functioned as moral and religious guides for their husbands. The "division between male and female worlds had a religious connotation, for the marketplace was considered dangerously amoral.

The men who operated in that sphere could save themselves only through constant contact with the moral world of the home, where women acted as carriers of the pure values that could counteract the destructive tendencies of the market" (74). This construction, which placed women firmly in the home and men in the marketplace, developed within the middle-classes. Lower class families that depended on two incomes for survival clearly could not conform to this construction. Hall argues that, while working-class families could not operate according to the middle-class construction of the family, they did accept many of the ideals of middle-class domesticity. The notion that the home provided a moral centre and a place of comfort for the husband was particularly popular with the working-class family.

As Michael Slater illustrates, Dickens subscribed to the bourgeois construction of femininity and domesticity. He, like most Victorians, imagined men and women as having different, yet complementary, natures. The place where these two natures come together most "naturally" is, of course, the bourgeois home. "This idea of virtuous womanhood as possessed of innate, God-given powers to uplift, regenerate and redeem, which is so ubiquitous in Dickens's writing, is inextricably bound up with his celebrated idealization of the domestic. It is always in terms of personal relationships, especially within a family grouping, that woman, for him as for most Victorians, realised her full moral and spiritual potential." (309) *Great Expectations* strikingly lacks female characters that fit this womanly ideal. The only female character in the novel that comes close to fitting this ideal is Biddy. Most other female characters are horribly deficient at performing the duties, which Victorian culture prescribes to them. Miss Havisham, for example, raises Estella as a heartless femme fatale, rather than as a virtuous, self-effacing "angel of the house." As we shall see, conflict in the novel emerges when its characters do not conform to this Victorian gender construction.

The first woman Pip describes in the novel is his dead mother. Because he has never seen his parents, nor any likenesses of them, he imagines his mother as "freckled and sickly" (35). The novel thus begins with a negative image of motherhood. Absent mothers and deficient mother substitutes are integral to the narrative from its very beginning. The next female character Pip introduces is his sister/mother substitute, Mrs. Joe Gargery. He describes his sister as harsh and unapproachable, far from the loving mother of Victorian fantasy. "She was tall and bony, and almost always wore a coarse apron, fastened over her figure behind with two hoops, and having a small impregnable bib in front, that was stuck full of pins and needles." (40) Mrs. Joe is clearly the opposite of the ideal Victorian woman. Pip depicts her more as a monster than as a woman. U.C. Knoepflmacher points out a humorous scene from Chapter Four which illustrates Mrs. Joe's lack of a feminine identity. After Mr. Wopsle claims, "What is detestable in a pig, is more detestable in a boy," Mr. Hubble adds, "Or a girl." Mr. Wopsle then responds: "'Of course, or a girl, Mr. Hubble,' assented Mr. Wopsle rather irritably, 'but there is no girl present.'" (58) Mr. Wopsle thus presents the Gargery household as operating without any sort of feminine influence (78-79).

Since Mrs. Joe is the antithesis of the womanly ideal, Pip must look elsewhere for maternal nurturing, which he finds not in another woman, but in his brother-in-law, Joe Gargery. Throughout the novel, Dickens presents Joe as a maternal figure in Pip's life. Like the ideal wife in Victorian culture, Joe neglects his own comfort and well-being rather than disturb the family setting. Joe has internalized the beatings his father gave his mother to such an extent that he refuses to return the blows Mrs. Joe deals to him and Pip with the Tickler.

I see so much in my poor mother, of a woman drudging and slaving and breaking her honest hart and never getting no peace in her mortal days, that I'm dead afeerd of going wrong in the way of not doing what's right by a woman, and I'd fur rather of the two go wrong the t'other way, and be a little ill-conwenienced myself. I wish it was only me that got put out, Pip; I wish there warn't no Tickler for you, old chap; I wish I could take it all on myself. [80]

Dickens's depiction of Joe is like that of the self-effacing mother who sacrifices her own well-being for the sake of her children. Joe re-assumes his role as mother substitute towards the novel's end, when Pip is recovering from his illness. Pip states that he "was like a child in [Joe's] hands," and that Joe "did everything for me except the household work, for which he had engaged a very decent woman" (476). While Joe's role as a mother stops at his performing strictly feminine household chores, he still functions as a maternal figure in his caring for Pip.

What, then, are the consequences of this reversal of gender roles?

Certainly, Dickens would not advocate an arrangement like the Gargery's, in which the woman is characterized by her masculinity and the man by his femininity. For Dickens, the only possible result of a situation in which gender roles are confused is violence and disorder. Pip is the victim of this gender inversion. Growing up in the Gargery household, as Carol Siegel claims, leads Pip to internalize the belief that "it is either beat or be beaten in marriage" (7). Siegel characterizes Pip as a masochist, as one who has so internalized the beatings from his sister that he comes to identify female love with violence and pain. Thus, when it comes to choosing a sexual-object, Pip chooses the heartless Estella over the compassionate and loving Biddy. Although Pip recognizes that Biddy is clearly the more suitable love-object of the two, his desire for pain overwhelms his sense of reason. He comes to realise, when walking with Biddy on the marshes, that "Biddy was never insulting, or capricious, or Biddy to-day and somebody else to-morrow; she would have derived only pain, and no pleasure, from giving me pain; she would far rather have wounded her own breast than mine" (157-58). Despite this realization, Pip masochistic tendencies lead him to over-value Estella and to hope that, "perhaps after all Miss Havisham was going to make my fortune when my time was out" (160).

Dickens's solution to the problem of women who do not act in accordance with Victorian gender construction often involves a violent taming of them: Mrs. Joe is beaten into submission by Orlick, Molly is tamed by Mr. Jaggers, and Estella is beaten by her husband, Bentley Drummle. Any deviance from gender norms on the part of women in *Great Expectations* is greeted with violence. It is interesting to note that all women, whatever their class background, are forced to submit to Dickens's bourgeois construction of gender. Thus Dickens, like many Victorians, held up the middle-class definition of gender as the ideal, which the lower- and upper-classes should emulate. This ideal woman, then, is one who is firmly rooted in the home and who subordinates her own self in favour of her husband and children.

Q. Do you agree that Dickens has taken care of children and their needs?

Or

Q. What picture does he create of Pip's childhood?

The first part of Dickens' novel, *Great Expectations,* is an account of the childhood of, Pip, the main character of the novel. In these beginning chapters, Dickens paints an extremely vivid picture of childhood. The reader is able to enter Pip's mind and see the world through the eyes of a child. This is possible because Dickens understood the thoughts and feelings of children and applied this to Pip's every thought and action when he wrote the novel. Dickens had an obvious gift for creating child characters in his works. The word "pip" itself refers to a seed from a plant. Seeds need to be nurtured if they are to grow and flourish. In order to understand both Dickens' talent and his compulsion to write about children it important to realise that through the characters in his novels he took up the plight of all children. In Dickens' view of childhood, he felt that children have certain needs: guidance in a nurturing home, to be free from emotional and physical abuse, to have a good education, and to be allowed to use their imaginations. In order for children to succeed in life he felt these needs must be met. Through his portrayal of child characters in the novel, *Great Expectations*, Dickens' demonstrates how adults rarely, nor adequately provided for these particular needs that children have.

Dickens often wrote about children in his stories who were crippled, such as Tiny Tim in *A Christmas Carol*. However, Dickens chose to create most of his main child characters with no physical maladies. As Collins points out, these characters were impeded emotionally in some way: "Most of his child heroes and heroines are born sound in wind and limb, to whatever early graves their sufferings may bring them, but a loving home is what they most obviously lack and need" (182). Pip is one of the characters who fits that description. He is healthy enough physically but he is severely crippled emotionally. In "Parents and Children in *Great Expectations*," Vereen Bell explains Pip's affliction:

Like any little boy Pip would like to be loved and pampered....In the absence of parents there are plenty of people who tell Pip what to do, to bully him, in a self-satisfied, self-enhancing way, but there is no one to shield him or guide him, or give him the special kind of love that he seeks. (23)

Pip is an orphan. Orphans were another one of Dickens' favourite subjects. What could be more crippling emotionally than to come into life without the crucial support of a mother and, or that of a father?

The opening chapter of the novel shows just how alone Pip is, as he sits on the gravestones of his father, mother, and brothers in the churchyard:

At such a time I found out for certain, that this bleak place overgrown with nettles was the churchyard; and that Philip Pirrip, late of his parish, and also Georgina wife of the above, were dead and buried; and that...infant children of the aforesaid also were dead and buried...and that the low leaden line beyond, was the river; and that the distant savage lair from which the wind was rushing, was the sea; and that the small bundle of shivers growing afraid of it all and beginning to cry was Pip. (24, chapter1)

Pip seems as if he is an island completely unto himself. His only blood relative is his sister, Mrs. Joe. After their parents die, she brought Pip up "by hand." One meaning of being "brought up by hand" is that his sister bottle-fed Pip since he was a baby (27, chapter2). But, what Dickens was really saying is that Pip was raised with constant abuse from his sister. Pip tells us that because "[his sister had] a hard and heavy hand" and that she was "much in the habit of laying it upon her husband as well as upon me," he felt that the expression meant that both he and Joe were "brought up by hand" (28, chapter2).

Pip is not only physically abused by his sister but he also suffers emotionally from her as well. In the novel she treats him more like a pebble in her shoe than a brother, or even a human being. Mrs. Joe explains all of the pain she had to endure in raising Pip:

And then she entered on a fearful catalogue of all of the illnesses I had been guilty of, and all the acts of sleeplessness I had committed, and all the high places I had tumbled from, and all the low places I had tumbled into, and all the injuries I had done myself, and all the times she had wished me in my grave, and I had continually refused to go there. (45, chapter2).

His sister talks about him openly as if he had no thoughts or feelings of his own. Rawlins refers to Pip's experience as that of a "Dickensian childhood - he is stripped of his rights, found guilty of being himself, and rendered invisible..." (673).

Pip has no one to turn to for guidance, no one but Joe, who is his sister's husband. However, Dickens does not really consider Joe an adult in the novel; at least not mentally or emotionally. Pip even thinks of Joe, "as a larger species of child, and as no more than [his] equal" (29, chapter2). Because of his childlike qualities, Joe also suffers the wrath of Mrs. Joe. She both physically and emotionally abuses him; for instance, she frequently "knocked his head...against the wall" (31, chapter2). Like Pip, he is treated as less than human.

Another need that Dickens felt children had was a good education. Dickens himself was in and out of several different schools throughout his childhood. Eventually, he was forced to educate himself because of his family's financial problems. Dickens had great expectations for himself and he believed that a good education was the means by which he could achieve his goals. Dickens believed that all children should have the opportunity to receive a good education. He believed that it was the responsibility of the church, of the parents, and of the state. He gave very freely to educational institutions, those that were exemplary schools and also those that were called "Ragged Schools" (Collins 71). In the novel, *Great Expectations*, Pip did receive an education from Mr. Wopsle's great-aunt. It was a very poor education and Pip learned more from his friend Biddy than he did in school. Another factor that deterred Pip's education was that his sister was opposed to it. Joe explained to Pip that she was not "over partial to having scholars on the premises" (63, chapter7). His sister was afraid that school would make Pip rebellious. Pip only receives a decent education when he goes to London in search of his great expectations.

Children frequently suffer at the hands of their adult guardians in Dickens' novels. As Collins points out: "The adult world is generally hostile, vicious, uncomprehending or indifferent; or the child has to minister to, instead of being supported by, it" (182). Pip, for instance, is brought up by his harsh, even abusive sister, and has no other stable adult figures in his life. He is constantly demoralized by all those who should be nurturing him in his youth. This may be a reflection of Dickens' own feelings of neglect and abandonment toward his parents as a result of the blacking house episode.

Estella also is a victim to her guardian in the novel. She too is never given the chance to be her own person. Estella is conditioned by her guardian to make men suffer, and in return it is Estella who will be made to suffer for her guardian's actions. Bell notes that:

Pip and Estella have in common the fact that they are both instruments of someone else's vengeance, that both - either actually or in effect orphans - have their true natures distorted and corrupted by a foster parent's selfish purpose. Miss Havisham is a severely disturbed old woman who has adopted Estella.

Miss Havisham was abandoned on her wedding day and as a result she forever harbors hatred toward men. In fact, she wants revenge on men and uses Estella to meet this purpose. Pip concludes that Miss Havisham "had done a grievous thing in taking an impressionable child [Estella]" and had manipulated into "the form that her wild resentment, spurned affection, and wounded pride, found vengeance in" (365, chapter49). Miss Havisham programmes Estella to have a fear of men being close to her and not to allow herself to become attached to them emotionally.

In contrast to both Pip and Estella's restrictive upbringings is the way in which the Pocket children are raised. Pip observed that "they were not growing up or being brought up, but were tumbling up" (181, chapter22). Here Dickens comically describes the large family with seven young children "tumbling" in the literal sense, as they "bounce in bushes" and nearly drown in the river (182, chapter22). They seem to have no guidance of any sort as they trip over themselves and one another. On a more serious note, Dickens is demonstrating how an upbringing without any guidance is unfair to children as well.

It seems as long as they remain children, that the child characters in *Great Expectations* will be unhappy. One may wonder why Dickens always seemed to make the world weigh so heavy on the little shoulders of so many of his characters. One reason is that Dickens appears to have created these suffering characters was that he wanted to protest the injustices toward children that he saw in Victorian society. He illustrated what these children needed and what they were missing. Just as a "seed" that is not nurtured cannot grow, children who are not loved and cared for can not grow up to live happy lives.

Q. Describe the different genres in Great Expectations.

One may attempt to position *Great Expectations* within the context of the Victorian novel (1837-1901), or within the history of Dickens's artistic output (1834-1870). The thirteenth of his novels, it is one of three relatively short novels designed for weekly magazine serialisation rather than monthly "part" publication, the other two being *Hard Times* (1854) for *Household Words* and *A Tale of Two Cities* (1859), the first novel serialised in *All the Year Round*. It is also his third major work to employ the first-person narrative point of view, the other two being the quasi-autobiographical *David Copperfield* (1849) and (at least, in part) *Bleak House* (1852). The modern reader sees this novel as a retrospcctive, first-person confessional. Alternatively, one may attempt to classify *Great Expectations* in terms of the various subgenres of the Victorian novel, for, unlike his earlier attempt at pseudo-autobiography, *David Copperfield, Great Expectations* does not fit so neatly into the German-inspired *Bildungsroman* (novel of development, or growing up).

Social Satire

To counter the lack of humour in *A Tale of Two Cities,* Dickens set out to provide character comedy, situation comedy, and especially (like W. M. Thackeray's *Vanity Fair*) social satire. Dickens makes us laugh at a society that values wealth and class, that condones snobbery and social injustice, that transports felons for relatively minor crimes, and that has allowed a great national institution, the theatre, to deteriorate. Although the utterances and actions of many of the characters make us laugh, each character evokes a different kind or quality of laughter.

The Novel of Crime and Detection

A relatively new form (probably an outgrowth of the Newgate Novel of Ainsworth, Thackeray, and Bulwer-Lytton), the Novel of Crime and Detection (sometimes mislabeled "The Murder Mystery") has influenced the characterization and the plot of *Great Expectations*. Like many of Wilkie Collins's novels,

Great Expectations introduces us to figures from the criminal underworld, in this case a lawyer and his nefarious clients, in particular, the escaped convict Abel Magwitch, the swindler Compeyson, and the murderess Molly Magwitchapter The reader must puzzle out what the relationship of such characters is to Miss Havisham, and if her eccentricity about Satis House's clocks and her wedding dress is somehow associated with them in the past.

Silver Fork Novel

Charles Lever's *A Day's Ride,* which began in *All the Year Round* in July, 1860, concerns a class and a lifestyle that Dickens personally held in contempt but that fascinated many of his readers. We may, at one level, regard *Great Expectations* as an "Anti-Silver Fork" novel, a satire upon the pretentiousness and money morality of the aristocracy, as represented by the brewery heiress Miss Havisham, her grasping relatives the Pockets, and the fatuous Uncle Pumblechook. Indeed, the very title of the novel may be meant ironically because the collapse of Pip's great expectations leaves him with no alternative but the bourgeois course of working for a living.

Newgate Novel

A form of fiction pioneered by Thackeray in *Catherine,* Ainsworth in *Rookwood,* and especially by Dickens himself in *Oliver Twist* (1837), this subgenre involves underworld types such as the fence (receiver of stolen goods), the pickpocket, the criminal mastermind, the highwayman, the housebreaker, the prostitute, the murderer, and the thief-taker (informer). This aspect of *Great Expectations* is embodied in the relationship between Magwitch and Compeyson, and in the plot gambit regarding the fate of Magwitch should the authorities discover that he has returned to England. This aspect is reinforced by references to George Lillo's George Barnwell in *The London Merchant* and Pip's feelings of guilt and betrayal, ironically stemming from his theft of the brandy, the pie, and the file to aid Magwitch (who rewards Pip for what he misinterprets as compassion rather than his actual motivation: fear).

The Gothic Novel

The tradition of the novel of suspense, horror, fear, and superstition that began with Horace Walpole's *The Castle of Otranto* (1764), continued into the nineteenth-century with the novels of Anne Radcliffe (notably, *The Mysteries of Udolpho*), Sir Walter Scott's *The Bride of Lammermoor*, Jane Austen's *Northanger Abbey* (a satire on the form), and Mary Shelley's *Frankenstein*. The melancholy ruin of Satis House, the bride frozen in time, the domineering aristocrat Bentley Drummle, the child (young Pip) and the young woman in distress, the monster (Orlick), and the suspenseful entrapments of Pip and Magwitch are all Gothic aspects of *Great Expectations*.

Serial Fiction

Each part or installment both advances the action, resolves previous problems, and poses fresh difficulties for the protagonist. Each part must be coherent and complete in itself, yet make connections (through continuing, easily recognized characters and settings) to what has gone before. Customarily, each part will end at a moment of crisis (for example, Pip's running off to the marshes to deliver the food and file to the convict at the end of part one) which the next will resolve—these complementary closings and openings are termed "curtains."

Romance

An older form than the novel, this genre continued into the nineteenth century with Hawthorne's *The Scarlet Letter*. Romance subordinates realism to emotion, and offers intensely personal rather than rational or objective responses. Pip's hopeless obsession with Estella ripples all the way through *Great Expectations*, and is in fact his chief motivation for becoming a "gentleman." The fairy-tale patterns derived from "Hansel and Gretel" and "Cinderella" contribute to the novel as romance.

Novel-with-a-Purpose

Many of the novels of Wilkie Collins, Dickens's protégé, fall under this heading since they advocate legal and social change—his *Heart and Science,* for example, attacks animal vivisection. Since Dickens described himself as "first and last, a reformer," *Great Expectations'* exposing the need for penal and educational reforms is consistent with this subgenre and Dickens's agenda throughout his works. His higher "purpose" is connected with the simple question, "What is a gentleman?" If we read the text properly, humble Joe Gargery rather than arrogant Bentley Drummle and his frivolous Finches of the Grove should be our answer.

Historical Novel

Although the pattern of a story's originating in the past and moving forward to the year of publication is not uncommon in Victorian fiction, *Great Expectations* begins just after the Napoleonic Wars and proceeds to recount events in detail until approximately 1830-35 before jumping ahead eleven years (1840-5, the major period of England's railway construction) to close the story.

Dickens carefully implants details in the text of the narrative to suggest that events therein described are very much "of the past." For example, since the one-pound notes mentioned in Chapter 10 were out of circulation from 1826 until 1915, the story must open prior to 1826. Since the death sentence which hangs over Magwitch as a transported felon was eliminated in 1835, and since the very end of the story transpires eleven years after Magwitch's death, Dickens concludes the story no later than 1846. The paddle-wheeler, a species of which mortally wounds Magwitch, was supplanted by the screw-propeller in 1839, thereby reinforcing a terminal date sometime in the mid-1840s.

The gibbet specifically noted at the opening reflects the practice abandoned in 1832 of leaving condemned criminals to rot where they were hanged. The king specifically mentioned at the beginning of the novel is George III, who died in 1820, when Pip was seven or eight. Thus, Dickens, born in 1812, seems to be identifying himself with his protagonist. The guinea, mentioned in Chapter 13, went out of circulation in 1817, yet young Charles Dickens arrived in London by coach from Chatham, the marsh country of the tale, at the age of ten (1822). Pip is about 23 in the middle of the book, and about 34 at the end; since Dickens turned 34 in February, 1846, he seems to be inviting his readers to connect the author and the narrator.

Q. Describe the Comic-Ironic Narrative of the novel Great Expectations.

When reading novels such as *David Copperfield* or *Great Expectations,* we come to see Dickens as a true master of narrative voice. Here, always the textual body reveals itself as an all-encompassing entity in which we find the protagonists' perspectives forever joined with authorial commentary. It is, furthermore, within this kind of double narrative that we find various other strange textual dichotomies, and we come to see the Dickensian world as one which is at once both sentimental and cynical, playful and severe, absurd, imaginative, and realistic. Part of these stylistic tensions are due to shifts which take place in the novel. For example, as the character matures his narrative voice likewise undergoes various changes. The Pip in the first chapters of *Great Expectations,* of course, is not the Pip of chapter twenty, and so forth. Nevertheless, often in Dickens' works these juxtaposing narrative tones coexist within a single scene, and one very predominant instance of this technique appears in Dickens' use of comic irony. The comic-ironic narrative in novels such as *Great Expectations,* however, is not so easily defined. At times, it manifests itself merely in the ironic undertone of the text indicative of an outside authorial voice, and this undertone may become humorous simply because it places the reader in a position in which he or she knows more than the character speaking.

The most common examples of such double-voiced narratives occur in Dickens' portrayals of children in which the young characters' innocent outlooks or naiveties attribute a certain playfulness to the author's knowing, matter-of-fact, and often tragic vision of adult society. However, this comic irony perhaps appears most vividly when Dickens simply throws a bleak or awful situation into comic relief. We see a very clear example of this latter form of comic irony in chapter twenty-three of *Great Expectations* when Pip has his first, somewhat absurd encounter with the Pocket family:

After dinner the children were introduced, and Mrs. Coiler made admiring comments on their eyes, noses, and legs — a sagacious way of improving their minds. There were four little girls, and two little boys, besides the baby who might have been either, and the baby's next successor who was as yet neither. They were brought in by Flopson and Millers much as though those two non-commissioned officers had been recruiting somewhere for children and had enlisted these: while Mrs. Pocket looked at the young Nobles that ought to have been, as if she rather thought she had had the pleasure of inspecting them before, but didn't quite know what to make of them.

"Here! Give me your fork, Mum, and take the baby," said Flopson. "Don't take it that way, or you'll get its head under the table."

Thus advised, Mrs. Pocket took it the other way, and got its head upon the table; which was announced to all present by a prodigious concussion.

"Dear, dear! Give it back, Mum," said Flopson; "and Miss Jane, come and dance to baby, do!"

One of the little girls, a mere mite who seemed to have prematurely taken upon herself some charge of the others, stepped out of her place by me, and danced to and from the baby until it left off crying, and laughed. Then, all the children laughed, and Mr. Pocket (who in the meantime had twice endeavored to lift himself up by the hair) laughed, and we all laughed and were glad.

Despite the fact that in the above passage the characters' laughter may have some impact upon the reader's reaction to the scene, we may not know whether to laugh, cry, or merely feel shocked after playing audience to the above occurrences. Clearly, Dickens is placing us in the same uncomfortable situation as Pip. However, there may be other reasons for Dickens' use of comic irony here. At this point in the novel, Pip and the reader have been introduced to two middle- or upper-class families or households: the Pockets and Miss

Havisham's home. How do we relate these two family settings to Pip's own family (Joe, Mrs. Joe, and Biddy), and is this above passage merely a farce on the upper-class household, or is it indicative of something more?

Mrs. Pocket's treatment of her baby and her reactions to her children in the above passage expose her as the incompetent mother and the self-important upper-class lady. Nevertheless, her character seems to fit into a whole slew of characters who are dysfunctional within their settings or roles. How do we juxtapose such characters with a man like Joe who seems to be both aware of and competent in his station in life? Do characters such as Joe or Biddy become the moral markers within the novel, and if so is their moral superiority due to their satisfaction with their appointed place?

A certain hierarchy of power is comically inverted in the above passage and in general throughout chapter twenty-three. Here, the young Jane is described as "taking charge" of both her siblings and her parents, and earlier in the chapter Pip states. "Both Mr. and Mrs. Pocket had such a noticeable air of being in someone else's hands, that I wondered who really was in possession of the house and let them live there, until I found this unknown power to be the servants." This comment seems to act as a direct attack on the upper-classes. However, if it is Pip who is judging the Pockets or noting this class irony, then he does not seem to heed his own warnings or observations. Who is truly speaking here? Is it Pip or Dickens or both?

Finally, the entrance of the children in the above paragraphs becomes something of a burlesque or a comical parade. Both the servants and the mother seem to be focused on the appearance of the children and it is their external qualities which are meant to give them a noble or sagacious air. Of course, nothing about the children (think of Jane's dance) or the negligent parents really seems regal. This scene, perhaps, fits right into Dickens overall commentary about superficiality or appearances in the novel, and how it is not necessarily the dress which makes the man, so to speak. Pip, if it is Pip here who is truly speaking, seems to notice this irony in this passage.

Nevertheless, he once again fails to relate these realizations to himself. How does Pip's preoccupation with dress reveal his own moral deficiencies or immaturities, and does Pip's ability to see in others what he cannot see in himself attribute to some of the comic-ironic tone apparent in the above passage?

Q. Critically analyse the character of Miss Havisham.

One of the strangest and most memorable characters in fiction, Miss Havisham's tragic story leads to her tragic life. But does she have a reason to feel sorry for herself? What is her function in the novel? All that and more: Miss Havisham hates men, and that causes her to live alone and never love anyone. Because she was hurt once, she can never love again. She never wants to see visitors, and she only uses the people she does see. Her relatives are not allowed to see her ever, except once a year or so. And only little girls that she uses to make her revenge plan and little boys that she uses to teach them. I will try to find some quotes, but Herbert describes her as a lifelong recluse, and Pip can tell that from when he first sees her. When she asks him (and the world in general) to forgive her, I think that is important. Her effect on people is quite clear- especially the effect she has on Herbert, Estella, and Pip. She sets the course of the novel by giving Pip Estella.

How she used Pip?

She needed someone to train Estella to break hearts. She was using Estella to get her revenge on men, and Pip was her toy. She trained Estella to tease and be hard and harsh while flaunting her beauty. She man Pip love Estella when she was never meant for him, as Pip was only a lab rat.

Childhood

Her unhappiness stems from her experience with Compeyson later in life. She did have a rotten half brother, and from his story we do get an idea of what her childhood must have been like. Arthur was Miss Havisham's father's son with the cook.

Q. In what ways does Miss Havisham changes?

In many ways Miss Havisham does change. In the beginning of the boot she is hellbent on revenge, because she was jilted on her wedding day by Compeyson. She takes little girls and makes sure that they have no heart, and then trains them to break the hearts of little boys. Miss Havisham does eventually realise what she has done to Estella. When she understands that it was as bad as what was done to her, she starts asking for forgiveness. She asks Pip and Estella to forgive her. She is dumbfounded and destroyed, beyond the point of repair, and she just kind of fades away.

The Complexity of her story- Miss Havisham and Magwitch

Magwitch was married to Molly and they had a daughter. Molly killed a woman (strangled her with her bare hands) and Jaggers managed to get her acquitted but then took her to be his housekeeper, and sent her daughter, Estella, to live with Miss Havisham. Magwitch had to go into hiding and lost track of his daughter. He caught up with Compeyson, a career criminal who had been responsible for scamming Miss Havisham with her brother Arthur, leaving her on their wedding day. Magwitch never knew that his daughter was living with Compeyson's ex-fiance. Compeyson set him up to take the fall for their illegal activities, smoothtalking the jury into believing that he- a gentleman- could never do it. Magwitch was then deported, but he escaped from the prison ship in the marsh and ran into Pip, scaring him into bringing him food and help. He owned up to stealing the supplies so that Pip would not be blamed, and he was sent to Australia. There he made a successful career as a sheep farmer and sent his money to Jaggers to give to Pip, not wanting Pip to know where the money came from. However he grew lonely, and had to return in disguise to see his dear boy as a gentleman. Compeyson learned that he was in London and followed him, hoping to tip the police off. He did that, and they all followed Pip, Herbert and Magwitch's boat on the river as they attempted to escape. Compeyson attacked Magwitch and both men fell overboard, Compeyson was drowned. Magwitch was tried for returning to England and he was sentenced to death, and his fortune was usurped by the crown. He died next to Pip before he could be executed, for the injuries sustained while fighting with Magwitchapter

Q. Pen down the quotes that describe Miss Havisham character.

A Recluse, Trapped In Time

"Miss Havisham is described as a recluse, and a somewhat crazy old lady. "She was dressed in rich materials- satins, and lace, and silks- all of white. Her shoes were white. And she had a long white veil dependent from her hair, but her hair was white... I saw that everything within my view which ought to be white, had been white long ago, and had lost its lustre, and was faded and yellow. I saw that the bride within the bridal dress had withered like the dress, and like the flowers, and had no brightness left but the brightness of her sunken eyes. I saw that the dress had been put upon the rounded figure of a young woman, and that the figure upon which it now hung loose, had shrunk to skin and bone." (Chapter 8)

Wants Revenge Against All Men

"Also, when we played at cards Miss Havisham would look on, with a miserly relish of Estella's moods, whatever they were. And sometimes, when her moods were so many and so contradictory of one another that I was puzzled what to say or do, Miss Havisham would embrace her with lavish fondness, murmuring something in her ear that sounded like, "Break their hearts my pride and hope, break their hearts and have no mercy!" (Chapter 12)

Joe Gargery

Q. Who is Joe Gargery? What is the importance of his character? How come he is the only friend of Pip?

Joe as an Important Character

Joe derives his strength by NOT changing throughout the novel. He is one of the only constants in the book, which is what makes him important as a character. In the beginning of the story, Joe is brought up "by hand" by Mrs. Joe, Pip's sister Georgiana. He is a simple, but kind and loving man who protects Pip in his heart if not physically. He is Pip's brother by marriage even though he is old enough to be his father. He is kind, sweet, simple, honest, good and caring. He allows Pip to go to London because he assumes it is the best thing for him. This is the same reason why he lets him to go to Miss Havisham's and lets her apprentice Pip to himself.

When Joe visits Pip in London, Pip treats him horribly. Pip does not understand beyond a barrel of oysters how important Joe is to his life. He is embarrassed to show him to his friends, and he really hurts his feelings. Pip is trying to leave everything behind to become something he is not. Joe understands this, and leaves him to realise his wrongs. He treats him with respect and calls his "sir", realizing that he has been raised beyond his old station in life. This kind of treatment makes Pip feel bad, realizing that in raising himself he has lowered Joe.

When Pip loses everything and becomes sick, Joe is there at his side without question. he helps him through it all despite everything. Joe does not care that Pip is no longer a rich gentleman. He does not care that Pip's benefactor was a convict. All that he knows is that Pip is sick and needs someone, so he is there.

Joe remains strong when his wife is injured and then dies. He protects her and helps her through it with the kind of unconditional love that only he displays throughout the novel. Biddy helps him through it, of course, and afterwards he marries her- which is what Georgiana would have wanted.

Joe's Family

Pip's sister wishes he had never been born and treats him accordingly, raising him "by hand" which means routinely beating him with a cane called "Tickler". She also hits her husband and abuses him. Joe is unable to help Pip, and although he is sweet and good he is also simple.

Pip and Joe's Relationship

Their relationship is interesting. Because Joe is Pip's sister's husband, he is more of a brother than a father figure. At the same time, he cannot protect Pip from his wife. He is even a little below Pip's level academically. Pip is ashamed of him somewhat. Later, he realises that he was wrong, and tries to reconcile.

Joe in London

This is important, because when Pip feels guilty he regrets what he has become, and he has a moment of awakening. Here he is, a wealthy "gentleman" with no care in the world, and this sweet old man who helped raise him and protect him has come all the way to see how he is, and he is ashamed to see him! Shame on Pip for treating him that way! Pip realises this of course, and when he is sick and Joe cares for him he has a new appreciation for the poor guy.

Quotes

"Joe was a fair man, with curls of flaxen hair on each side of his smooth face, and with eyes of such a very undecided blue that they seemed to have somehow got mixed with their own whites. He was a mild, good-natured, sweet-tempered, easy-going, foolish, dear fellow — a sort of Hercules in strength, and also in weakness."

"Pip, dear old chap, life is made of ever so many partings welded together, as I may say, and one man's a blacksmith, and one's a whitesmith, and one's a goldsmith, and one's a coppersmith. Diwisions among such must come, and must be met as they come. If there's been any fault at all to-day, it's mine. You and me is not two figures to be together in London; nor yet anywheres else but what is private, and beknown, and understood among friends.

It ain't that I am proud, but that I want to be right, as you shall never see me no more in these clothes. I'm wrong in these clothes. I'm wrong out of the forge, the kitchen, or off th' meshes. You won't find half so much fault in me if you think of me in my forge dress, with my hammer in my hand, or even my pipe. You won't find half so much fault in me if, supposing as you should ever wish to see me, you come and put your head in at the forge window and see Joe the blacksmith, there, at the old anvil, in the old burnt apron, sticking to the old work. I'm awful dull, but I hope I've beat out something nigh the rights of this at last. And so GOD bless you, dear old Pip, old chap, GOD bless you!"

"I had neither the good sense nor the good feeling to know that this was all my fault, and that if I had been easier with Joe, Joe would have been easier with me. I felt impatient of him and out of temper with him; in which condition he heaped coals of fire on my head."

MRS. JOE (GEORGIANA)

Q. Who is Mrs. Joe? Why is she shown as a cruel woman? What is the importance of her role in the novel?

Notes on Mrs. Joe

Mrs. Joe is a cruel and witchy woman. She regrets that Pip lived when all of her other siblings died, and she treats him accordingly, having been charged with his care. She beats Pip with "Tickler" and does not treat her husband very well either. Given that, however, she does not get what she deserves. She is attacked by Orlick and her head injuries are so bad that she never recovers and then dies.

Quotes

HOUSEKEEPING

"Mrs. Joe was a very clean housekeeper, but had an exquisite art of making her cleanliness more uncomfortable and unacceptable than dirt itself." "Some medical beast had revived tar-water in those days as a fine medicine and Mrs. Joe always kept a supply of it in the cupboard; having a belief in its virtues correspondent to its nastiness. At the best of times, so much of this elixir was administered to me as a choice restorative that I was conscious of going about, smelling like a new fence."

OPINION OF PIP

"I was always treated as if I had insisted on being born, in opposition to the dictates of reason, religion, and morality, and against the dissuading arguments of my best friends".

"Drat that boy," interposed my sister, frowning at me over her work, "what a questioner he is. Ask no questions, and you'll be told no lies."

CHILD-REARING PRACTICES

"My sister, Mrs Joe Gargery, was more than twenty years older than I, and had established a great reputation with herself and the neighbours because she had brought me up `by hand`. Having at that time to find out for myself what the expression meant, and knowing her to have a hard and heavy hand, and to be much in the habit of laying it upon her husband as well as upon me, I supposed that Joe Gargery and I were both brought up by hand. She was not a good-looking woman, my sister; and I had a general impression that she must have made Joe Gargery marry her by hand."

DOLGE ORLICK

Q. Who is Orlick? Why does he hate Pip so much? Who did he kill and why? What is his importance to the novel?

Orlick is Joe Gargery's journeyman blacksmith. He has a grudge against Mrs. Joe and attempts but fails to kill her. With Compeyson, he plots to murder Pip by drawing him to the limekiln, but his plan is foiled by Pip's friends.

Orlick's Character

Orlick did have some bad luck, and did not entirely escape justice. Orlick does go to jail, but for assaulting Pumblechook not for the other stuff he was involved in. Pip does get him dismissed from Miss Havisham, after all. When he attempted to kill Pip he was really just doing Compeyson's bidding. It is true that nothing ever happens to him, and he never gets caught for aiding and abetting or attempted murder.

Most of the stuff that Orlick does at the end is actually at Compeyson's bidding. Compeyson is a sly, smooth-talking crook who could just as easily have talked Orlick into doing things for him as he did Compeyson. Orlick hated Joe and his wife because he felt treated poorly by them, and he hated Pip for getting him dismissed from his position with Miss Havisham. Clearly, Orlick was involved in criminal activities and should have been punished. While Compeyson was drowned, Orlick seems to have gotten away. Whether we should sympathize with him because he had a hard life is not clear, because he definitely has murderous intentions.

Orlick's Revenge

Orlick attempts to get revenge on both Mrs. Joe and Pip. He cannot get revenge on Pip, because Pip has done nothing wrong to him. Pip also has friends that rescue him. He cannot even kill Mrs. Joe correctly, as she lives the attack as a vegetable. Basically, you know how well Mrs. Joe treated Pip- not very well. She beat Pip, she beat Joe, she might as well have beaten Orlick. At any rate, he felt that he was mistreated by her- he is a very unstable person, did you notice? His hatred of Pip is partly provoked by this, partly by his dismissal from Miss Havisham and partly by his joining Miss Havisham.

Orlick's Role

If you want to look at this from the point of the writer, Orlick is like Pip's alter-ego. He is there during Pip's worst moments, and in this way we can think of Orlick's role in the novel as Pip's wake-up call.

Quotes

Mrs. Joe describes him as a "great idle hulker"

"He pretended that his Christian name was Dolge — a clear impossibility — but he was a fellow of that obstinate disposition that I believe him to have been the prey of no delusion in this particular, but wilfully to have imposed that name upon the village as an affront to its understanding. He was a broad- shouldered loose-limbed swarthy fellow of great strength, never in a hurry, and always slouching. He never seemed to come to his work on purpose, but would slouch in as if by mere accident. And when he went to the Jolly Bargemen to eat his dinner, or went away at night, he would slouch out, like Cain or the Wandering Jew as if he had no idea where he was going and no intention of ever coming back."

"He always slouched, locomotive, with his eyes on the ground; and, when accosted or otherwise required to raise them, he looked up in a half resentful, half puzzled way, as though the only thought he ever had, was, that it was rather an odd and injurious fact that he should never be thinking."

"I suppose he was about five-and-twenty, but he usually spoke of himself as an ancient person."

Q. Why Orlick found the need to revenge Pip?

"Old Orlick felt that the situation admitted of nothing less than coming on, and was on his defence straightway; so, without so much as pulling off their singed and burnt aprons, they went at one another, like two giants. But, if any man in that neighborhood could stand up long against Joe, I never saw the man. Orlick, as if he had been of no more account than the pale young gentleman, was very soon among the coal-dust, and in no hurry to come out of it."

The attack on Mrs. Joe- who was it?

'The house seems to have been violently entered when

Joe Gargery was out. Supposed by con- victs. Somebody has been attacked and hurt.'

Biddy: "Don't you see? It's him.! Orlick, without a doubt!"

He explains as he attempts to kill Pip

'I come upon her from behind, as I come upon you to-night. I giv' it her! I left her for dead, and if there had been a limekiln as nigh her as there is now nigh you, she shouldn't have come to life again. But it warn't Old Orlick as did it; it was you. You was favoured, and he was bullied and beat. Old Orlick bullied and beat, eh? Now you pays for it. You done it; now you pays for it.' "Somehow or another I'll have him!"

Abel Magwitch

Q. Who is Abel Magwitch? What is his role in the novel? Who was he sent by to horrify Pip? Describe his complicated yet significant life.

Abel Magwitch is the convict who frightened Pip as a boy in the first chapter of this book. He was deported and made a fortune in Australia that he secretly sent to Pip through Jaggers. Pip wants to help him because he feels obligated, given that Magwitch is his benefactor. Magwitch's story is long and complicated.

Magwitch's Complicated Life

Magwitch was married to Molly and they had a daughter. Molly killed a woman (strangled her with her bare hands) and Jaggers managed to get her acquitted but then took her to be his housekeeper, and sent her daughter, Estella, to live with Miss Havisham. Magwitch had to go into hiding and lost track of his daughter. He caught up with Compeyson, a career criminal who had been responsible for scamming Miss Havisham with her brother Arthur, leaving her on their wedding day. Magwitch never knew that his daughter was living with Compeyson's ex-fiancé. Compeyson set him up to take the fall for their illegal activities, smooth-talking the jury into believing that he- a gentleman- could never do it. Magwitch was then deported, but he escaped from the prison ship in the marsh and ran into Pip, scaring him into bringing him food and help. He owned up to stealing the supplies so that Pip would not be blamed, and he was sent to Australia.

There he made a successful career as a sheep farmer and sent his money to Jaggers to give to Pip, not wanting Pip to know where the money came from. However, he grew lonely, and had to return in disguise to see his dear boy as a gentleman. Compeyson learned that he was in London and followed him, hoping to tip the police off. He did that, and they all followed Pip, Herbert and Magwitch's boat on the river as they attempted to escape. Compeyson attacked Magwitch and both men fell overboard, Compeyson was drowned. Magwitch was tried for returning to England and he was sentenced to death, and his fortune was usurped by the crown. He died next to Pip before he could be executed, for the injuries sustained while fighting with Magwitchapter

Magwitch's Capture

Pip and Herbert hired a boat to sneak Magwitch out of the country. They were going to meet a steamer at the ocean. Compeyson was following them, and called the police. While the police in a boat and Compeyson in a boat chased Pip and Herbert and Magwitch, Compeyson and Magwitch got into a tussle, and fell into the water. Compeyson drowned, Magwitch was captured and that was that. There was a trial, at which Magwitch was condemned to death. All of his money was usurped by the crown, leaving Pip broke and in debt. Magwitch died in Pip's arms before he could be hung. He explained his story to Pip, and Pip realised that he had a daughter and that daughter was Estella. Pip told Magwitch before he died that his daughter was well and richapter Magwitch died as happy as could be expected.

Pip's obligation to Magwitch

Pip expects Magwitch to want him to become a gentleman. Pip regrets what he has done in wasting away the money he was given when he sees how hard Magwitch has worked. Technically, Pip owes Magwitch nothing because he is pleased when he sees that Pip is well, is surrounded by luxury, has wealthy friends, and seems happy. Pip does not tell him how he has spent the years away, not wanting to disappoint him.

It is your opinion whether or not you think Pip owed Magwitch enough to hide him and then sneak him out of the country. He could have turned him away. But because of the experiences he did have, he learned how to be a better person and would have never done that. Pip is obliged in some ways to care for Magwitch, to help him, to refrain from hurting him (by not telling him what he has become) and to look after him like a father when he lies dying in the hospital and try to make his final time happy (by telling him about Estella).

Magwitch does return, and expects Pip to take him in. Pip does not know who the money is from, obviously, but when he finds out he realises that he has not fulfilled his obligation, even though he did not know he had one -if that makes sense- and feels bad about it. He does try to make it up to him. Whether Pip likes it or not, or even if he does not realise it, Magwitch has taken on the role of a second father in his life, and he should be grateful.

Magwitch as a Catalyst for Pip's Growth

This is a good way to describe it. Magwitch comes into Pip's life when he is young and immature. At this stage, they are at similar levels of development. Pip is just a scared little boy, and Magwitch is just a rough outlaw. Both are not as developed as they could be. However, when Magwitch gives Pip the money, Pip goes to London and grows up. There, he becomes a gentleman and is no longer a scared little kid. Given Joe's maturity level, it can be determined that there is little hope for Pip's growth if he were to remain in his present life. However because Magwitch removes him from it, he has a chance to grow.

I am not implying that Pip's condition in London is that of a mature, grown man- far from it. But when Magwitch returns, he shocks Pip into realizing that he has been living a lie. He will never marry Estella, and Miss Havisham never intended to advance him. With this realization, and the loss of the money when Magwitch is caught, Pip stops living on borrowed time and returns to an honest life in a counting house- more a gentleman than he ever was when he had all the money he ever needed.

Due to Magwitch's generosity, Pip has his wish granted. Due to Magwitch's sentimentality, Pip has all that was granted taken away. He realises that if all he ever really wished for had come true, and it had not made him a better person, there must be more to life than money and social status.

Q. Describe the similarities between Joe and Magwitch

Joe and Magwitch were both instrumental in raising Pip. Joe protected and educated him as a child, Magwitch gave him the opportunity to grow up and become something. Both men are kind and generous, but also simple and uneducated. Pip is ashamed of both of them because he does not see that they fit into the new life he has created- he is above them. Yet both men forgive him when he hurts them and love him despite his faults.

Quotations

Magwitch's first appearance

"The man, after looking at me for a moment, turned me upside down, and emptied my pockets. There was nothing in them but a piece of bread."

Magwitch and Compeyson

The following quotation summarizes why Magwitch hated Compeyson:

"... And when it come to character, warn't it Compeyson as had been to the school, and warn't it his schoolfellows as was in this position and in that, and warn't it him as had been know'd by witnesses in such clubs and societies, and nowt to his disadvantage? And warn't it me as had been tried afore, and as had been know'd up hill and down dale in Bridewells and Lock-Ups? And when it come to speech-making, warn't it Compeyson as could speak to 'em wi' his face dropping every now and then into his white pocket-handkercher - ah! and wi' verses in his speech, too - and warn't it me as could only say, 'Gentlemen, this man at my side is a most precious rascal'? And when the verdict come, warn't it Compeyson as was recommended to mercy on account of good character and bad company, and giving up all the information he could agen me, and warn't it me as got never a word but Guilty?... "

JAGGERS' HANDS

You caught on to a very important symbol- Jaggers attempts to get "uninvolved" even when he IS.

"My guardian was in his room, washing his hands with his scented soap" "he would wash his hands, and wipe them and dry them all over this towel, whenever he came in from a police-court or dismissed a client from his room. When I and my friends repaired to him at six o'clock next day, he seemed to have been engaged on a case of a darker complexion than usual, for, we found him with his head butted into this closet, not only washing his hands, but laving his face and gargling his throat"

"I found him in his dressing-room surrounded by his stock of boots, already hard at it, washing his hands of us." (chapter 26)

"What I suffered from, was the incompatibility between his cold presence and my feelings towards Estella. It was not that I knew I could never bear to speak to him about her, that I knew I could never bear to hear him creak his boots at her, that I knew I could never bear to see him wash his hands of her; it was, that my admiration should be within a foot or two of him— it was, that my feelings should be in the same place with him — that, was the agonizing circumstance" (chapter 29)

"As a necessary sequence, I asked him if he would favour us with his company, and he promptly accepted the invitation. But he insisted on walking home with me, in order that I might make no extra preparation for him, and first he had a letter or two to write, and (of course) had his hands to wash." (chapter 36)

Q. Briefly explain the implicit conflict in the novel Great Expectations.

Or

Q. Does it differ with different characters?

There are internal conflicts in which characters battle with their own motivations and desires. They have conflicting needs or choices. Pip's first internal conflict stems from a very real external threat- he must choose whether to help the convict or not. Later, Pip faces the conflicts of lying, which manifests itself in his guilt. This continues and strengthens later in the story when he lies to his family about what goes on at Miss Havisham's house. Throughout the novel, Pip's greatest internal conflict continues to be guilt over some choice he makes. Ultimately, his guilt over choosing to take Magwitch's money without knowing where it came from leads him to realise that he had been selfish and cruel to someone who helped him. It took a great internal struggle that lasts for most of the novel for Pip to realise that he had to do the right thing.

Pip's struggle to learn right from wrong begins early. He is conflicted over his choices to lie and steal and his motivations, which are pure. Like most children, Pip has to learn the fine line between which of society's rules to accept. He makes the choice again when he breaks the law to sneak Magwitch out of the country. Pip does not always make moral choices. He takes money from an unknown benefactor (which may or may not be immoral) and then spurns the benefactor when he reveals himself. He lives a lifestyle that breeds corruption, and he corrupts others including honest Herbert while allowing himself to be corrupted. It is at this point that he gets into debt and denounces his family, especially Joe, out of shame.

Pip has an even greater internal conflict with love. He must decide whether or not he truly loves Estella. He cannot stand her, yet he cannot be away from her. Though she is clearly bad for him and, as she tells him, has no heart to give him, he is in love. Much of his internal pain comes from her presence, her spurning of him and his longing for her.

Pip experiences external conflicts with other characters and with society. He struggles with his sister, who physically and mentally abuses him, but he really does not care for her and she does not dramatically affect him. Most of his struggles are with Joe, whom he loves and cares for but is ashamed of because of his status. Pip feels a sense of entitlement once he gets money, and he pushes humble Joe away. Later, when Joe saves him and comforts him in his illness, he regrets the way he treated Joe. When he returns, fallen, and wants to marry Biddy he finds himself humbled when he learns Joe already has her. Here the secret rivalry with Joe, who is essentially Pip's brother (his brother-in-law actually), manifests itself to Pip. Pip also struggles with Biddy, because he does not want to accept her advice. He considers her sweet and good, but beneath him. When his own idea of his social role is reduced he returns to marry Biddy, but she has already married Joe.

Pip struggles with Estella throughout the book. She tells him as a child that he is plain and simple, coarse. She belittles everything from his boots to his vocabulary and treats him like a dog. Pip realises that she is this way because Miss Havisham is teaching her, but he cannot draw himself away. He believes that she is his betrothed, and in fact is led by Miss Havisham to think so. As she grows older, Estella pushes away more and more. She explains to him one day when he asks if she remembers their childhood:

'You must know,' said Estella, condescending to me as a brilliant and beautiful woman might, 'that I have no heart — if that has anything to do with my memory.' (chapter 29)

Estella continues to taunt him as she tries for her own gains. She marries Drummle, a rival of Pip's (Pip's external conflicts with Drummle are secondary in the novel). Later, after he has died, she says that she will raise her child alone. In one version of the ending, she may marry Pip, but it would be a loveless marriage. Miss Havisham is Pip's nemesis. She has had her heart broken (by Compeyson, Magwithch's former partner) and seeks to raise young girls so that theirs may not break also. To do this, she teaches them to break hearts instead. At a very young age, she goes for Pip's:"' What do I touch?' `Your heart.' `Broken!' She uttered the word with an eager look, and with strong emphasis, and with a weird smile that had a kind of boast in it." (chapter 9)

Later, Miss Havisham regrets what she has done to Estella. As she explains to Pip: "But as she grew, and promised to be very beautiful, I gradually did worse, and with my praises, and with my jewels, and with my teachings, and with this figure of myself always before her a warning to back and point my lessons, I stole her heart away and put ice in its place.' `Better,' I could not help saying, `to have left her a natural heart, even to be bruised or broken.' (chapter 29).

From the first chapter, Pip has a conflict with Magwitchapter He is afraid of him when he first meets him.

When he learns that he has been taking his money, he is repulsed. When he learns of Magwitch's life, and how he has been ill used he softens. He helps Magwitch try to escape England and when they are caught and Magwitch is dying, he tells him that Estella is a fine, successful woman. Pip's conflict with Dolge Orlick cannot be forgotten. Orlick tries to flaunt him throughout the book and at one point tries to kill him.

Q. When Pip sees the "shadows" around Estella, is he seeing Miss Havisham's influence, or is it a second-sight type of thing? Why is there still no shadow in the original ending?

Among Dickens's short novels, a subdivision that ranges from *A Christmas Carol* (1843) to *Great Expectations* (1861), the word "shadow" and its cognates "shadows," "shadowy," "shadowed," and "shadowing" are most concentrated in the two Christmas Books, *The Haunted Man* and *A Christmas Carol*. The occurrence of this cluster of terms is much lower proportionately in *Great Expectations*, and yet several appearances of the word "shadow" in a figurative sense are extremely important. Like many other writers, Dickens often uses the word "shadow" and its variants to describe a literal interruption of light, particularly in phrases such as "When the shadows of evening were closing in" (*Great Expectations*, Chapter 35). He also uses "shadow" in a quasi-figurative or not-quite-literal sense in such expression as "the heavy shadow of Temple Bar" (*A Tale of Two Cities*, Book II, Chapter 1) since shadows have no weight, but this shadow is more ominous because it is associated with capital punishment. Finally, Dickens often uses "shadows" allegorically to imply memories, premonitions, or foreshadowings, as in Scrooge's question to the Spirit of Christmas Yet to Come: "Are these the shadows of things that Will be, or are they shadows of things that May be, only?" (*A Christmas Carol*, Stave III).

Exactly what is the sense, then, of the shadows that Pip sees around Estella? Is he seeing the influence of Miss Havisham (the past imposing itself upon the present), or is he having a premonition (seeing a projection of the present in the future)? The words "shadow" and "shadows" occur a total of fifteen times in *Great Expectations*, but only two of these occurrences involve Estella. While eleven of the fifteen occurrences of these words are literal, the instances associated with Estella are allegorical. The first is justly famous since it is part of a deliberate attempt to generate suspense at the very end of a chapter:... when I saw her face at the coach window and her hand waving to me. What was the nameless shadow which again in that one instant had passed? (Chapter 32)

Since at the beginning of the next chapter (still within the 13 April 1861 installment, and therefore not a serial "curtain") Pip comments that he "saw Miss Havisham's influence in the change" in Estella's manner towards him, many readers would be inclined to conclude that the "nameless shadow" implies an imprinting of Miss Havisham's personality upon Estella's. However, as the discussion of the two Richmonds reminds us, there are two fairy-godparents who cast their shadows upon their adopted children. The influence Pip detects may be Miss Havisham's, but the word"shadow" in the sense of "reflection," "phantom," or "copy" is pointing towards her natural parents, Molly, Jaggers' maid, and the convict on the marshes, Magwitch, for in Estella's face and hand he sees their reflections.

This recognition is not conscious, of course, since Pip the protagonist (not be confused with the Pip the narrator, who knows all even from the first) does learn the identity of benefactor until Chapter 39. Does not receive confirmation that Molly is Estella's mother until Chapter 48: "I thought how the same feeling had come back when I saw a face looking at me, and a hand waving to me, from a stage-coach window...." By the close of Chapter 50, Pip has pieced together the identity of Estella's parents. In a moment of epiphany, "like lightning" the knowledge has "flashed" upon him, dispelling the mysterious shadow that has hung about Estella. Thus, in Chapter 32 the word "shadow" is both obscuring darkness, dim recognition, and premonition of a truth to be revealed later. Since in dining with Jaggers at his Gerrard Street 26, his beginning to connect Molly and Estella in Chapter 32 is subconscious deduction on the part of the protagonist but conscious manipulation of the reader on the part of the narrator, for in that moment Pip is preparing us for the revelation of Estella's parentage, a mystery of importance equal to that of his benefactor's identity and motivations.

The "shadow" in Chapter 32 that Pip is trying to penetrate challenges conscious thought and temporarily defeats it. The "shadow" which has blocked the light of recognition is also a fleeting impression and a reflected image. The hand is the objective correlative that has prompted the (as yet) unconscious recognition, so that it constitutes a symbol, prefiguration, or foreshadowing. In that it connects present with past, the hand has momentarily summoned up a spectral form. Thus, like Ebenezer Scrooge in A Christmas Carol, Pip has connected "the shadows of things that have been" with "the shadows of things that Will be" revealed in time. "Readers of the novel may perceive Pip's inability to name this a shadow' as just one example of his struggle to understand the riddles of his past" and how these riddles will affect his romantic longings for Estella in the future.

However, that Pip in his capacity of narrator does not "name" the shadow in Chapter 32 is not a mark of ignorance but of guile; if the explosive truth of Estella's parentage is to flash like lightning upon us, we must be kept in a state of anticipation." Dickens uses a convention he perfected in serial fiction to engage reader interest and expectations, and to advance the plot" (Guiliano and Collins, II: 985). He leaves both his readers and his narrator in the dark in Chapter 32, although his narrator-protagonist is in fact withholding the truth from us, his readers, as it was so long withheld from him. The question which closes chapter 32 places us as readers in doubt and suspense for another nine chapters, and, in fact, is not fully answered until Jaggers puts the case' in Chapter 51. If we regard the deluded protagonist and deluding narrator as opaque rather than transparent, as manipulative and unreliable rather than wholly honest, then the "shadow" at the close of Chapter 32 is "The faint appearance of something seen through an obscuring medium" (*OED* IX: 591) such as a stage scrim, as well as a prefiguration and spectral form of past incidents that, if only apprehended, would confer present identities.

Part II

The second significant association of Estella and shadows occurs at the very close of Dickens's revised ending of the novel, the validity of which has been much debated by twentieth-century readers and critics. In the first or original ending, there is a carriage, Estella's face and hands — but no shadow. After all these years, despite Pip's failure to name the Shropshire doctor whom Estella has married (and thereby acknowledge that she has taken another man's name), everything seems perfectly clear — or should one say "prosaically" clear? There is nothing in the ending that Dickens read to Ellen Ternan and Bulwer-Lytton that connects either of the story's principal characters to the novel's Manichaean conflict between the forces of darkness (of retribution, ignorance, of willfulness, of self-interest, of class and gender exploitation, of Id-like Orlick and egotistical Drummle) and those of light (of spiritual and emotional resurrection, human sympathy, of justice, of compassion, of Jaggers' secret altruism, of Pip's love for those closest to him, of the developing superego that is Pip).

And the power that Dickens's novels continue to exert upon readers is that these stories sweep us up in this whirlwind struggle, then deposit those readers upon the moral high ground of a better world, a world where Uncle Scrooge can join in the party games at Nephew Fred's and restore Tiny Tim to health; where the children and children's children of Charles Darnay and Lucie Manette play in the light of freedom; where young Pip growing up under the loving guidance of Joe, Biddy, Uncle Pip, and Aunt Estella will not make the errors his namesake made; where Milly and the children, Tetterbys, and Swidgers join hands in a circle that encompasses not only England but all people in all times and places.

As Edgar Rosenberg and others have noted these last twenty years, there are in fact six endings, the first of which Dickens cancelled following the promptings of a fellow writer and the young woman who was his lover, and his own intuition as a populist writer. The remaining five, the textual history of Dickens's fine-tuning what he knew to be the right ending, all involve a resolution to the conflict of light and shadow. The walls of Satis House have been torn down, so there are no shadows in the desolate place at sunset, and no shadows as the post-lapsarian moon rises:

as the morning mists had risen long ago when I fist left the forge, so, the evening mists were rising now, and in all the broad expanse of tranquil light they show to me I saw.... (Chapter 59)

But precisely what Pip saw Dickens laboured over, like Leonardo with *The Mona Lisa*. In the serial, Dickens had written "the shadow of no parting, but one" and then cancelled "but one," realizing that there must be no more shadows between Pip and Estella if they have really escaped Miss Havisham's teachings and can approach each other upon an equality of intellect and sentiment. Dickens maintained this reading in the 1861 first volume edition, wishing to suggest, perhaps, that Pip "now realises that he, not some shadowy other, controls his actions, and [that] he can see Estella for who she is, not as the fiction of great expectations" (Thomson 95). Syntactically and logically, however, Pip does not see a shadow at all if "but one" does not conclude the sentence.

The shadow of death, "of another parting," is tantalizingly ambiguous here because Pip avoids "naming" it — or is he still the flawed, ignorant first-person narrator who cannot see it, though its shadow would be detectable to a superior consciousness? If Pip has really stepped into the light of self-knowledge and mutual understanding with Estella, no such ambiguity should exist. "Death may have its dominion over Pip and Estella, but is not to be mentioned here and now" (Rosenberg 94) — or rather, like the love of Eloise and Abelard or that of Romeo and Juliet, this love will utterly disavow Death's dominion.

Consequently, in the 1862 Library edition and the 1868 Charles Dickens edition, the line reads "no shadow of another parting from her" — a reading followed by all modern editions because it represents the novelist's final intention. If Pip sees "no shadow," Dickens is affirming that Pip has freed himself from the legacy of the past, of egotism, of the class system, so that he can see Estella as herself rather than extension of Miss Havisham or the scion of a convicted felon and a dubiously exonerated murderess. The emphatic, adjectival "no" before "shadow" may be indicative, as Rosenberg posits, of Dickens's effort "to stress the intensity of Pip's emotional response to someone not only capable of evoking but of deserving it" (97). However, when the Miltonic mists rose before, at the close of the "first stage" of Pip's Expectations, Pip was still in the dark of self-delusion as well of an ignorance imposed by others, so that the mists had only seemed to rise — who is to say that, after all, Pip is not still an unreliable narrator as he sees the mists rise again?

Q. Discuss the different endings of the novel.

Or

Q. Is the second ending appropriate or not?

I think that given the fact that Dickens intended for Pip and Estella to go their separate ways in the first place, the ending that you have described (where they are married) is inappropriate. There are several reasons for this. First of all, it is contradictory to the theme of the novel. Pip is supposed to realise that he was wrong in acting the way that he did toward those that loved him. He is supposed to return to an honest living and forget about the money. If he marries Estella, it is to close to a marriage for what he once had. He could have loved her genuinely, but I feel that Dickens intended for Pip to realise that he did not really love her but loved her money and her lifestyle. Estella also is to learn that she can be comfortable (if not happy) on her own, and because of what she has been through could likely never be happy in a mature relationship with Pip.

His love for her is pure childish fantasy, and she needs to take some time to herself until one day she can marry for love and not money (as she did with Drummle) or simplicity (as she would with Pip). Dickens changed the ending because a friend suggested that it might be better for his readers to accept- a readership that was reeling from the storybook ending of David Copperfield and the symbolically happy ending of his last book, A Tale of Two Cities.

Q. Is the second ending possible? Is the ending appropriate? What is the best ending?

I think the first ending is better because it is more believable, I think. It is also the one Dickens intended. You should see my post on the Oliver Twist Spark Note referring to this subject, because I included a quote from Dickens on why he chose to alter the ending. He claimed that his friend convinced him, and had good reasons for why Pip and Estella should be together. I would not state that the first ending is better just because it was Dickens' first choice, however, because he did change it.

I think that ending one is more believable because the whole premise of the book is that Pip and Estella cannot be happy together. Dickens spends the whole book talking about how she has no heart, how she leads him on, how she is miserable and marries for money- and then suddenly we are supposed to believe that she can change enough for them to live happily ever after together? If you ask me, ending #2 is just wishful thinking on Pip's part, and the marriage would probably end up like Paul and Edith's marriage in "Dombey and Son" (if you have not read that one, let me just tell you that it was NOT a happy marriage)! Pip is too immature regarding love, and regarding Estella, for their relationship to work. He grows up enough to realise that "they" will never be.

Another reason that the first ending is more believable is that Dickens does not give us any reason to even hope that Pip and Estella will be happy in their life together. He just sort of throws it suddenly at the reader without any real proof. Estella has just gotten out of a disastrous marriage, she has been hurt too many times, and she has a little daughter. She may be desperate, but is she that desperate?

You should note that there is another side to this argument. Estella is able to forget Miss Havisham's teachings. She does gain heart, and even in the original ending she shows affection for Pip combined with sorrow. She may have loved him all along, and have been actually hoping that whole time she was leading him to his ruin. It is also possible that Pip and Estella have been hurt so much by their hopelessly demented childhoods that neither of them will ever be able to love anyone else, and each other is all they will ever know. In this case, even if they do not live happily ever after, they will be together and that might mend some of the hurt of their childhood days.

You decide which argument you agree with most. You should also look at past messages, because this subject comes up A LOT! Look at the other pages to get some other viewpoints.

The Original Ending of Great Expectations

I was really surprised, because I looked at all of the online e-texts that I could find and none had the original ending! If you want to read it, try the version by Signet Publishing that's paperback, I am pretty sure it has it.

By the way, you were right about the carriage! For now, here is what I have: Here's why he changed it:

"You will be surprised," Dickens wrote to Forrester, "to hear that I have changed the end of Great Expectations from and after Pip's return to Joe's, and finding his little likeness there. Bulwer, who has been, as I think you know, extraordinarily taken by the book, so strongly urged it upon me, after reading the proofs, and supported his view with such good reasons, that I resolved to make the change...."

Here's what he changed:

There was no chapter 20, but the sentence which opens it ("For eleven years" altered to "eight years") followed the paragraph about his business partnership with Herbert and led to Biddy's question whether he is sure he does not fret for Estella ("I am sure and certain, Biddy" was altered to "O no- I think not Biddy". After that, this was the closing statement:

"It was two years more, before I saw herself. I had heard of her as leading a most unhappy life, and as being separated from her husband who had used her with great cruelty, and who had become quite renowned as a compound of pride, brutality and meanness. I had heard of the death of her husband (from an accident consequent of ill-treating a horse), and of her being again the Shropshire doctor, who, against her interest had once very manfully interposed, on an occasion when he was in professional attendance on Mr. Drummle, and had witnessed some outrageous treatment of her. I had heard that the Shropshire doctor was not rich, and they lived on her own personal fortune. I was in England again- in London, and walking along Piccadilly with little Pip- when a servant came running after me to ask would I step back to a lady in a carriage who wished to speak to me. It was a little pony carriage, which the lady was driving; and the lady and I looked sadly enough on one another. "I am greatly changed, I know; but I thought you would like to shake hands with Estella too, Pip. Lift up that pretty child and let me kiss it!" (She supposed the child, I think, to be my child). I was very glad afterwards to have such an interview; for, in her face and in her voice, and in her touch, she gave me the assurance, that suffering had been stronger than Miss Havisham's teaching, and had given her a heart to understand what my heart used to be."

Chapter 15

Further Study Questions

Stage I of Pip's Expectations: Chapter I to IX

Chapter 1

- How does Dickens use setting to convey the mood right at the opening?
- What does Dickens' description of the first convict tell us about him?
- What is surprising about the narrative point-of- view Dickens has adopted?
- How does Dickens contrast the convict and Pip?
- But in what ways are these two characters similar?
- What objects does the convict want brought to him?
- What personal circumstance of Pip's is convenient for the convict?*

Note: This is the first coincidence of a plot that comes to depend on coincidences.

Vocabulary: "wittles" = vittles (food); "battery" = gun enplacement, in this case probably dating from the Napoleonic Wars, which ended at Waterloo in 1815.

Chapter 2

- How does Dickens arouse our sympathies for certain characters?
- Why does Pip live with village blacksmith Joe Gargery?
- What is the nature of the relationship between these two characters?

- What object that Pip takes the convict makes him feel guilty and nearly gets him discovered?

Vocabulary: "bolting" = swallowing without properly chewing (probably an indication of Pip's apprehensiveness at the dinner table); "hulks" = former naval vessels now being used as temporary prisons.

[The first installment (1 Dec. 1860) ended here.]

Chapter 3

- What is surprising about the attitude of the two convicts towards one another?
- What object in this chapter leads to a real mystery later on?

Vocabulary: "rimy" = frosty.

Chapter 4

Note Mr. Wopsle's self-righteous biblical allusion: "Swine were the companions of the prodigal" (see *Luke* XV:11-32).

- Explain the expression "like monumental Crusaders as to their legs."
- What special occasion is being celebrated and how?
- And yet why does Pip feel apprehensive and miserable?

Vocabulary: "penitentials" = possibly a reference to prison uniform; also, clothing worn as a sign of repentance or sorrow for sin; "banns" = announcement of impending marriage made in church; "thrown open" = Wopsle is ineligible for the post of clergyman in the Church of England because he is not a university graduate — the profession has not been made accessible to members of the lower classes.

[The second installment (8 Dec., 1860) ended here: is Pip about to be arrested?]

Chapter 5

- How was the suspense of the previous chapter explained? (Note the effect of the serialized format on the novel's structure; this sustaining of suspense from the end of one installment through the beginning of the next involved careful plotting to coincide with the closing and opening of "curtains.")

- How did the first convict show his appreciation for Pip's loyalty at this point?
- What apparently is the cause of the hostility between the two convicts?
- Explain: "like a wicked Noah's ark" at the very end of the chapter.

[The third installment (15 Dec., 1860) ended here.]

Chapter 6

- Who is Pumblechook, and how does he get Pip into Satis House?

Chapter 7

"I was to be apprenticed to Joe"—a seven-year apprenticeship was the usual way of entering a trade.

- How does Dickens satirize public education in this chapter?
- Note that Pip describes his alphabet as "a bramble bush" and his fingers as "thieves"; how do these references contribute to the book's imagery?
- Explain: "steam was yet in its infancy" (most British cities were connected by railways in 1860).
- What is implied about England's government when Dickens has Joe tell Pip that Mrs. Joe, being given to government, does not want him to be able to read and write?

[The fourth installment (22 December 1860) ended here.]

Chapter 8

- Note the connection between the vegetation and the prison imagery in the descriptions of both Pumblechook's shop and Miss Havisham's house; how is Pip's very name involved in this imagery?
- Note the description of Satis (Latin, meaning "enough' or plenty" as in satisfaction) House: "old brick, and dismal and had a great many bars to it."

What other type of building does the derelict mansion seem to resemble?

- Miss Havisham behaves like an aristocrat; by ________, however, her father made his fortune, which passed to her.
- What does Miss Havisham's appearance remind Pip of? How is this analogy apt?
- What about Pip does Estella criticize?
- What does his reaction to her criticism tell us about Pip?
- The key image for English society of the nineteenth century is the "rank garden with an old wall". God started our world, Dickens seems to say, as a paradise (The Garden of ________), but sinful and careless men have made a "rank garden" of it. Once again, the "old wall" suggests a prison. Early nineteenth-century Britain had so many prisoners that there weren't prisons enough to hold them. Hence there are improvised prisons, the "________" at the end of the "Meshes"; later, the convicts will be "transported" by prison ships to ________. Return means death.

[The fifth installment (29 December 1860) ended here.]

Chapter 9

- Why does Pip "embroider" his account of his visit to Satis House?
- Why do Pumblechook and Mrs. Joe believe this far-fetched account?
- Note the admonition to the reader at the very end of the chapter; how does this passage further connect the story's vegetation and the prison imagery?

Chapter 10

- How do we know the bank notes come from the convict?
- What does this incident with the bank notes indicate about Joe?

[The sixth installment (5 Jan., 1861) ended here.]

Chapter 11

- Why does Miss Havisham scorn her relatives?
- Explain how "toadies and humbugs" applies to the Pockets.
- What strange epergne does Pip see on the table? How does this object relate to Miss Havisham's dress?

[The seventh installment (12 Jan., 1861) ended here.]

Chapter 12

- What kind of punishment does Pip expect for striking the young gentleman?
- Instead, Miss Havisham rewards Pip later: how?

Chapter 13

- Why does Pip feel uncomfortable when he and Joe visit Satis House?
- Who takes most of the credit for Miss Havisham's generosity? Who takes the money?
- Explain: "I should never like Joe's trade. I had liked it once, but once was not now."

[The eighth installment (19 January 1861) ended here.]

Chapter 14

- What fear involving Estella "haunted" Pip now?
- Pip is ashamed of his home, and is unhappy there: why does not he run away?

Chapter 15

- Describe the two new characters introduced here and Pip's relationship with them.
- How does Joe get into a fight with Orlick?
- How does this fight become important later on?
- What becomes of Estella?
- Why does Pip identify himself with George Barnwell in George Lillo's play *The London Merchant*?

[The ninth installment (26 January 1861) ended here.]

Chapter 16

- Who is suspected of the crime committed here, and why?

- What does Dickens convey through Pip about the police?
- Whom does Biddy suspect of Mrs. Joe's assault, and why?

Chapter 17

- What additional reason does Pip now have for disliking Orlick?
- What is the relationship between Pip and Biddy now?
- What is the mental and emotional conflict Pip undergoes here?

[The tenth installment (2 February 1861) ended here.]

Chapter XVIII

- Where had Pip encountered the mysterious stranger before?
- What were the conditions upon which Pip would receive his "great expectations"?
- What reason does Pip have for thinking Jaggers is Miss Havisham's agent in terms of his suddenly receiving "great expectations"?
- Though he now is to have wealth and education, why is Pip discontented?

Chapter XIX

- Why have Trabb and Pumblechook changed their attitude towards Pip?
- What clue are we given as to Trabb's true character?
- Why does Miss Havisham fail to correct Pip when he thanks her for his fortune?
- Compare "and the mists had all solemnly risen now, and the world lay spread before me" with the conclusion of John Milton's *Paradise Lost*, an epic poem based on the opening of "The Book of Genesis" in the Bible:

The World was all before them, where to choose
Thir place of rest, and providence thir guide:
They hand-in-hand with wand'ring steps and slow,
Through Eden took thir solitary way.

This is the end of the first stage of Pip's Expectations and the end of the twelfth installment (16 February 1861).

Note on Symbolism: A literary symbol extends the meaning of a word or phrase beyond its usual literal or denotative meaning by bringing in its many associative or connotative meanings. How are the following Symbolic? Pip, Estella, Pocket, Hubble, meshes.

Stage II of Pip's Expectations

Chapter XX

- What kind of lawyer is Mr. Jaggers? (That is, what is specialty?)
- What is Pip's first impression of London?

Chapter XXI

- Who is Pip's room-mate? By coincidence, when did we meet him previously/
- Why does the selection of this young man as his companion confirm Pip's suspicions that Miss Havisham was his benefactor?

The thirteenth installment (23 Feb., 1861) ended here.

Chapter XXII

"Half-price to the theatre" — at an evening performance, after the first play, admission was reduced in most Victorian theatres.

- What does his new friend tell Pip about Miss Havisham's past?
- Why has she ordered Herbert's father out of her house?
- What is Herbert's occupation? What does "cut into the Direction" suggest about his goals?

[The fourteenth installment (2 March, 1861) ended ended here.]

Chapter XXIII

Mr. Pocket aspired to "the Woolsack" (the seat of the Lord Chancellor in the House of Lords) or the "mitre" (a bishop's hat).

- What is Herbert's father's chief fault? Why is he especially suitable to educate Pip?
- In what way are Mrs. Pocket and Pip alike?
- How do Drummle and Startop differ?

Vocabulary: "grinder" = private teacher or tutor of children of the rich; "blades" = fashionable young men; "baronet" = hereditary aristocratic title above the degree of knight, although both are addressed as "Sir" followed by Christian and surname.

Chapter XXIV

Note: The Old Bailey was London's criminal court.

- What kind of training is Mr. Pocket to give Pip?
- What earlier impressions of Jaggers are confirmed?
- What is Wemmick's highly pragmatic philosophy?

[The fifteenth installment (9 March, 1861) ended ended here.]

Chapter XXV

The Gothic Revival in architecture was at its height in the 1860s.

- What does Pip share with Herbert besides the Barnard's Inn Chambers and the home in Hammersmith?
- What other side of Wemmick does Pip find at his Walworth "Castle"?

Vocabulary: "Cracksmen" are housebreakers or burglars; "Britannia metal" is a cheap substitute for silver; "Walworth," now absorbed into Greater London, was still a village in the mid-nineteenth century; "Greenwich time" is the standard for British time, calculated from the meridian running through the Greenwich Observatory.

Chapter XXVI

The "Witches' cauldron" is a reference to the apparitions that rise from the Weird Sisters' cooking-pot in *Macbeth*, IV, i.

- What is Jaggers' warning to Pip concerning Drummle?
- What is mysterious about Molly?

[The sixteenth installment (16 March, 1861) ended ended here.]

Chapter XXVII

"I had made this monster" is a humorous allusion to Mary Shelley's 1818 Gothic novel *Frankenstein,* in which a young scientist creates a highly destructive and resentful monster.

- Why is Joe's visit not a success?
- Why does Joe come to London?
- Which play by Shakespeare is indicated by "the highest tragic walk of our National Bard"?

Vocabulary: "Roscian" = in the manner of Roscius, a famous actor in ancient Rome.

Chapter XXVIII

A "Half-way House" is a roadside inn that is the mid-point of a coach journey. Dickens may mean the Earl of Warwick at Welling, Kent.

- How is the convict theme re-introduced?
- *"Verb. Sap."* is a Latin abbreviation meaning "To a wise man, a word is enough." Why is this expression used here?
- Who is famous in his hometown as Pip's earliest companion, patron and friend? What is Pip's attitude to this supposed fact?

Vocabulary: "Lifer" = sentenced to prison or transportation to Australia for life; "Mentor" = the avuncular advisor of Prince Telemachus, son of the hero Odysseus, in the early books of Homer's *Odyssey*; "Quintin Matsys" = a Flemish painter (1466-1530) who was (supposedly) apprenticed to a blacksmith in his youth.

[The seventeenth installment (23 March, 1861) ended ended here.]

Chapter XXIX

"Tag and Rag and Bobtail"—a mob or rabble wearing ragged clothes.

- In what role does Pip see himself as he returned to Miss Havisham's?
- In his feelings for Estella, how does Pip come to follow Miss Havisham's teaching?

- Why does Pip not visit Joe?

[The eighteenth installment (30 March, 1861) ended ended here.]

Chapter XXX

- How did Pip "get even with" Orlick?
- How did Herbert's "love life" show a contrast with that of Pip?
- Why does Pip refer to the codfish and barrel of oysters he sends to Joe as "penitential"?
- Why does Herbert use the nick-name "Handel" for Pip?
- Why does Herbert accuse Pip of "looking into our gift-horse's mouth with a magnifying glass"?

Vocabulary: "sour grapes" is an allusion to a fable by the Greek Aesop (c. 620-c. 560 BC) in which a fox consoles himself for a crow's unwillingness to help him obtain a bunch of grapes. The term indicates Herbert's wide reading, and suggests that he feels Pip is deluding himself about being intended for Estella.

Chapter XXXI

- How does Pip's night at the theatre only increase his anxieties instead of easing them?

[The nineteenth installment (6 April, 1861) ended ended here.]

Chapter XXXII

- Why does Dickens include a picture of Newgate Prison?
- How does Estella appear to Pip in contrast to his visit to the prison?

Chapter XXXIII

- Why has Estella come to London? 2. Why is Pip so full of misery after seeing her?

Vocabulary: "Moses in the bulrushes" is certainly a humorous way of describing the small quantity of butter in relationship to the surrounding parsely. In the Old Testament, Pharaoh's daughter discovers the infant Moses in a basket by the margin of the Nile River (*Exodus* II: 3-6).

The twentieth installment (13 April, 1861) ended here.

Chapter XXXIV

- Why does Pip's life in London make things difficult for Herbert? 2. What Club did they join? What is the narrator's attitude towards this club?

Covent Garden = at the time, a disreputable part of London frequented at night by prostitutes.

Chapter XXXV

- How does Mrs. Joe's death affect Pip? 2. Why does her death not bring Pip and Joe any closer together?

Vocabulary: "Mummery" is suggestive of play-acting, namely that the Victorian mourning rituals accompanying Mrs. Joe's funeral are farcical.

[The twenty-first installment (20 April, 1861) ended ended here.]

Chapter XXXVI

- How do Pip's fortunes improve on his twenty-first birthday? 2. What does Pip still not find out?

Chapter XXXVII

- What plan does Wemmick propose for Pip's desire to help Herbert? 2. What humorous touch concerning Wemmick is shown?

[The twenty-second installment (27 April, 1861) endedended here.]

Chapter XXXVIII

- Why is Miss Havisham so pleased with Estella's behaviour?
- How does the success of Miss Havisham's teaching cause her grief? 3. What happened to cause Pip even more pain in his pursuit of Estella?

[The twenty-third installment (4 May, 1861) ended ended here.]

Chapter XXXIX

- Who is the strange visitor?
- Why has he come?
- What is Pip's reaction to this revelation
  a. In regard to himself?
  b. In regard to Estella?
  c. In regard to Joe?

Vocabulary: "A Game One" is a lively, eager, daring fellow; Magwitch pronounces "vermin" (a repulsive creature such as a rat) "warmint," indicating his low-class speechapter

[The twenty-fourth installment (11 May, 1861) ended ended here.]

Stage III of Pip's Expectations

Chapter XL

- What is the new problem that Pip faces?
- What is his frightful but rich patron's name?
- How does Pip's discussion with Jaggers disabuse him of the notion that Miss Havisham has been his patron?

Vocabulary: "I'm a heavy grubber" (voracious eater), admits Magwitchapter Fresh from his voyage from "New South Wales" (the British colony in Australia) or "Botany Bay" (the harbour of present-day Sydney, where transported convicts disembarked), he wears a pea coat" (a sailor's heavy blue woolen jacket). The "Calendar" to which Pip alludes is the infamous *Newgate Calendar* (1771) containing the biographies of notorious criminals. Finally, Pip compares himself to Mary Shelley's Victor Frankenstein, "the imaginary student pursued by the misshapen creature who made me" for he sees Magwitch in terms of both the creator and the persecutor in the 1818 novel.

[The twenty-fifth installment (18 May, 1861) ended ended here.]

Chapter XLI

- Upon his return, what solution does Herbert suggest?

Vocabulary: "muzzled" = restricted, confined, suggesting that Magwitch is trying to be "genteel" for the sake of Pip and Herbert.

Chapter XLII: "Magwitch's Story"

- What kind of life had Magwitch had as a child, and then as an adult?
- What do we learn of the cause of Magwitch's hatred for Compeyson (the second convict)?
- What do we learn about a certain "mad lady"?
- What was the result of Magwitch's assault on Compeyson after their escape from the prison ship?
- What details does Herbert add?

Vocabulary: "traveller's rest" = a tramps' shelter; "taturs" = potatoes; "Epsom" = famous racecourse; "dab" = expert; "the horrors" = violent fit of shaking caused by alcoholism; "Bridewells and Lock-ups" = prisons and jails (gaols).

[The twenty-sixth installment (25 May, 1861) ended here.]

Chapter XLIII

- What added danger do they now realise "Provis" to be in?

Chapter XLIV

- Why does Miss Havisham lead Pip on to believe she was his benefactress?
- What admission does Estella make to Pip?
- What is Pip's reply?

[The twenty-seventh installment (1 June, 1861) ended ended here.]

Chapter XLV

- Why is it necessary to move Magwitch?
- What does Wemmick advise Pip to get hold of?

Vocabulary: "Dover road" = road leading south to the port on the English Channel by which travellers made their way to France; "Divinely Righteous" = this satirical description of the four-post bedstead as a species of tyrant alludes to the doctrine of the Divine Right of Kings espoused by the Stuart monarchs in the 17th c.; "Argus" = monster from Greco-Roman myth that possessed a hundred eyes, and therefore was never completely sound asleep but always on watch; "shoot the bridge" = pass rapidly under the dangerous narrow arches of Old London Bridge in a small boat at ebb tide on the Thames.

Chapter XLVI

- Where is "Mr. Campbell" found by Pip?
- Why is Pip to obtain a boat?

Vocabulary: "Double Gloucester" = an orange- coloured cheese named after a city in the west of England; "Old London Bridge" was torn down in 1843 to make way for a new bridge, since transferred brick by brick to Havasu City, Colorado.

[The twenty-eighth installment (8 June, 1861) ended ended here.]

Chapter XLVII

- Why des Pip return Magwitch's unopened pocket book?
- Who sits behind Pip at the th:atre?

Vocabulary: "swab" = clumsy fellow; a term used by sailors to denigrate co-workers, originally pertaining to the labourer who mopped the ship's deck, from Dutch nautical term "zwabber."

Chapter XLVIII

- Who does Pip feel Molly to be?
- What reasons does he have for his suspicions?
- What sort of husband does Jaggers think The Spider would be to Estella?
- The phrase "over the broomstick" means "not legally married," and implies a common-law marriage. Who are the people who were "married" in this informal manner?
- Hounslow Heath, about twelve miles west of London, was a maze of footpaths: What event transpired there?

[The twenty-ninth installment (15 June, 1861) ended ended here.]

Chapter XLIX

- Why does Pip go to Satis House?
- What does Miss Havisham ask of Pip in return for the £900?
- What information does she give him about Estella?
- Although Pip has saved Miss Havisham from the fire, how is she when he leaves?

Chapter L

- From what Magwitch tells Pip, what does Pip deduce?

[The thirtieth installment (22 June, 1861) ended ended here.]

Chapter LI

- In confirming his conclusion, what side of his nature did Jaggers show?

Chapter LII

- What good thing does Pip complete?
- How has Pip's rescue of Miss Havisham delayed his plans?
- When do they plan to put their plan into action?
- Where does Pip go Monday night?
- What happens to the letter which concerns his uncle Provis?

[The thirty-first installment (29 June, 1861) ended ended here.]

Chapter LIII

- Who captures Pip in the old sluice house?
- Why does Pip feel he was doomed?
- How is Pip providentially saved?

Dickens wrote in a memorandum that Pip is now about 23, and that he was about 7 at the opening of the story. Magwitch, now 60, was about 40 when he first met Compeyson.

[The thirty-second installment (6 July, 1861) ended here.]

Chapter LIV

- What news disturbs Pip when they got Magwitch as far as the public-house on the river?
- How are his fears justified when they set out for the steamer?
- How does Pip's attitude toward Magwitch change after the convict had been rescued from the water?

Vocabulary: "coal-whippers" = workmen who unload coal from ships; "ballast-lighters" = Thames barges carrying stabilizing weight to be transferred to sailing ships; "thowels" = wooden pegs that serve oarlocks for rowing; "jack" = one who performs odd-jobs.

[The thirty-third installment (13 July, 1861) ended here.]

Chapter LV

A note of suspense "Don't go home". "Hummums," a hotel in Covent Garden, had once been a Turkish bath: "Hammam" is Arabic for "bathtub."

- What happened to Compeyson, who had prevented Magwitch's escape?
- What kept Pip from taking a job with Herbert?
- What is characteristic about Wemmick's wedding?
- The "Pool" is a particularly busy stretch of the Thames between London Bridge and Greenwich: why is Provis to be kept here?

Vocabulary: "The Red Book" gives the titles and addresses of the British aristocracy; "Hymen" is the Greco-Roman patron god of marriage seen at the close of Shakespeare's *As You Like It*; "provided by contract" means "paid in advance for goods or services."

Chapter LVI

- How does Pip repay his benefactor before Magwitch escaped his hanging sentence through death?

Vocabulary: "The Home Secretary" in the British cabinet had the power to commute a convicted felon's death-sentence.

[The thirty-fourth installment (20 July, 1861) ended here.]

Chapter LVII

- Who has nursed Pip through his illness and paid his debts?
- What does Joe tell Pip of Miss Havisham's generosity in death?

Vocabulary: Joe mispronounces "codicil" (a legally binding addition to a will) as "coddle shell," as if referring to coddled eggs, "coddle" meaning both "to boil gently" and "to treat as an invalid.

Chapter LVII

- What does Pip plan to do after Joe left?

[The thirty-fifth installment (27 July, 1861) ended here.]

Chapter LVIII

- What does Pip do when he found Joe and Biddy happily married?

Chapter LIX

- When Pip visited Biddy and Joe and their two children eleven years later, what did Biddy advise him to do?
- What had Pip heard of Estella?
- What change had come over Estella when he met her at the site of Ṣatis House?
- How does "a cold silvery mist" recall the end of the First Stage of Pip's expectations? Why is Dickens making this connection?
- In what ways does the revised ending seem as believable as the original one?

[The last weekly installment in *All the Year Round*, 3 August, ended here.]

Chapter 16

Critical Essays

Intimidation and Embarrassment in Conversations of Dickens' Novels

Introductory

The nineteenth-century novel hosts many villains who all seem to be experts in intimidating people around them. Dickens' novels too have many "bad" characters who all have their peculiar ways of oppressing the weak and the innocent. However, intimidation does not always occur through the explicit threats and practices of an evil character. Often "good" characters intimidate others, and characters intimidate each other even when they are polite and "nice" as well. Intimidation also occurs within social interactions which may have several other results and defining characteristics; for example embarrassment is another emotional state which often accompanies or replaces intimidation. In this paper I will first propose a definition of intimidation and later exemplify this definition by explicating some conversations, scenes and characters in several of Dickens' novels.

Definition of "Intimidation"

Although people may intimidate others in numerous ways, all intimidating actions impose a "face threat" to one or more of the parties involved in a social interaction. Erving Goffman defines the term "face" as "the positive social value a person effectively claims for himself by the line others assume he has taken during a particular contact" (5). By this definition Goffman also suggests that "face is an image of self delineated in terms of approved social attributes" (5). Penelope Brown and Stephen Levinson qualify Goffman's definition by attributing two aspects to "face": negative face and positive face (66). These two are defined in terms of the basic wants that an individual has; the negative face is "the want of every 'competent adult member' [of society] that his actions be unimpeded by others" whereas the positive face is "the want of every member that his wants be desirable to at least some others".

According to these two approaches, an individual's face is threatened whenever the public image, the desire to complete an act or the approval of society towards the wants of the person is challenged. There are roughly three ways a face threat may occur: the face threat may be unintentionally posed so that the offender may be "innocent." It may be maliciously and intentionally posed to intimidate someone. Thirdly, it may be incidental since it may come as the by-product of another action.

"Face Threats" in Dickens

Since these options cover a very wide range of social interaction and communication patterns, the focus of this paper is limited to the face threats that occur during conversations between two characters in Dickens. Before going into complicated social interaction models, which involve face threats at several levels, it may be practical to start with some simple face threats. I use this term with reference to all interactions in which one of the parties poses a face threat to the other without being challenged in return. Such threats, which cause intimidation often, occur in Dickens when people in different age groups and social positions meet. Professionals in their relationships with one another or with non-professionals usually intimidate others, since professionalism as a behaviour pattern differentiates people according to their status. This attitude results in the intentional neglect of some of the parties in a social interaction.

"Face Threats" in David Copperfield

An obvious example is observed at Mr. Waterbrook's dinner table in Chapter 25 of *David Copperfield.* In this scene two of Mr. Waterbrook's guests indulge in what David Copperfield calls a "mysterious dialogue" which includes many abbreviations, jargon and other hidden but implied information:

I observed that Mr. Gulpidge and Mr. Henry Spiker, who had hitherto been very distant, entered into a defensive alliance against us, the common enemy, and exchanged a mysterious dialogue across the table for our defeat and overthrow.

"That affair of the first bond for four thousand five hundred pounds has not taken the course that was expected, Spiker," said Mr. Gulpidge.

"Do you mean the D. of A's?" said Mr. Spiker.

"The C. of B's!" said Mr. Gulpidge.

Mr. Spiker raised his eyebrows, and looked much concerned.

"When the question was referred to Lord —I needn't name him," said Mr. Gulpidge, checking himself-

"I understand," said Mr. Spiker, "N."...

"So the matter rests at this hour," said Mr. Gulpidge, throwing himself back in his chair. "Our friend Waterbrook will excuse me if I forbear to explain myself generally, on account of the magnitude of the interests involved." (434-35)

The dialogue takes place in the company of several people who have no knowledge about the issues being discussed or the people being referred to.

As David comments, the dialogue intends to "defeat and overthrow" others by making them feel ignorant and out of place in company. Two men as well as the host have "an expression of gloomy intelligence" which makes all the others "outsiders" and "victims of a salutary awe and astonishment" (*David Copperfield* 435). The speakers obviously desire not to be understood, which endangers the feeling of belonging to the group for the listeners and undermines their social value in that interaction.

"Face Threats" in *Pickwick Papers*

Another example of professionalism as a means of intimidation may be seen in the court scene of *Pickwick Papers*. The scene, which also reflects Dickens' view of "justice-at-work" among other things, has long soliloquies by Sergeant Buzfuz, who uses his professional status in court to address the members of the jury and attempts to intimidate Mr. Pickwick by excluding him from the interaction.

"I say systematic villainy gentlemen," said Sergeant Buzfuz, looking through Mr. Pickwick, and talking at him; "and when I say systematic villainy, let me tell the defendant Pickwick, if he be in court, as I am informed he is, that it would have been more decent...-if he had stopped away... and let me tell him further, as my lord will tell you, gentlemen, that a counsel, in the discharge of his duty to his client, is neither to be intimidated nor bullied, nor put down.... (*Pickwick Papers 561*).

Mr. Pickwick is the intended hearer of this speech; however, since technically the jury ("gentlemen") is being addressed, Pickwick cannot respond. Moreover, he is being threatened by Sergeant Buzfuz's information about the possible consequences of his actions if he intimidates the Sergeant. Even that bit of information is not given to him but to the jury. Sergeant Buzfuz, though "looking through Mr. Pickwick," does not acknowledge his physical presence and accepts it only on the ground that he has been informed about it by others. Mr. Pickwick's obvious desire to be an active participant of the interaction is disregarded and suppressed, which poses several threats to his negative face.

"Face Threats" in The Old Curiosity Shop and Little Dorrit

Professionalism is only one attitude that may threaten people's desires to be a part of a social interaction or be unimpeded in their actions. Dickens' novels display such simple face threats very often when a villainous character has an interaction with a child or a weak figure. *The Old Curiosity Shop* provides several examples through Quilp's interactions with Nell, the Grandfather or Mrs. Quilp. At the end of Chapter

5, running also into the following chapter, Quilp and Little Nell have a conversation that is worth studying.

Quilp greets Little Nell "with his disheveled hair hanging all about him and a yellow handkerchief over his head" (*Old Curiosity Shop* 90) as well as a strong exclamation that startles the child. The conversation lacks formal greetings, salutations and farewells that conventionally indicate due respect to the interactants' faces. As Erving Goffman observes, greetings are significant indicators that the encounter "involves sufficient suppression of hostility for the participants temporarily to drop their guards and talk" (41).

In this case Quilp threatens the conditions under which a mutually controlled and balanced exchange of information can take place, and he instead establishes a superiority over the little girl. The style, direction, content and duration of the dialogue is determined by him, whereas Nell should ideally have the right and duty to determine those factors as well.

Dickens also notes that even the appearance of the man "was something fearful to behold" (*Old Curiosity Shop* 90), but Quilp makes the encounter even more difficult and unusual for Nell by asking her if she can see "a boy standing on his head" (90). For someone like Nell, who is not accustomed to Tom Scott's unusual way of protesting his boss, this question is out of context and thus confusing. Consequently, the reader is told that Nell stands "timidly by" and shows "some fear and distrust of the little man" (90). After the period of silence during which Quilp reads the letter Nell has brought, she is again startled by his loud "halloa here!" (92).

Quilp has already frightened Nell by his physical appearance, loud voice and total disregard for conventional forms of conversation; during the rest of the scene his insistence on learning if Nell knows anything about the contents of the letter takes on a physically intimidating nature: "Do you wish you may die if you do know, hey?" (*Old Curiosity Shop 92*), he asks her. His further inquiry about Nell's desire to be his second wife is also unexpected and completely out of place as he is already married and Nell is only a child. Nell is frightened by the question even when she does not understand its full nature. When she does understand, she "shrank from him in a great agitation, and trembled violently" (93). Although it is obvious that she is more frightened that anything else, the situation is also embarrassing for her. She is further intimidated by not being permitted to go home, which is literally an impediment to her desire to act freely.

In this scene Nell is severely harassed, but her fears and embarrassment do not lead to any reaction in order to change her position in the interaction. However, embarrassment may bring along an active protest of the intimidating and embarrassing face threat in an effort to get out of that situation through what Erving Goffman calls "face saving practices" (15-19).

The conversations that take place between Amy, Fanny and later William Dorrit regarding Amy's "infamous" conduct in Chapter 31 of *Little Dorrit* show face saving practices which arise after the face threats. This scene is very complicated in terms of face threats since it involves threats imposed by almost all parties on others and the subtle relationship between intimidation and embarrassment becomes very explicit.

Here Amy Dorrit is walking towards the Marshal sea Prison with Mr. Nandy, and as the running title of the page states, "she appears in public with a pauper" (*Little Dorrit* 417). Fanny meets the couple just before they reach the prison door and instead of the usual forms of greeting, she makes a curious observation: "Why, good gracious me, Amy!...You never mean it!" (*Little Dorrit* 417). Amy is confused by her sister's obscure comment and asks her what she means. The explanation she gets from Fanny is far from satisfactory, moreover insulting:

"Well! I could have believed a great deal of you," returned the young lady with burning indignation, "but I don't think even I could have believed this of even you!"

"Fanny!" cried Little Dorrit, wounded and astonished.

"Oh! Don't Fanny me, you mean little thing, don't! The idea of coming along the open streets, in the broad light of day, with a Pauper!"...

"O Fanny!"

"I tell you not to Fanny me, for I'll not submit to it! I never knew such a thing. The way in which you are resolved and determined to disgrace us on all occasions, is really infamous. You bad little thing!" (*Little Dorrit* 417)

One may object to Fanny's accusations of Amy's disgracing all Dorrits by stating that Amy does not have nor want a public image that may be endangered by her appearance with Mr. Nandy. However, Amy certainly wants her own desires, in this case her desire to please Mr. Nandy, to be shared by her family. Thus she has threatened her own positive face in this situation. At the same time she has (as Fanny explicitly states) disregarded her family's pretentious but nevertheless maintained public image of gentility. These two conflicting obligations put Amy in an awkward situation.

Fanny's treatment of Amy is intimidating, not only by the nature of the accusations but also by the language she uses for her sister. "Mean little thing," "bad little thing," (*Little Dorrit* 417, 418) and later "common-minded little Amy," "complete prison-child" and "prevaricating little piece of goods" (417, 419) are discouragingly accusing and belittling. Frightened and upset, Amy cannot even suggest that there is no essential difference in "social worth" between the Dorrits and Mr. Nandy. Instead, she is "wounded and astonished" (417, 418), "pale and trembling" and remorseful (417, 419). All these symptoms suggest that she is afraid of keeping in line with her conduct. Thus she tries to make up for the harm she has done to her family face and apologises.

Although Fanny's furious reaction to Amy's offence is disproportionate with the supposed crime, it is not totally unjustified; Fanny has, in fact, lost face: her public image has been threatened by Amy's action. Instead of the more expected reactions of intimidation and embarrassment, this face threat gives rise to a "burning indignation" in Fanny. As Christopher Ricks indicates, "Indignation stands interestingly to embarrassment; the one hot flush drives out the other, as fire fire, so that a common way of staving off embarrassment one would otherwise feel is by inciting oneself to indignation" (3). Thus, consciously or unconsciously, Fanny deals with her embarrassment by translating her upset emotional state from embarrassment to anger. As Ricks observes, indignation also attracts enough public attention to justify the attempts to heal the damage of the face threat just experienced (3). In this case, too, Fanny's behaviour provokes Mr. Dorrit's own embarrassment and he therefore accuses Amy of humiliating him. After Amy's apology, however, Fanny's indignation is replaced by embarrassment once again, this time for her own harsh attitude towards her little sister, and Fanny begins to cry "with a partly angry and partly repentant sob" (417, 420).

Amy is intimidated and confused not only by Fanny's cruel words but also by her father's gently expressed disappointment in her. Mr. Dorrit's claim that Amy has humiliated him is a threat to Amy's desire to be a perfect daughter. She is embarrassed for two reasons which may seem contradictory at first: for one, she is embarrassed at being the black sheep of the family and threatening the family's public image. But she is also obviously embarrassed by that pretentious public image of gentility as well. Therefore her first apology is for whatever she may have unintentionally done that has offended her family (*Little Dorrit 417, 419*). After Mr. Dorrit explains the nature of her offence, she attempts to explain her behaviour:

> I don't justify myself for having wounded your dear heart.... I do nothing but beg and pray you be comforted and overlook it. But if I had not known that you were kind to the old man yourself, and took much notice of him, and were always glad to see him, I would not have come here with him, father, I would not indeed. 417, 420)

This humble apology indicates that as much as she is sorry for what she has done, she is embarrassed and confused by the inconsistency in the family's relationship with Mr. Nandy.

Fanny's impoliteness obviously plays an important role in intimidating Amy; however, politeness itself may have similar consequences. Mrs. Quilp's tea party portrays a very polite Quilp who nevertheless intimidates his mother-in-law. Everyone with whom Quilp interacts is intimidated by his verbal or physical threats; on the other hand, his politeness is so obviously exaggerated and out of his public image that it is hard for Mrs. Jiniwin to cope with this new image as well.

His politeness makes it necessary foreveryone to adjust their attitude towards him although they know that his politeness is not genuine.

Mrs. Jiniwin has been discussing Quilp's rudeness and tyranny for some time when the man himself shows up as a "gentleman" to contradict her claims. Aware of Quilp's dislike for visitors, Mrs. Jiniwin tries to justify her daughter's tea party, and to her great surprise Quilp seems to agree with everything she says. Although Quilp does not explicitly intimidate her, to have to deal with a Quilp so out of face makes Mrs. Jiniwin uncomfortable. She starts "trembling, partly with anger and partly with a secret fear of her impish son-in-law" (*Old Curiosity Shop 80*). As in the case of Fanny Dorrit, Mrs. Jiniwin's indignation is the replacement for her embarrassment. Quilp has threatened her dignified mother-in-law image by contradicting her observations about his tyranny. He makes fun of her by being out of face, thus threatening the offensive stand she has taken against him.

The social interactions studied so far involve face threats posed unintentionally, as in the case of Little Dorrit's offence to her family's public image, intentionally due to justifiable (like Fanny's intimidating anger directed toward Amy) or unjustifiable reasons (such as Quilp's verbal harassment and intimidation of Nell). The examples of conversation studied in this paper are too few to offer a thorough analysis of the many ways characters intimidate and embarrass others or eliminate those feelings in Dickens' novels. Regardless of the nature or manner of these violations or threats of face, they all carry with them a vitality that enlivens the scene and provide extra tension for the reader. As a master of handling tension, Dickens no doubt benefits from these scenes and uses them as yet another trademark of his mastery.

Dickens' Great Expectations for Education in Victorian England

In 1864, in a speech to the Establishment of the Shakespeare Foundation Schools, Charles Dickens emphasized his public schooling philosophy in these words: "no where in this country is there so complete an absence of servility to mere rank, to mere position, to mere riches as in a public school. A boy there is always what his abilities or his personal qualities make him" (*Speeches* 336). This was Dickens' great expectation for the education of England's children. He was a leading middle-class advocate of reforming the existing low quality, variegated educational system that was scattered across England. He lobbied for a government-supported free public system that would enable all children to reach their potential regardless of their financial situation. Dickens utilized his art as a platform to promote these reforms. In *Great Expectations*, he depicted several educational opportunities that highlighted the lack of quality education available to the lower classes. His representation of an education given freely by someone who cares was the model he encouraged the government of England to use in create its own educational system.

Dickens' critiques of the existing educational system and the government's lack of support for it are found throughout his work. *Household Words*, a journal published by Dickens in the 1850s, was a common forum for his message. One article, published in 1851, gave a fictional but generally accurate visit to an old school. His final words reminded society that although they "had done much better since," they needed to "do far better yet" ("Our School" 52).

Later that same year, he co-authored an article criticizing the so-called free schools of England because they rarely accommodated free students. This programme proved to be insufficient and ineffective. The article pointed out that "in two thousand of them, there are not four hundred free pupils" (Dickens and Morley, "Free Schools" 169). Dickens, novels, however, proved to be a more effective platform by reaching a far wider audience. In his preface to *Nicholas Nickleby*, he comments on "the Monstrous neglect of education in England and the disregard of it by the state" (Dickens preface). It is in *Great Expectations*, however, that Dickens makes a strong case for his reforms. His depiction of early Victorian education was a reminder of how minimal options were for the poor, how far the system had developed and how much it still lacked. Dickens did not want society to endorse the "status quo" of education.

Great Expectations tells the story of Pip's pursuit of his great expectations and how they were hindered and helped by his educational options. Pip, like Dickens, encounters a great deal of frustration with the educational "status quo" of the early nineteenth century. Pip's first barrier is his sister, Mrs. Joe Gargery, who is the patriarchal figure in Pip's home. She embodies the fears and reluctance that the ruling class held toward mass education of the lower class. Throughout the entire story, she is referred to as Mrs. Joe or Mrs. Joe Gargery, while her counterpart is simply known as Joe. This is an obvious indication of her dominant position in the household. She makes the rules and enforces them, often in an abusive manner. Joe even describes her to Pip as the "government of you and myself" (63; chapter 7). Just as the government of the early nineteenth century allowed education but gave no support to it, Mrs. Joe allows Pip to attend school but never encourages it and even fears it in Joe.

Joe, on the other hand, represents the plight of the poorer classes. As a child, Joe encounters many "drawbacks" on his "learning" including an abusive father and work obligations (62; chapter 7). In a society that offers no protection for its children, Joe manages the best he can. He achieves the low expectations society had allotted him. As an adult, Mrs. Gargery further hinders his educational pursuits. Joe tells Pip that their tutoring sessions must be on the "sly" because "she ain't over partial to having scholars on the premises" and in "partickler would not be partial to my being a scholar, for fear as I might rise" (63; chapter 7). The ruling class needed education to civilize the working class but feared that too much education would allow them to rise above their station.

Society's tolerance provides a meager opportunity, but Pip eagerly pursues it. His formal elementary education, compliments of Mr. Wopsle's great aunt and her private Dame school, offers Pip little, if any education. This was typical of the time and reminiscent of a school briefly attended by Dickens. A typical day's lesson began as "pupils ate apples and put straws up one another's back" (84; chapter 10). When an actual attempt was made to teach, the children "buzzingly passed a ragged book from hand to hand," while the mistress would fall "into a coma" (84; chapter 10). Private Dame schools of the time offered a "ragged" education at best that provided a chaotic atmosphere and tidbits of knowledge for a small weekly fee.

Through his portrayals of teachers in *Great Expectations,* Dickens symbolized the varied educational opportunities and what they offered. Mr. Wopsle's great aunt illustrates the lack of education available to the working class. Like the education she offers, this old dame is "ridiculous," "of limited means," "and unlimited infirmity" (59, chapter 7). She is so insignificant, that she has no name. This emphasizes the insignificant amount of knowledge she offers her students. Pip later admits he learned "next to nothing" (83; chapter 10). Just as she is a distant relative of a church clerk, her school is a distant relative of the church's attempts at educating the poorer class. Dame Schools had been in existence a long time and offered a ridiculously limited education. A new option was needed. Dickens suggests the end of such enterprises in his description of the demise of Mr. Wopsle's great aunt. She "successfully overcame that bad habit of living" (131; chapter 17). Dame schools were society's "bad habit" that needed to be extinguished.

Other educational options existed in Victorian England but were reserved for those who could afford it. Pip is elevated to one such opportunity when a mysterious benefactor pays for his "gentleman's education." Matthew Pocket illustrates this type of education. As indicated by its tutor's name, this genre of education was reserved for those who had "full pockets." Unfortunately, it was bestowed upon many who would find little use for it. These "gentlemen" were not expected to work. Mr. Pocket, a Cambridge graduate, provides a scholarly education that like his own pursuits leads to "loftier hopes" that often fail (185; chapter 23). This type of education produced self-serving individuals who offered no benefit to society. Pip views his tutor and ultimately his "gentleman's" education as being "almost comic in his distraught way" (183; chapter 23). It costs a great deal of money for Pip to "contract expensive habits" (197; chapter 25). His expensive habits put him in debt, yet his scholarly education leaves him "fit for nothing" (316; chapter 41). Almost a comical situation, if you are not living it. Even an expensive education yields very little benefit for Pip and society.

The only quality education that Pip receives is free of charge. Biddy is the teacher who represents an education given freely and with care. When Pip requests Biddy to "impart all her learning" to him, she is "most obliging" and "immediately began to carry out her promise" (84; chapter 10). Biddy is a caring teacher who imparts her knowledge as a mother would to her child. Although she is not a mother until the end of the story, Biddy represents the only true mother figure. She cares for her grandmother, Mrs. Gargery, Joe, Pip and eventually her own children. It is part of her duties as caretaker to teach; she is the natural teacher.

Biddy represents the hopeful future of education. She is the granddaughter of the "old dame" who will carry her educational legacy into an era of quality opportunities for all. She provides Pip with the educational foundation that allows him to attain his great expectations. It is no coincidence that she becomes the schoolmistress of the working class town who freely and with great care teaches her pupils. She provides her students with the fundamental necessities to reach their goals. This is what a public education should do.

Dickens' educational philosophies were well defined in his art. In *Great Expectations,* he provides a vivid picture of the working-class struggles with the existing educational opportunities, the unsubstantial education of the affluent, and the benefits of an education offered freely and with care. *Great Expectations* was a magic mirror for England's Victorian society. It allowed them to look at their educational accomplishments since the early part of the century, view its present flaws, and see the possibilities of the future. Dickens' realistic depictions of schools and teachers emphasized the need for reform and the possibility of creating an educational system that provided an impartial quality education to all of England's children. England's public school system should be like a mother who freely teaches her children all she knows so that they may reach their potential and achieve their own great expectations. Ironically, in 1870, the year Charles Dickens died, England passed legislation that began a system for a free and compulsory education for all children.

An Unbridgeable Gap in "Great Expectations" The Necessity of the First Ending

Each of the two endings to *Great Expectations* has its own merits within the context of the novel. The revised ending more beautifully and symbolically concludes the text, while the original better utilizes the themes and absolute message of Pip's story. Thematically the novel follows the disillusionment and subsequent rise and fall of Pip into and out of a lifestyle that he did not properly fit into. For that reason I find it hard to accept the revised ending in spite of its vivid and carefully crafted imagery. It not only feels forced as a conclusion to the events comprising the last bits of Volume III, it attempts too carefully to partially reproduce bits of the Victorian methods of Austen or Bronte in tying up loose ends with romantic reconciliation. Despite the partial ambiguity of the revision's reconciliation, the allusion exists and fails to mesh with the rest of the novel. That which Estella represents in Pip's expectations requires that the two cannot reconcile fully in conclusion.

The novel's ending in either case reads as an epilogue of sorts, a bit tacked on to tie up the loose end of Estella. Necessary as it may be, it also highlights earlier moments as more proper and thematic endings for Pip. In relegating Pip's "great expectations" to lessons learned, finalizing his cycles of aspirations of grandeur and ill behaviour, the narrative cycles back upon itself to where Pip began. In this the thematic ending of the novel is the return of Pip to the forge. The forge, represented by fire and the "avenging coals" (41) reminding him of his guilt represent just that - a source of binding and of guilt. The avenging flames that he runs from plagued by guilt throughout the novel, he eventually must return to and face. As the owner of that forge and a blacksmith Joe represents honesty and acceptance of self. Throughout the novel blacksmithing as a motif represents the linking, bending, and twisting of different bits together:

"[L]ife is made of ever so many partings welded together, as I may say, and one man's a blacksmith, and one's a whitesmith, and one's a goldsmith, and one's a coppersmith. Diwisions among such must come, and must be met as they come" (246).

Joe understands those divisions and accepts them, and the key to Pip's rapprochement is doing the same. By returning to what his life originally demanded of him, having exhausted his attempts at the class conciliation with what he believes Estella to be, he closes that loop. Before visiting Miss Havisham and Estella, he had no aspirations for advancement nor shame in his upbringing, and was happy in his friendship with Joe, playing their games and eluding Mrs. Joe's injustices. Pip's love for Estella, far from requited receives only snobbish condescension in response. "She called [him] 'boy' so often, and with a carelessness that was far from complimentary" (70). Instead of accepting who he was internally and ignoring the external views of those like Estella, he created in her an impetus for greed and aspirations of greatness. The rapprochement of Pip with the life he lived before he met Estella occurs largely because of the relationship he develops with Magwitch, a representative of everything he flees up and through Volume III. The realization that money does not breed happiness and that appearances and class standing do not negotiate the relationship between one's self and the world solidifies with the death of his erstwhile benefactor. Upon returning to the forge Pip closes the loop he started when he first met Estella and Miss Havisham, finding happiness with those that he loves and that love him.

If Pip is required to meet again with Estella, it is most appropriate for them to meet from behind the veils of the worlds in which they originally met and with the gap that Pip spent the course of the novel attempting to bridge. Estella undergoes her own version of penance and learns to understand how the mannerisms in which she grew accustomed abused others and herself. Pip witnesses and accepts that her "suffering has been stronger than Miss Havisham's teaching, and ha[s] given her a heart to understand what [his] heart used to be" (496), creating the only sense of finality required between the two befitting the themes of the novel. Even with the realization that Estella has suffered as much as and learned the same lessons as Pip, she remains separated by class standards - as Pip and little Pip walk down the street, she rides in her carriage with a servant. As polarities of measuring personal and social character, Estella and Joe must end the novel at different ends of the spectrum to fulfill the division and understanding that Pip makes between the two. However, I think it appropriate that Estella in her own way successfully finds her way to happiness as well. Rapprochement of Pip should not exclude the same for Estella.

In contrast to the solitary breakdown of Pip's cycle of expectations, other cycles in Victorian literature allow complete reconciliation. Within *Emma,* a breakdown of barriers was required for a mutual understanding to occur between Emma and Mr. Knightley.

The cycle of miscommunication breaks down at a critical moment and the two are able to realise a hidden truth, their love for each other. One of the novel's key problems in regards to conclusion was surpassing this barrier and breaking that cycle, so when it happened that the cycle could be broken, the novel was permitted to end. In the case of Pip's conclusion, Estella represents that cycle which breaks and allows the ending of the novel. She constitutes the commencement of Pip's expectations, and to properly reconcile himself with whom he is he must reconcile the necessity of forgoing those expectations. As a representative of that broken cycle, Estella cannot return and establish a role within Pip's new life as that would cheapen and partially obscure what he accomplishes.

For this reason, I find the presence of little Pip perfectly fitting, especially with Estella offering physical contact to him rather than Pip. As Pip states, " sitting on my own little stool looking at the fire, was - I again!" (490). The son of Joe and Biddy represents a new cycle born of the values that Pip realises after Magwitch's death. Pip is given another chance, a new opportunity to explore a childhood destroyed by unrealistic expectations.

The two walking together, Pip and an untouched form of himself act as both ending and new beginning. Estella's affection towards little Pip returns the wheel to the beginning where Estella mocks and talks down to our Pip. Realistically this is the extent of their reconciliation. Taken in context with the rest of the novel, the ending must properly address and appropriate the themes in relation to both Pip and Estella. Realistically there exists no reason for either to be unhappy. But because of the role Estella played in breeding the unhappiness that plagued Pip, they cannot be happy together. Pip, realizing the folly in his appreciation for external definitions of human worth, allows for his final rapprochement with Joe and Biddy and reflectively, Estella undergoes a similar situation in which she comes to understand the nature of her actions and the cruelty bred by Miss Havisham. This allows her to find happiness. By reseparating these worlds of inequity both parties are capable of finding peace of a sort.

Bibliography

Chesterton, G. K. Appreciations and Criticisms of the Works of Charles Dickens. New York: Dutton, 1911.

Collins, Philip. Dickens and Education. New York: St. Martins, 1963.

Dickens, Charles. Great Expectations. New York: Bantam, 1986.

Leavis, F. R., and Q. D. Leavis. Dickens the Novelist. London: Chatto and Windus, 1970.

Manning, Sylvia Bank. Dickens as Satirist. New Haven: Yale University Press, 1971.

Wilson, Angus. The World of Charles Dickens. New York: Viking, 1970.

Wilson, Edmund. The Wound and the Bow: Seven Studies in Literature. Boston: Houghton Mifflin, 1941.

Bradbury, Nicola. *Charles Dickens's "Great Expectations."* New York: St. Martin's Press, 1990.

Brooks-Davies, Douglas. *Charles Dickens: Great Expectations*. London: Penguin, 1989.

Calder, Angus. Introduction to *Great Expectations*. Penguin, 1981.

Carlisle, Janice, ed. *"Great Expectations" by Charles Dickens*. Bedford Books of St Martin's Press, 1996.

Connor, Steven. *Charles Dickens*. London: Basil Blackwell, 1985.

Cotsell, Michael, ed. *Critical Essays on Charles Dickens' "Great Expectations."* Boston: G.K. Hall, 1990.